M

Free People of Color

Inside the African American Community

James Oliver Horton

Smithsonian Institution Press

Washington and London

93 466

Chapter 5 is reprinted from *Feminist Studies* 12, no. 1 (Spring 1886): 51–76, by permission of the publisher, *Feminist Studies,* Inc., c/o Women's Studies Program, University of Maryland, College Park, MD 20742. Chapter 6 is reprinted with permission from *Afro-Americans in New York Life and History* (July 1984). Chapter 9 was first published as "Race, Literacy and Occupations in Reconstruction Washington, D.C.," in *Toward a New South,* edited by Orville Burton and Robert McMath (Greenwood Press, Westport, CT, 1982); reprinted with permission. Grateful acknowledgment is also made for permission to quote from the following sources: "Blacks in Antebellum Boston: The Migrant and the Community, an Analysis of Adaptation," *Southern Studies* (Fall 1982). "Weevils in the Wheat: Free Blacks and the Constitution, 1787–1860," *this Constitution,* Fall 1985, published by Project '87 of the American Historical Association and the American Political Science Association. "Generations of Protest: Black Families and Social Reform in Antebellum Boston," *New England Quarterly* 49:242–56.

Copy Editor: Karin Kaufman
Production Editor: Jenelle Walthour
Designer: Alan Carter

Library of Congress Cataloging-in-Publication Data
Horton, James Oliver.
Free people of color: inside the African American
community / James Oliver Horton.
　　p.　　cm.
Includes bibliographical references and index.
ISBN 1-56098-203-9 (alk. paper)
1. Afro-Americans—History—To 1863. 2. United States—
Race relations. I. Title.
E185.9.H67　　1993
973'.0496073—dc20　　　　　　　　　92-16446

British Library Cataloguing-in-Publication Data is available

Manufactured in the United States of America
00 99 98 97 96 95 94 93　　5　4　3　2　1

∞ The paper used in this publication meets the minimum requirements of the American National Standard for Permanence of Paper for Printed Library Materials Z39.48-1984

Contents

Preface

This book emerged from a series of studies on a variety of aspects of free black life in the nineteenth-century North. Six of the ten chapters have been published elsewhere in one form or another, although most have been revised for inclusion in this volume. It was begun as a comparative investigation of African American community, and it is far from complete. Rather, it is a progress report, a preview of work that is ongoing. It is intended to contribute to the work of fellow researchers and to inform those to whom this research is new. It has been and continues to be an exciting and surprising undertaking.

In some ways this has been a difficult book to write, for despite my best efforts at detached scholarship, many of the issues contained here carry personal significance beyond their intrinsic academic value. In attempting to examine the interior of black community, I have often been forced to come to grips with my own experiences growing up in that community. As I learned in the course of the research for this project, the distance between the black world of the antebellum North and that of my youth in the Newark, New Jersey, of the 1950s is not as great as it might appear.

My familiarity with my world alerted me to the markers of that historic world, and although specific issues were different, sometimes incomparable, those markers helped me in my attempt to negotiate my way into a social interior seldom visited by historians. In the cooperative efforts among blacks of that early time, I recognized those of a later time and comprehended that cooperative efforts did not always signal agreement on means or even on some short term ends. At the same time, I understood that internal conflict did not mean disunity, for during times of crisis in mid-twentieth century Newark I had seen those who routinely disagreed, sometimes to the point of violence, stand together in the name of community action.

It may seem contradictory to suggest parallels, especially as I argue in the following pages for important variations over time and space, yet the interior issues of the nineteenth century remain relevant to African American communities of the late twentieth century, even if there are important differences to be acknowledged.

This project could never have been completed without the support, assistance, and cooperation of a host of friends and colleagues. Ira Berlin and Stanley Engerman read the complete manuscript and offered invaluable advice for significant revision. A list of those who have read and commented on individual chapters of this book is long. It includes Phyllis Palmer, Sharon Harley, Noralee Frankel, Elizabeth Pleck, Maurine Weiner, Jo Ann Argersinger, and Rayna Green, who provided me with a critical reading of various chapters and critical advice on gender issues and theory. Joel Williamson, Laurence Glasco, Theodore Hershberg, and Monroe Fordham provided important comments on issues of color and racial identity. My colleague Clarence Mondale counseled me on the importance of region in studying American culture and suggested the concept of the "lower North" as an important cultural division in the antebellum period. Hartmut Keil, who coauthored "African Americans and Germans in Mid-nineteenth Century Buffalo" as a conference paper given at the annual meeting of the Organization of American Historians in Washington, D.C., in 1990, contributed his expertise as both historian and linguist. James Mohr's suggestions on issues of gender and violence were very helpful in shaping many of the arguments advanced here, and Spencer Crew, who read parts of the manuscript in various states of completion, contributed not only his expertise but also his warm personal support at critical points in ways that not even he knows.

Manuela Thurner provided thoughtful advice on the substance and structure of the manuscript, and Cynthia Stout was both supportive and extremely efficient in assisting with the manuscript's preparation. The research assistance of Rama Ramakrishna and Shira Nichaman and the editorial assistance of Catherine Kreyche also were extremely important to the completion of this project.

I express my gratitude to the George Washington University, the National Endowment for the Humanities, and the Scholarly Studies Program of the Smithsonian Institution for partial funding of this project. And I owe a special debt to two scholars at opposite ends of the country, Roger Kennedy in Washington, D.C., and Idus Newby in Honolulu, Hawaii, for listening to my ideas and frustrations and providing valuable insights into history and American culture. I wish to publicly thank them for their patience. I benefitted enormously from their experience and support.

My greatest debt by far is to Lois E. Horton, who interrupted her own projects at various times during the last decade to read, edit, and critique this manuscript at every step of its development. She coauthored two of the chapters, one of which, "Race, Occupation, and Literacy in Reconstruction Washington, D.C.," was published and the other, "Violence, Protest, and Identity: Black Manhood in Antebellum America," given as a conference paper. Her scholarly perception, her historical and sociological expertise, and her warm and loving support have made this book possible.

Free People of Color

Northern Free Blacks

The Scholarly Discussion

By the mid-eighteenth century, the shimmering waters and crisp air of the Narragansett region of Rhode Island had attracted tiny settlements to its scattered islands. Where a century before Roger Williams had taken shelter with the Indians, now stood a few small farms and a sprinkling of larger estates. London Hazard was born on one of the more sizable parcels in 1761. He, like the land itself, was the legal property of George Hazard, family man, estate owner, and slaveholder. London was one of more than sixteen thousand blacks then in New England, many clustered in South Kingston township where at the time of his birth almost one in every three inhabitants was of African decent, and most of those were slaves.

Sold as a teenager to Godfrey Hazard, one of his master's relatives, London spent most of his older adolescence in South Kingston proper. It was from South Kingston that he enlisted in the Rhode Island militia to fight in the American Revolution. London served in place of one of his master's relatives who had been drafted into the Continental army but, under the law allowing substitutions, sent London in his stead. During the next three and a half years, London served in the cause of national independence, replacing several in the Hazard family who found the call of the military too onerous and dangerous to answer personally. London received no monetary compensation for his service, but he was rewarded with something far more precious than the devalued Continental scrip paid to American soldiers. His service brought him his freedom at the end of the war.[1]

Thousands of slaves like London won their freedom through their service in the Continental army. In the aftermath of the Revolution, in a movement justified by the language of freedom and liberty and appeals to natural rights, states north of Delaware abolished slavery outright or through plans for gradual emancipation. Unlike the South, agricultural slavery had never been as economically significant in the North, where conditions of soil and climate discouraged the large plantations assumed most suitable for slave labor. In the northern cities, young artisans pressed master craftsmen not to purchase slaves as workers in their trades. Traditional views that bound labor devalued free labor persisted throughout the eighteenth century, contributing to the potency of abolition sentiment after the Revolution. Then, too, northern merchants, many of whom had built their fortunes in the Atlantic slave trade, were economically freer to heed the idealistic call of abolition than planters further south, whose economy and "way of life" rested on slave labor.[2]

By the second quarter of the nineteenth century, slavery had become a largely southern institution. In the North a free black society took shape. These African Americans clustered in small urban communities in sizable cities. During the early years of the century, they established stable families, built their own institutions, and, although most of them were legally denied full citizenship, they nevertheless became a vigorous force in regional and national politics. Free African Americans represented only about 10 percent of the total black population at the time of the Civil War, but their role in the issues that led to southern secession was far disproportionate to their numbers.

This book is about these northern free people of color during the mid-nineteenth century. It is not a survey of their community development, nor is it a comprehensive analysis of their political activism. Rather, it is a series of discussions about many of the major concerns that animated their private deliberations and structured their relationships. The African American community has never been monolithic. Gender, national identity, color, leadership, and the relationships between free blacks and slaves or with various immigrant groups have all been issues of disagreement. Even basics, such as the selection of an identifying name for the race, were hotly debated. This study will examine the interior of free black society during the period to view many of the concerns that often rent the community.

Here also is a people who, despite their differences, were bound by a shared oppression and the power of a collective history. At crucial times, at points of crisis, this diverse people united to support common goals. It was not necessary that they walk in lockstep in order to form a community of common direction. There were many black experiences, yet one overwhelming common black history. The contradictions implicit in this statement form the fundamentals of this study.

Many historians have studied African Americans in the years before the Civil War, but most have concentrated on southern slaves. In the 1970s, influenced by the civil rights movement and the policy debates about the causes of contemporary black poverty, several scholars offered important historical studies of the black community. Implicitly or explicitly they reacted to social scientists who claimed that black problems in contemporary America were due to traditional weakness and the accelerating disintegration of the black family set in motion by the slave experience. Some questioned the historical viability or even the existence of black community.[3]

The notion of blacks as historical victims grew during the post–World War II years. Liberal historians revised the historiography of the early twentieth century, which posited slavery as a benevolent institution and African Americans as the morally and intellectually limited beneficiaries of its guidance. In 1956 Kenneth Stampp disputed descriptions of a mild American slavery and the docile black slave, highlighting instead slave resistance to a brutal institution. It was not a peculiar racial heritage he emphasized, but a more general humanness that governed the reaction of black slaves to this institution of bondage.[4]

Three years later Stanley Elkins, marshalling the weapons of social psychology, expanded this view to suggest that the evidence of racial inferiority the early scholars had found (stereotypical happy, infantile slave behavior that Elkins called the *Sambo personality*) was in fact a result of the personality distortion brought on by the harsh oppression of a closed system of bondage. Comparing the victimization of the slave to that of Jews in Hitler's concentration camps, Elkins found parallel circumstances producing parallel human disabilities. The Sambo stereotype carried validity, Elkins believed, only as a consequence of the destructive slave system, not as an expression of racial heritage.

Both Stampp and Elkins successfully discredited the racial justification of slavery, but in doing so they encouraged an analysis that focused on African Americans as relatively powerless victims of white oppression. This historical picture of blacks as victims carried special significance for a debate moving into a broader arena during the mid-1960s as social scientists sought to assess the underlying causes of the persistence of black urban poverty. In 1965 then Assistant Secretary of Labor Daniel Patrick Moynihan offered an influential theory that drew on Elkins's work. "It was by destroying the Negro family under slavery," Moynihan argued, "that white America broke the will of the Negro people."[5]

Moynihan was attempting to focus federal social policy on the economic and social-psychological needs of poor urban blacks, but his approach so offended African Americans, and many whites as well, that it incited more than a decade of rebuttal. He had written on these issues before, and many found his theories on the subject of race suspect. It was not only the message but also the tone and the assumptions offered as fact without substantiation that fired the anti-Moynihan forces. In a study published three years before his report on black families, Moynihan and coauthor Nathan Glazer assumed what many took to be a condescending tone in their inquiry into race and ethnicity in New York City. Although contrary evidence existed, Moynihan and Glazer unquestioningly accepted conventional beliefs. Whereas they recognized a variety of distinct national cultural heritages among the city's ethnics, they assumed that slavery had so destroyed African cultural heritage that "the Negro [was] only American and nothing else." As such, they contended, "He has no values and culture to guard and protect." They went on to assert that slavery had created a tradition of dependency that remained a problem. African Americans, they believed, did not cooperate among themselves and were too often content to look to others to solve their problems. This situation was supposedly exacerbated by the "shame of being black": "He [the black man] finds nothing positive in it [his race]."[6]

In the politically charged atmosphere of the 1960s, such statements seemed yet another attempt to exonerate white America from responsibility for its racially oppressive and restrictive past. Psychologist William Ryan dubbed this *blaming the victim,* that is, attributing the failure of blacks, especially black men, to benefit fully from the opportunities offered by American society to weaknesses and failures in African American society. Reaction to these charges prompted many historical studies of African American familial relations and institutional development as scholars sought to test the theory of black community "breakdown" against the historical record.[7]

Slave-community studies led the way. Important work by John Blassingame, Herbert Gutman, Eugene Genovese, Leslie Owens, and others provided powerful evidence of collective strength among slaves.[8] The intricacies of the slave community and the character of the black family became the chief focus of investigation. To varying degrees these historians and others challenged the theory of "breakdown" and the notions of black victimization, which had taken center stage during the preceding decade. Scholars brought new methods to their work, some using the computer technology of the "new social history," to study the structure of African American society.[9]

Although the new slave-community studies dominated the historians' attentions in the 1970s, the study of free blacks also occupied an increasing number of scholars. The standard historical treatment of free African Americans in the northern states before the Civil War was Leon Litwack's *North of Slavery,* written a decade before. It was a groundbreaking book in several ways. Published during the early years of the modern civil rights movement, when the focus was on southern racial injustice, Litwack's study reminded readers that racial discrimination was neither limited to the South nor a recent phenomenon. At a time when many in the North expressed shock and contempt for the blatant expressions of southern racial bigotry codified in state regulations and institutionalized at all political, economic, and social levels, Litwack cautioned northern liberals against feelings of regional superiority. *North of Slavery* set the issue of race in a national and historical context. It warned that although "the inherent cruelty and violence of southern slavery require[d] no further demonstration . . . this does not prove northern humanity." As political scientist Howard Zinn suggested for the twentieth century, Litwack demonstrated for the nineteenth century: racial injustice was a national characteristic. Not limited by region, it was an American disgrace.[10]

Litwack traced the impact of "white supremacy" in the northern states from the abolition of slavery in that region in the early decades of the nineteenth century. He described the legal and extralegal limits imposed on black people by northern state and local regulations and the social customs and predilections of the region. In his account the antebellum North sounded much like the twentieth-century South. His work illustrated the obstacles African Americans faced and attacked traditional assumptions that blacks were passive non-actors on the nation's historical stage. Although Litwack's was not a social history, it suggested the complexities of the relationships among northern free blacks, relationships fundamental to the structure of African American community.

By the late 1960s, a few historians were building on Litwack's foundation. In 1969 Benjamin Quarles highlighted black activism in *Black Abolitionists,* a full-length treatment of the role of African Americans in the antislavery movement. In this detailed and thoroughly documented study, which became a classic of the next generation, Quarles fleshed out earlier suggestions of the significant role played by blacks not only as antislavery speakers but also as initiators, leaders, and shapers of the movement. *Black Abolitionists* told the story of blacks and whites allied in antislavery activities and insinuated the outlines of the free black community that served as the basis for reform activity. It suggested a relationship between the configuration of black society and the nature of its political action.[11]

The late 1960s saw the rise of the new social history, with its emphases on community studies "from the bottom up." Its impact on black history was evidenced by Theodore Hershberg's establishment of a research group, the Philadelphia Social History Project, which profoundly affected the course of free-black studies in the next generation. Using many techniques he and his colleagues had pioneered, Hershberg began the collection and computerization of census and other quantifiable data on the African American, German, and Irish populations of mid-nineteenth century Philadelphia. The data gathered on blacks was especially interesting as it included the statistics from the Quaker and abolitionist censuses of 1838, 1847, and 1856. This information, originally compiled by Quakers to combat claims of degradation among free blacks and to forestall efforts to disenfranchise Pennsylvania blacks, offered unique information on black households in the city.[12]

From this project came several important publications that integrated the social history of African Americans with analyses of their political activism. Hershberg's 1971 article, "Free Blacks in Antebellum Philadelphia: A Study of Ex-Slaves, Freeborn, and Socioeconomic Decline," raised important questions about the long-lasting effects of slavery on the slave. Comparing those born free with those who obtained their freedom after spending time in slavery, it indicated that those who won freedom by their own efforts made greater progress in freedom than those who had never been slaves. It also found that the economic status of free blacks in Philadelphia declined in the decades before the Civil War. The particularities of Philadelphia as an urban setting and the nature of slavery in the surrounding areas of the upper South suggested caution in generalizing from these findings. Yet they furnished a bench mark for others in the study of urban free black life in the North and contributed social and economic data to assist our understanding of black political activism.[13]

In succeeding years the Philadelphia Social History Project produced studies of mulattoes and black intergroup relations and the nature and structure of free black families in Philadelphia. These inquiries illustrated several issues interior to the black community—issues generally reserved for sociological studies but which became of greater interest to social historians during the 1970s. They also used computer analysis and adapted social science techniques to the data of social history.[14]

During the 1970s several important studies focused on aspects of free black life in the antebellum North, although few were as quantitative as the Philadelphia project. A 1971 anthology edited by John Bracy, August Meier, and Elliott Rudwick brought together several previously published articles on African Americans in the antislavery movement, and in 1974 Jane and William Pease published *They Who Would be Free,* a study of pre–Civil War black activism. Both these works emphasized the active roles played by African Americans functioning alone and in concert with white reformers.[15]

In their analysis the Peases painted a grim picture of community, of black abolition and the ability of black leaders to formulate and implement a concerted plan of action. Basing their study on an array of primary and secondary materials, the Peases explored the different approaches of black and white abolitionists and growing black frustration with the slow pace of progress. They concluded that despite a noble effort, "whether assessed by its goals or its organizational efficiency, black abolitionism was a failure."[16] They saw its leaders as detached from the masses of ordinary blacks, overly concerned with self-aggrandizement, and preoccupied with bickering among themselves. In their condemnation of antebellum black leadership, the Peases were undoubtedly influenced by the earlier analysis of Frederick Cooper, who believed that black leaders were more interested in the moral uplift of free blacks generally, and in broadening of opportunities for the black middle class in particular, than in the abolition of slavery.[17] These cynical views reflected the racial pessimism felt by many in the early 1970s. The fragmentation of the civil rights movement after the assassination of Martin Luther King, highly publicized black quarrels over calls for separatism and the rejection of nonviolence, and attacks on the black middle class by some black nationalists for, it was charged, having isolated themselves from the black masses seemed to some a tragically futile finale to the hopeful civil rights decades.[18]

The Peases' historical vision of black society seemed to mirror these contemporary concerns. They saw free blacks as active and articulate but hopelessly divided and "powerless," a people who in the decades before the Civil War had clearly perceived that their situation was getting worse. Here the Peases supported Hershberg's finding in Philadelphia that economic and political life declined for blacks during the 1850s.[19] African Americans, they argued, could not be independent of white-controlled resources but could only plead for rights that white society often refused to grant. They saw scant returns for the decades of black struggle, save a few isolated successes and the rise of a small, divided group of black leaders. As some argued in the early 1970s that revolution was the only route to black freedom, so the Peases seemed to suggest that only through violence could the goals of black abolition have been achieved. They speculated that the escape from slavery of many of those who later became black leaders may have "lured potential insurrectionary leaders from the South."[20]

As the 1970s produced black nationalism debates within the black community, several scholars presented important studies of its nineteenth-century antecedents. Several biographies of key figures in the antebellum movement were introduced, including two significant treatments of Henry Highland Garnet and a biography of Martin Robinson Delany. All of these broadened the contemporary discussion of black nationalism and raised timely questions about the feasibility of interracial cooperation on basic reforms in American society.[21]

Floyd J. Miller took a longer and more general view of these issues in his *Search for Black Nationality*, which detailed the interest in African colonization, the rise of the American Colonization Society and its rejection by most free blacks, and, finally, the development of increasingly militant black nationalist movements in the 1850s. Miller studied the thoughts and actions of the pioneers of black nationalism. He viewed African American activism in the decades before the Civil War as a dynamic force that influenced political events rapidly taking shape in American society.[22]

Miller's book was one of several political and intellectual studies that presented a context for issues being raised by social historians at the time. These studies helped to lay the basis for a new look at antebellum free black life.[23] One of the most influential examinations of free blacks in the pre–Civil War years focused on the South. Published in 1975, employing many of the methods and asking the questions of the new social history, Ira Berlin's study *Slaves Without Masters* blended a concern for black community structure with significant observations on black political activism. It was a major achievement, for it expanded the ground for understanding the complexity and diversity of free black society in the antebellum period as few historians had done.[24]

Berlin explored the dynamics of class, color, and gender as they influenced the development of African American institutions and communities. His work served as a bridge between the slave-community studies, with their emphasis on social structure, and cultural formation and free-black studies, which tended toward a concentration on political activism. Especially important was Berlin's argument, later enlarged to include the North, which treated the impact of change over time and regional differences on race relations and the character of black life. With the publication of this work, the study of antebellum free blacks moved to a new, more social history–oriented phase.[25]

It was that social complexity and the ongoing debate over the historical existence and the nature of black community that inspired my interest during the 1970s. In 1979 in *Black Bostonians*, sociologist Lois E. Horton and I focused on a single antebellum free black community. Like most scholars of the period, we were deeply aware of the contemporary significance of our undertaking. Influenced by the early quantitative community studies of Hershberg and others, we sought to combine both quantitative and qualitative sources, to "humanize" the numbers by emphasizing the ordinary black people of antebellum Boston. Our study included but did not magnify the presence and importance of black leaders. We hoped that our work would help to inform the discussion concerning not only the discrimination African Americans faced in the antebellum North but also their response to that discrimination, and the formal and informal community structures they established for mutual support and social action. Our concern was the nature and function of the black community and its relation to black political action.[26]

We saw the black community as the foundation for black activism, and thus we were as interested in the structure of black households and the character of black family relations as we were in the formation of black protest organizations. The social dimensions of black Boston, especially its statistical presentation, had not been studied before, and we intended our detailed picture of that community as a context for the activism we also illustrated. Our assumption, which proved correct, was that the patterns of community organization would be reflected in the character of its political activism. It was clear that black Boston was a diverse community, but as we studied its interior relations and started to understand the depth of cooperation and mutual support even in the face of individual disagreements and political quarrels, we were more impressed with the strength and cohesion of black community life than some earlier scholars. We found some of the same weaknesses that the Peases had described, but we were less discouraged by the obstacles to black abolitionist goals, in part because from inside the black community the view of progress was more long-term and complex, often measured by one successful slave rescue or one relative sheltered at a time. From inside black society, black anger and frustration was clearly visible—but so too was black hope and determination that failure would never be the final word. Much more distressing were our findings that the economy was deteriorating for blacks in Boston during the 1850s. This substantiated Hershberg's observations concerning economic conditions for Philadelphia blacks during the same period. It was this economic crisis, which strained the facilities of the Boston community to it limits, that gave us greatest concern.

The 1980s saw the continued expansion of approaches to the study of free black society. Leonard Curry, in a valuable analysis of fifteen of the largest black communities in the North and South, provided extensive comparative statistics on demographics, occupation, and residential patterns. He also surveyed educational opportunities, crime, and poverty within free black communities. Drawing on some of the demographic questions Hershberg had raised, Curry focused more comparatively than anyone had before. In this respect he also drew on Berlin's notion of the importance of comparative regional approaches to the study of free black life. Although Curry ended his study in 1850, he added critical information to the growing body of knowledge on antebellum blacks.[27]

In 1982 Robert Cottrol studied the social and political life in antebellum black Providence, Rhode Island, confirming the pattern of community activism and organization among free blacks found in other cities. His extensive treatment of unlikely interracial political alliances struck during the period was instructive and suggested that historians should pay greater attention to issues of race and class in attempting to understand the dynamics of black community life. Here again region was a critical factor in accessing the options open to black people in creating community support apparatus.[28]

As quantitative historical analysis had influenced the study of free blacks in the preceding decade, the 1980s witnessed the rise of folklore and material culture as two of the most significant methodological directions. Several important works paved the way for this development. Joseph P. Reidy, through his investigation of slave celebrations and ceremonies begun in the eighteenth century, focused attention on the intersection of African and American cultures and its significance in encouraging black resistance in New England. Of all the black culture/folklore studies, Lawrence Levine's *Black Culture Black Consciousness,* published in 1977, was the most influential. Tracing the cultural connections between Africa and America, using folktales, slave songs, and spirituals, Levine documented the development of a distinctive African American culture. He also propounded the usefulness of historical folklore in illustrating and analyzing black community and cultural life. These sources were employed most immediately and with greatest success by scholars studying the slave community, but several have found them helpful for analyzing free black society as well.[29]

During the 1980s the study of free blacks matured still further with several important and sophisticated publications. Emma Jones Lapsansky stressed the importance of examining the extensive social networks and shared values in order to understand class structure within the black community. Her's was an especially significant contribution, for it underscored personal relationships as the building blocks of community. Richard Blackett placed that community and its political protest in an international context, exploring the connections between the American and British abolition movements through a study of black abolitionists who traveled abroad speaking on behalf of their brothers and sisters in slavery. Their efforts to expose American hypocrisy to Britain and Europe was a major project involving scores of African Americans and provided black American society with an international perspective on American prejudice.[30]

Gary Nash deserves special attention for both the quality and quantity of his contributions during the last decade. His *Forging Freedom: The Formation of Philadelphia's Black Community* (1988) built on his earlier work, combining quantitative analysis of census data with a close reading of public and private records and secondary sources to sketch free black life in a major northern city with striking historical detail. His story of community formation analyzes the growth of black Philadelphia from the colonial period to the antebellum era. Its focus is multilevel, from the family to the major institutions of black society, and is the most complete picture yet produced of the largest northern African American community of the period.[31]

Nash and others helped move the scholarly discussion forward to more complex and ultimately more important ground. No longer simply the passive objects of reformer zeal or vigilante terrorism, black people were now viewed as major actors in America's historical drama. Their views and opinions were acknowledged, as was the significance of their cultural, economic, and political presence. Most recently the work of Shane White on the transition from slavery to freedom in New York City has pointed the way to more sophisticated uses of folklore, linguistics, and material culture. White added to these sources an impressive array of eighteenth- and nineteenth-century magazines and newspapers to produce a most intriguing interpretation of northern slavery and the development of the urban free black community. This study and other highly suggestive and imaginative work presently underway—by scholars such as W. Jeffrey Bolster on the community and culture of black seamen and Lonnie Bunch on the nineteenth-century cultural interaction of blacks and Mexicans in Los Angeles—place interracial contacts in a new context. Emphasizing the importance of shared circumstances and concerns in bridging racial divides at specific times, in specific places, they set out promising new directions for future study and furthered comprehension of the puzzle of black society.[32]

A review of recent contributions to the study of northern free black life before the Civil War would not be complete without special mention of several editorial projects that have made primary documents available. Building on the early offerings of Carter G. Woodson, Herbert Aptheker, Philip Foner, Dorothy Porter, and others, these projects have provided the raw material for in-depth investigation. There are several collections that make available slave narratives, which often shed a personal light on black community life. Notable among these are John Blassingame's *Slave Testimony,* Charles Blockson's *The Underground Railroad,* Bert James Loewenberg and Ruth Bogin's *Black Women in Nineteenth-Century American Life,* and Ann Allen Shock-

ley's *Afro-American Women Writers, 1746–1933*. These collections and
the many reissued narratives of hundreds of other blacks who attained
their freedom and recorded their experiences in the antebellum North
are the closest approximation to personal diaries available for the plain
people of color. They provide a window into personal thoughts and
family life, and although many were issued for specific abolitionist purposes, sometimes transcribed by white abolitionists, they remain useful
as eyewitness testimony.[33]

The political thoughts of free blacks are accessible through collections compiled by Dorothy Sterling in *Speak Out in Thunder Tones,*
which brought together newspaper articles, letters, and speeches by and
about free blacks from the late eighteenth century through the Civil
War, and through the minutes of the black state conventions edited by
Philip Foner and George Walker, which is a worthy complement to
Howard H. Bell's collection, *Minutes of the Proceedings of the National
Negro Conventions, 1830–1864*. Together these last two collections
provide a close-up of the concerns and actions of free blacks acting in
concert at the regional and the national level.[34]

The most extensive published primary source collection on antebellum black activism is *The Black Abolitionist Papers,* compiled by a
team of scholars headed by C. Peter Ripley and Roy E. Finkenbine. This
collection is on seventeen rolls of microfilm and includes written material produced by and about black abolitionists gathered from libraries
around the world. Although the documents concentrate on political issues, they are also a major source of social data on free blacks. Approximately 10 percent of the microfilmed documents are to be included in a
five-volume series covering black abolitionist activities in Great Britain,
Canada, and the United States. These volumes contain substantive historical essays and editorial notes, providing historical context for the
documents. As is evident, this is a massive undertaking and the field is
greatly indebted to the editors for providing access to this vast array of
primary sources.[35]

Clearly the study of free northern blacks has progressed a good
deal in the last generation. Today almost all scholars accept the historical existence of a highly structured and dynamic community among antebellum free African Americans. The task now is to understand the variety, diversity, and nuances of that community. In an important critique
of recent research on the black urban experience, Kenneth Kusmer has

suggested a general theoretical framework for such study. He argues that there were three types of forces that gave shape to black urban life:

1. External forces. These include white attitudes toward blacks and how these attitudes were expressed, that is, the existence of, or the extent of, racial restrictions, discrimination, and violence at all levels of racial contact. These encompass racial discrimination (or lack of it) expressed not only in the structure of law but also through custom and tradition.
2. Internal forces. These refer to the variety of black individual and institutional responses to the restrictions, threats, or violence imposed by external forces. Black response should be broadly interpreted to include individual and family relationships, community life-styles, the construction of community secular and religious institutions, and the development and preservation of cultural folklore.
3. Structural forces. These factors are associated with the geographical location of the black community and the wider society in which it was located. They include components such as the type and stage of development of the local economy; the nature of the political structure; the traditions that helped to determine the social arrangements; and the relevant demographic factors, including the age, regional origins, and ethnic composition of the local population.[36]

Viewing antebellum free black communities in this way helps to emphasize the complexity of black life. An African heritage transformed by European and Native American cultural influences and combined with the effects of black protest and resistance to racism created African American culture and society. Since the early 1980s, under grants from the National Endowment for the Humanities, the National Museum of American History of the Smithsonian Institution, and the George Washington University, I have been trying to understand that process as it shaped free black communities in several northern cities and towns. Much of my work has focused on the last two of Kusmer's theoretical categories, internal and structural forces. I have attempted to locate and illustrate issues internal to black society that were part of the complexity of African American life before the Civil War.

These internal issues often determined the nature and range of community responses to the external and structural factors. They were also sometimes the cause of divisions among African Americans, which bubbled to the surface as controversy. In a recent and highly provocative book, *Deromanticizing Black History,* Clarence Walker argued that historians have ignored these divisions, tending instead to "romanticize" the black historical experience, unduly emphasizing the strength of African American unity. "In dealing with black people," Walker charged, "historians must get beyond the romantic notion that oppression produced a class of people who were inevitably kind and generous to their peers." Instead he pointed to the "racial self-hatred and oppositions based on color that have historically divided black America."[37]

I agree with some of Walker's argument. Oppression does not necessarily produce group cohesion, although historical evidence suggests that it often did, in some places for varying periods. If historians have placed great significance on evidence of cooperation in the black community (and there is plenty of it), it is partly as a corrective to earlier assumptions about black community disorganization. For those of us schooled on the 1960s notions of black community "breakdown," the abundance of countertestimony is sticking. Our eagerness to make others aware of our "discovery" is understandable. Still, Walker is correct to suggest that there have always been significant divisions among black people. An absence of complete unity among human beings is hardly surprising. But his call for a more "realistic" examination of black history demands that internal divisions and tensions be analyzed and understood. They must be seen, however, in the context of racial complexity imposed by American society. It is difficult to explain or even to characterize the unity and the divergence that often coexisted among various groups of black people. Yet these characteristics were the result of internal matters that were frequently divisive, even as external and structural forces encouraged a unified response.

A further complication is the regional variation of these coexisting characteristics, an issue discussed in two seminal articles, "The Structure of the Free Negro Caste in the Antebellum United States" and "Time, Space, and the Evolution of Afro-American Society," by Ira Berlin. Economic, political, and social differences created very different local and regional environments to which black communities had to adjust, creating unique societal arrangements and political strategies.[38] Local structural factors—such as size and proportion of the African American community, proximity to the South, the influence of slaveholding culture, and the degree of local dependence on Southern economics, to name a few—may have not only determined race relations but also may have influenced structures, discussions, and potential divisions within the black community. Simply put, black people, like all Americans, developed communities that reflected the national, regional, and local issues affecting their well-being. The relationships among African Americans were partially dependent on the needs of a particular black community and its response to these specific issues and the local political, economic, and social conditions.

In the antebellum era, the abolition of slavery, the protection of free blacks from slave kidnappers, and the promotion of civil rights and equality of opportunity were the fundamentals that drew almost total African American support. There was general tolerance for differences of opinion on a broad range of topics, but the assumption was that all blacks agreed on the necessity for the abolition of slavery and the acquisition of the full rights of citizenship. Strategy and tactics were constantly at issue but generally African Americans differed less over ends than over means.

One issue which encouraged considerable debate among free northern blacks during the pre-Civil War years was African colonization. In 1816 the American Colonization Society was formed by several prominent white citizens, many of them slaveholders, to promote the colonization of blacks in Africa. With federal support (the organization was in fact formed in the halls of the U.S. House of Representatives) they established the colony of Liberia in 1820. That year the *Mayflower of Liberia,* carrying eighty-six African Americans, sailed out of the port of New York bound for West Africa. By 1830 the vast majority of free blacks in the North opposed this venture because they saw it as a deprivation of their rights as Americans and because the removal of the free black population would have the effect of isolating slaves from their most steadfast allies. There were, however, a few free blacks who saw colonization as one means of securing self-government and self-determination. A few saw a black-governed Liberia as a place of personal opportunity as well as general black advancement. Although some, a small minority, saw emigration to West Africa, the West Indies, or Canada as the only way to secure these ends, and others, the vast majority, would struggle within the American context, all agreed on freedom, equality, and full citizenship as the desired ends. The argument was over where these ends could best be realized.

Although emigration never attracted more than a small fraction of African American support, the establishment of black-controlled institutions to serve black people gathered a much larger following. Historians have tended to see both these positions, emigration and black institutional separatism, as a part of the philosophy of black nationalism. On the one hand, the "nation" would be external to the United States; on the other hand, it would be internal, "a nation within a nation." Although most prominent black leaders during this period supported the integration of blacks into American society, some, a larger number than supported emigration, endorsed a separate African American institutional life—what the twentieth-century system of racial segregation professed but never provided: separate but equal facilities.

Yet if black separatists opposed integrationist efforts, it was not because they espoused different ends but because they had lost faith in integration as a means to those ends. Believing that only black-controlled institutions could actually serve the needs of black people, and smarting from displays of paternalism and more blatant racism by white abolitionist allies, these separatists pushed for black schools, black social service organizations, black entertainment centers, and black social-protest and political-action groups. In almost all cases, those who stood on separatist ground did so out of a loss of faith in the ability of white institutions to serve black needs or the political will of white society to care.

These divisions within black society—divisions that encouraged these varying approaches to black problems—must be seen in the context of matters internal to black community, matters exacerbated by external pressures but understood in reference to personal, family, and community relations. The chapters in this volume attempt to do more than view blacks as active agents of social change or as important shapers of their own lives and destinies. They mean to suggest the internal complexity of African American community.

This book is divided into three sections. The first, "A Community of Commitment," considers the role of ordinary black people in social protest and cooperative efforts to deal with the special handicaps created by the burden of slavery and racial prejudice. It focuses on the concerted action African Americans took as they confronted the racial issues limiting their opportunities and threatening their freedoms. African Americans agreed on what was needed: an end to slavery; full citizenship in American society, including black political rights and power; and educational and economic opportunities for black people sufficient to secure and sustain their families and their communities. Their actions assumed a variety of forms, from formal organized efforts to informal, individual acts of human kindness and family support. The theme of this section is solidarity.

The second section, "Multiple Identities: Gender, Color, and Nationality," presents three of the most pressing and long-standing issues of debate among blacks: gender roles, color significance, and national identity. These issues are inextricably bound and have been controversial and often confusing to Americans of African heritage. Indeed, they have been major flash points within the black community. Frequently white America presumed to define black Americans in ways most convenient to its purposes and most profitable to its fortunes. But it was easier to define black people than to force their acceptance of that definition. Questions of black identity have carried critical political and economic implications and have been hotly debated within the black community for generations, demonstrating the variety of African American opinion and reflecting the diversity of black community. Debate was influenced, but not totally controlled, by white racial assumptions. It was not unaffected by the actions of the world outside, for the presence of slavery and racial discrimination were inevitably complicating factors, but it was most likely to concern internal matters, generally obscured from the white world.

Section three, "Race and Ethnicity," devotes attention to the relations between blacks and nineteenth-century immigrants in an effort to suggest the complexity of race relations in northern cities. Economic competition and the relative opportunities available to individual Americans depended in large part on racial and ethnic restrictions. Black people understood that all whites were not alike. Nor were their relationships with white people monolithic. The chapters in this section attempt to shed light on some of the differences that blacks understood and used to shape their strategies of alliance and their perceptions of opportunity.

What follows, then, is an attempt to contribute to and encourage the historical inquiry into the unifying and divisive issues among African American people. Many of the conclusions reached here are of necessity tentative. Much research remains to be done. We still know very little about the interior of free black life in the shadowy world of the antebellum North. Important studies are on the way, but for now we can concentrate on the issues at hand—that free people of color were a multifaceted people with lives complicated by forces outside their community, forces that restricted their opportunities and limited the fulfillment of their dreams. Then, as now, African Americans were burdened by America's obsession with race, a burden that will continue to weigh heavily until it is honestly faced, fully addressed, and finally resolved. It is to that eventuality that this book is dedicated.

1

A Community of Commitment

Americans like to think of themselves as individualists. The nineteenth-century image of the "rugged individualist" was immortalized in twentieth-century popular culture and came to symbolize the quintessential American. In reality the interdependence symbolized by community is more descriptive of American life, especially the lives of most working people. Community has been central to the lives of black people, for few could stand alone against the assaults of poverty and racism omnipresent in their experience.

This section discusses some of the many ways that African Americans united in acts of mutual support. It examines three interconnected issues of community: migration, protest, and outreach. Chapter 1, "Blacks in Antebellum Boston: The Migrant and the Community," demonstrates how formal and informal networks helped to integrate migrants into the black community.

Chapter 2, "Generations of Protest: Black Families and Social Reform," shows the enduring strength of black activism. Entire African American families participated in a variety of social and political actions geared toward mutual support and protection. No less than white families, black Bostonians developed patterns of social activism that passed from parent to child to grandchild, making involvement truly a family tradition.

The third chapter, "Links to Bondage: Free Blacks and the Underground Railroad," details an informal, cross-regional network of blacks who formed the backbone of the movement to aid and protect slaves fleeing the South. Free northern men and women, often at risk to their own safety, offered safe havens and physical and emotional aid to strangers as well as to friends and kin fleeing slavery. But even more significant, this chapter shows the connections between those on either side of the "cotton curtain," connections maintained for years, even under the most difficult of conditions, through a system of underground communication networks. This chapter discusses regional differences in underground railroad action. San Francisco blacks, lacking the immediacy of personal contact with slavery eastern blacks had, appeared to be less militant on the issue of direct action against slavery, preferring instead to attack local issues of racial prejudice and discrimination. The affect of region on community is a continuous theme throughout this book.

CAUTION!!

COLORED PEOPLE

OF BOSTON, ONE & ALL,

You are hereby respectfully **CAUTIONED** and advised, to avoid conversing with the

Watchmen and Police Officers of Boston,

For since the recent **ORDER OF THE MAYOR & ALDERMEN**, they are empowered to act as

KIDNAPPERS

AND

Slave Catchers,

And they have already been actually employed in **KIDNAPPING, CATCHING, AND KEEPING SLAVES.** Therefore, if you value your **LIBERTY**, and the *Welfare of the Fugitives* among you, *Shun* them in every possible manner, as so many *HOUNDS* on the track of the most unfortunate of your race.

Keep a Sharp Look Out for KIDNAPPERS, and have TOP EYE open.

APRIL 24, 1851.

In black communities across the North, special vigilance committees were formed to protect fugitive slaves who migrated to northern cities. Such protection was especially important after the passage of the federal Fugitive Slave Law of 1850. (Library of Congress)

Chapter 1

Blacks in Antebellum Boston

The Migrant and the Community

JAMES OLIVER HORTON

The dynamics of slavery and freedom shaped black life in such diverse ways that scholars rarely treat northern and southern free blacks in tandem; but viewed from the perspective of the antebellum years, the distance between free black life in the North and in the South does not appear as great. In fact, some free blacks traveled south to find work and occasionally to settle, and—more important—many southern free blacks migrated north so that by the time of the Civil War, they made up a large portion of the black population in the free states.

The migratory patterns and experiences of antebellum free blacks throw new light on free black life, North and South, and provide an opportunity to understand the process of black migration before the "Great Migration" of the twentieth century.[1] The city of Boston is an especially good place from which to view the movement of black people. The relatively small size of Boston's black population and their self-conscious desire for community reveal the ways newly arrived immigrants influenced the development of black society and the ways the established community shaped the lives of the newly arrived.[2]

In 1638 slave traders first brought African Americans to Boston. They came as servants from the West Indies. These first black migrants eventually replaced native American Indians held in slavery. Religious beliefs and environmental limitations ensured that Boston never became a great slaveholding center. Boston merchants were generally slave traders rather than slaveholders after the mid-seventeenth century.

Boston's black population grew slowly. On the eve of the American Revolution, fewer than one thousand blacks resided in the city.[3]

The principles and ideals expressed in revolutionary Boston, the important role Boston's blacks played in the war effort, and the declining economic importance of local slavery combined to give rise to a strong abolitionist spirit among Boston's revolutionary generation, whites as well as blacks. This spirit created the climate for the 1783 decision by the Massachusetts Supreme Court that slavery was inconsistent with the provisions of the 1780 state constitution. With the state's abolition of slavery, Boston's blacks could expand their efforts to build their community.[4]

By 1800 more than eleven hundred blacks lived in Boston, composing less than .4 percent of the residents. This number more than doubled by the outbreak of the Civil War, when blacks numbered 2,261, about 1 percent of the city's population.[5] The migration of blacks from outside Massachusetts accounted for most of this increase. At no time during the antebellum years did the influx of blacks compare to that of the Great Migration of the twentieth century when in a single decade major northern cities increased their black populations manyfold. Yet the pre–Civil War black migration to Boston has its own importance in the study of the adjustment of newcomers to a new environment. Because there were fewer migrants during this period, the agencies and institutions that aided them in their adjustment can be studied more easily. The smaller number of these early black migrants allowed them to be assimilated into the established black community with less difficulty, yet the mechanisms by which this was accomplished were similar to those of the larger, twentieth-century migration. These adaptive mechanisms are important to the understanding of the development of urban black society.

By the mid-nineteenth century, more than 55 percent of black Bostonians had been born outside of Massachusetts. The proportion of migrants among Boston's blacks was greater than among other black populations in the state. In 1850 less than 40 percent of all blacks living in Massachusetts had been born out of state. By 1860 the gap between Boston's black migrant population and that of the state as a whole had widened: the proportion of blacks living in Massachusetts who had been born out of state had risen to about 44 percent, whereas the proportion of Boston blacks born out of state had jumped to more than 61 percent.[6] Clearly, the economic and social opportunities of the urban environment and the presence of a sizable established black community in Boston were attractive to blacks migrating to Massachusetts. Throughout the antebellum period, Boston's black migrant population grew faster than its native black population.

Many of the blacks born in Boston were personally familiar with the migrant experience and its attendant difficulties. Some, such as William Cooper Nell, were the sons and daughters of migrants. Nell, the historian, abolitionist, and community leader, was born in the black section of Boston's Beacon Hill in 1817, but his father, William G. Nell, a sailor, had come to Boston from South Carolina on a British brig in which he was imprisoned during the War of 1812.[7] Like William Cooper Nell, many members of Boston's black community developed an empathy for the problems of newcomers.

The diverse origins of these migrants attest to the cosmopolitan character of the antebellum black community. Many black migrants had been born abroad. In 1850, 179, or 16 percent, of these migrants came from outside the borders of the United States. More than half of the foreign born were from Canada, and almost one-fourth had been born in Europe. In contrast to the migration pattern of the twentieth century, in which West Indians composed the majority of foreign-born blacks, less than 20 percent of antebellum black migrants to Boston had been born there. In addition to the Canadians, the West Indians, and the Europeans, a few blacks migrated from South America, and even a few from Africa. Most of the African-born migrants were probably brought to the New World as slaves and came to Boston after obtaining their freedom, but some had never been slaves and had come to Boston via Britain and Canada. Almost one-third of Boston's black migrants had been born in the South. Two hundred seventy-one, or more than 80 percent, of these southern-born men and women were from Virginia, Maryland, and the District of Columbia. The migration of blacks out of the South to antebellum Boston probably followed the path of the Atlantic coastline, as in 1850 only about 4 percent of the migrant population had been born in the central or western South.[8]

Most southern blacks probably did not come directly to Boston. The birthplaces of their children indicate that Boston was one of a number of cities along the Atlantic coast in which they had lived. The ages and birthplaces of the children of southern migrants suggest that many of these families moved relatively short distances over the course of decades to Boston from their southern birthplaces. This pattern would seem to parallel that of white families moving from the East to the Midwest during antebellum years.

The 1850 census listed 369, or slightly more than one-third, of the city's black migrants as having been born in northern states other than Massachusetts. Forty-four percent of these northern-born migrants had been born in New England; most of the rest had come from New York and Pennsylvania. Like southern migrants, most Northerners hailed from Atlantic seacoast states and had traveled relatively short distances to come to Boston.

The census of 1860 indicates a gradual shift in immigration from neighboring northern states to more distant places. By that year the percentage of migrants from outside the country had risen by 10 percentage points to more than 26 percent, with most of these from Canada. There was also an 8 percentage point rise, to more than 40 percent, in the number of southern-born migrants, with the majority from Virginia and Maryland. The significant number of southern migrants in Boston led one black southern-born woman to observe that the Boston black community looked like "the old country."[9] By 1860 more southern than northern migrants resided in Boston. Only one-third of the black migrants in that year had been born in the North. Almost one-half of the northern migrants had come from New York and Pennsylvania, with slightly more than 40 percent from New England.

This pattern of increasing migration from the South was even more pronounced than census figures indicate, because one category of southern migrant, fugitive slaves, was generally not included in the census enumerations. This group, not anxious to have their whereabouts officially recorded, often composed a sizable portion of the city's black community. Theodore Parker, a white abolitionist and Congregational minister, estimated in October 1850 that four hundred to six hundred fugitives lived in the city.[10] There is no way to judge the accuracy of Parker's figure, but immediately after the passage of the federal Fugitive Slave Act in 1850, two hundred fugitives left Boston for the safety of Canada.[11]

By the mid-1850s, the exodus slowed as it became clear that black Bostonians and their white abolitionist allies would protect fugitives. By 1860 many unrecorded southern-born migrant fugitives remained in the city. Census figures do not adequately reflect the importance and influence of these southern migrants, and as census data are least accurate for the most mobile segment of the population, it is likely that there was a general underenumeration of the migrant population. The growth in the migrant population, especially the southern-born, increased after the Civil War, when Southerners came to dominate the city's black community.[12]

Like other immigrant groups, blacks often traveled to cities where relatives and friends had gone before. Deeply concerned with the racial climate of areas in which they lived, they were sensitive to the reputation of various northern cities. The experience of Peter Randolph, a black minister and ex-slave, illustrates the importance of communication between blacks in the development of migration patterns. Randolph had been told by proslavery whites in Virginia that the North generally, Boston particularly, was a dangerous place. They tried to convince him that he would be killed, imprisoned, or pressed into forced labor there. Yet Randolph knew of Boston's favorable reputation among the free blacks and the slaves in Virginia. Boston, by reputation, was "foremost in advocating the Negro's cause and vouchsafing to him the immunities of citizenship."[13]

Boston's reputation among blacks attracted Randolph and hundreds of other migrants to the city. One key element in Boston's reputation as a center for radical reform was William Lloyd Garrison's *Liberator*, which was published in the city. This abolitionist journal and its crusading white editor helped convince many that the city was a safe haven for people of color. But Boston was also the city of the "Garrison mob," which in 1836 attacked the young crusader and almost ended the city's militant abolitionist press. Life in Boston never matched its reputation for racial egalitarianism, yet compared to most other northern cities, largely through the efforts of dedicated white abolitionists and the black community, Boston was a racially tolerant place. If blacks did not find complete racial equality there, they did at least find opportunities for education, employment, and community.[14]

Most influential Bostonians did not view the small, proportionally declining black population as a threat to order and stability, despite the prominence of black civil rights and abolitionist protests in the city. They were more concerned about the dramatic growth of Irish immigration to Boston after the mid-1840s, which severely taxed the resources of the city and threatened the traditional sociopolitical order. These concerns overshadowed the race problem in the minds of many and helped promote racial tolerance among native-born white Bostonians.[15]

The existence of an established and active black community also attracted migrants to Boston. Black newcomers, barred from many city facilities, found support within this community. With hotels and white boardinghouses closed to them, job opportunities severely limited, and sections of the city unsafe for them, migrants relied on the established blacks. They sought out friends or relatives in the Boston area, who provided housing and social contacts. Blacks migrants to antebellum Boston had many of the same problems as other immigrants, and they used many of the same techniques to aid their adjustment to urban life.

As a result of their connections, prominent blacks seemed to have a relatively smooth transition to Boston. There were networks of relationships among blacks in major northern cities, especially Philadelphia, New York City, Boston, and a few other New England cities, which accounts for some of the migration between these cities. Charlotte Forten, the daughter of a prominent and wealthy black Philadelphia family, boarded with her father's friends—black abolitionist Charles Lenox Remond and his family—in Salem, Massachusetts. Forten, who attended normal school in the Boston area, found adjustment to her new home considerably easier because of the efforts of her host family.[16]

These networks were maintained by communication through black newspapers, personal contacts, and letters. The national antislavery movement, the national Negro convention meetings, religious associations, and conventions held by black fraternal organizations all provided contacts and lines of communication between black communities. Thus when in 1853 John S. Rock, a black doctor, moved his practice from Philadelphia to Boston, his adjustment was eased by Boston contacts he had made through his social and political activism in Philadelphia.[17]

Similar mechanisms of adaptation eased the difficulties of poorer migrants. Black unskilled and semiskilled workers who traveled frequently in search of employment also developed a network of acquaintances and contacts in northern cities. The statements of black workers who came to Boston in the years before the Civil War and an analysis of their birthplaces and the birthplaces of their children suggests that by the 1850s a travel circuit had developed. For East Coast black migrants, this circuit included Philadelphia, New York City, Providence, New Bedford, and Boston. Often a black worker was drawn from one of these cities to another by favorable reports from a friend who had gone before. Washington Perkins completed the route from the Southeast through Philadelphia and New York City to Boston by the early 1850s.

He came at the urging of a Philadelphia acquaintance then living in Boston. Later, both migrants persuaded James Weed, then in Philadelphia, to move to Boston. Thus when Weed arrived, he found friends who helped him get a job and boarded him for six months while he got settled.[18] Such acquaintances were extremely important in the adaptive process for black migrants in antebellum Boston.

Although those without contacts in the community found the transition to Boston life more difficult, even they usually could find a low-cost room to rent in a black household. One unskilled migrant from Virginia who had no such contacts wandered around the city in search of shelter and work until he was befriended by a black laborer who spent a day taking him to prospective employers.[19]

Blacks, unable to support independent households, often boarded with other blacks. At times of economic crises or social disruption, migrants and nonmigrants boarded with friends and relatives. Economic pressures exacerbated by the depression of 1857 and the growing job competition from Irish immigrants increased the instances of boarding and the proportion of nonmigrants who boarded. In 1850 about one-third of black households in Boston included boarders, 70 percent of whom were migrants. Ten years later, although the percentage of households taking in boarders had risen to 40 percent, the proportion of boarders who were migrants had fallen to 60 percent. Migrants continued to board in large numbers, but they were joined by increasing numbers of Massachusetts-born blacks, who also faced substantial economic difficulties.

The decrease in the proportion of boarders who were migrants may also have been affected by the increase in the proportion of black migrants coming from the South by 1860. Southern-born migrants were more likely than northern ones to be skilled workers. Many of them entered Boston with skills such as carpentry, blacksmithing, or tailoring, and could maintain independent residences. Because boarding was most important to those with the fewest financial resources, southern-born migrants tended to board less frequently than other migrants, and their increased presence among migrants lowered the percentage of migrants who boarded. It also masked the actual rise in boarding by 1860 for northern-born migrants, who, like their Massachusetts-born counterparts, boarded in partial reaction to growing economic pressure.

The proportion of black households in Boston with boarders in 1850 and 1860 appears to be high when compared to non-black households in other cities. In 1855 only 20 to 25 percent of all native-born white households and 13 to 15 percent of all Irish households took in boarders in Buffalo.[20] For the same period in Hudson Valley communities, the rate of boarding was only 17 to 22 percent.[21] Although some nineteenth-century reformers feared that the presence of outsiders would lead to "incipient family disorganization [and] a helter-skelter piling of individuals upon one another without regard for privacy," this was not a problem for blacks.[22] The augmented family had, by the mid-nineteenth century, become common in black households. In part this may reflect African tradition as well as an adaptation to the conditions of African American life.[23] Thus it is not surprising that boarding was an important means of migrant adjustment to pre–Civil War Boston.

Hosts introduced boarders to employment opportunities, to the church, and to friends. John Porter of Virginia came to Boston in the late 1840s without skills or employment. In 1850 he was boarding with the Gardner family, who introduced him to the Twelfth Baptist Church. He also found work in a clothing store owned by Coffin Pitts, a member of that church. Porter was active with the Boston Vigilance Committee, a group established by black and white abolitionists to aid fugitive slaves. In this venture he joined the Gardners, their neighbor Pitts, and other church members. For Porter, as for other migrant boarders, the host family provided entry into the activities of the black community.[24]

The host family also eased the fears and loneliness of the newcomer in a strange environment. For the 60 percent of migrants who were single adults, boarding was an ideal arrangement. They needed little living space, meals were often included, and with the help of the host family a successful adjustment could be made to the city. About half of the migrant boarders were single men. For many, especially for seamen and dock laborers, the black-operated boardinghouses in the North End provided even more than food and shelter. These boardinghouses were small communities, offering fellowship in card games and friendly conversation.

Joseph Green and Frank Hamilton lived in the same boardinghouse in the North End. They became friends when they discovered their mutual interest in music. At a church meeting in the late 1850s, they met Thomas Plotner, a musician who had recently arrived from New York City. The three soon formed a musical trio, and for the next few years they played in various boardinghouses in the evenings. They were only part-time musicians, playing mainly for their own enjoyment, but they were apparently quite popular in the North End. In this way, Plotner was introduced to the boardinghouse society. Soon he became a boarder himself, and lasting friendships were formed. When blacks enlisted in the Union army during the Civil War, the trio volunteered together. They served together in the black Fifty-fourth Massachusetts Regiment until Green died of "fever" and Plotner was killed at the Battle of Fort Wagner, leaving Hamilton as the lone survivor.[25]

Friendships formed among boarders meant that each could be called upon for help by fellows in need. John Tidd was a regular tenant in Arthur Jones's North End seamen's boardinghouse during the 1830s. In 1834 Tidd was jailed in New Orleans and was in danger of being illegally sold into slavery. He smuggled a letter to Boston asking for aid from Jones and other boardinghouse residents. Tidd's friends convinced the Massachusetts authorities to intercede on Tidd's behalf.[26] Boardinghouse residents often acted together to register protest or to aid one of their members. Boardinghouse groups were prominent in several fugitive-slave rescues. Thus the boardinghouse was a place where migrants mixed with natives, shared mutual concerns, and participated in group action.

Single women were more likely to board with families than in large boardinghouses. Nineteenth-century social customs, which dictated greater supervision for women than for men, meant that it was common for a young woman or teenage girl without parents to board with a family. Susan Hall came to Boston as a teenager in the early 1850s. Although she moved frequently in the late years of the decade, her first few years were spent at the home of Lydia Potter, who lived on Phillips Street on Beacon Hill. In exchange for work in the household, this arrangement provided both food and shelter—and a friend, as Sara Potter, Lydia's daughter, was about Susan's age. Through Sara, Susan was introduced to the world of Boston's black teenagers. She also was warned against becoming too friendly with the black sailors and dock laborers of the North End. For migrants like Susan, boarding provided the necessities of life, friendship, social contacts, and parental protection.[27]

For migrant black women, work opportunities were limited. Many provided services for their host families to help defray their living expenses. Such work could support some female boarders, but others were forced to look for work in the white community. Domestic service was important for black women. Almost all black women who worked outside their homes were domestics for white families. This was sometimes demeaning and always difficult work, but it was generally stable employment. Many jobs held by black men were seasonal. Dock laborers were idle during much of the winter when the harbor froze over, and seamen often were forced to leave their families to ship in warmer waters. During these periods the steady salary of domestic service often sustained the household. A host family with contacts among the city's wealthy whites was a valuable resource indeed for boarding families as for single women seeking domestic work.

As the single most important institution in the free black community, the church was also one of the most important agencies of adaptation for black migrants. It was common for boarders to attend church with their host families. Because many of the most desirable jobs for blacks were in black-owned businesses, the church was a particularly good place to make contacts. Black businessmen, such as Peter Howard and Lewis Hayden, hired blacks whenever possible, and they could usually be found at the church services. At church a migrant also could find friends. Single men often met their future wives at church, and, for some young women, it was often the only acceptable place to socialize with men. Although the Potter family would not allow their daughter Sara or their young tenant Susan to see single men in the North End, both noted that they could always associate with these men in church.[28]

For recent arrivals, the church provided both a means for entering black society and a continuity with their previous experience. There were great similarities between Boston's black churches and churches in other black communities. Black churches in Boston, Cleveland, Detroit, Philadelphia, Baltimore, and other cities were social, political, and cultural centers as well as spiritual institutions. Sermons in Hartford, New York City, or Boston were usually based on Old Testament lessons, interpreted for contemporary significance with a message to sustain oppressed people. The style of preaching was familiar to blacks no matter where they lived. The preacher built to an emotional crescendo, and the entire congregation responded both verbally and physically, finding at least temporary relief from the common pressures of black life. Religious music was an important part of any black church experience. The songs were the same and the singing style varied little from one urban church to another. The black churches of Boston seemed entirely familiar to migrants and made a strange city seem less foreign.

The black church also provided the political base that supported social protest and activist movements. The church, almost entirely responsible to the community, was generally the black institution most in-dependent of white society. It sheltered civil-rights groups, antislavery organizations, and various agencies of social reform. When William Lloyd Garrison and other abolitionists could find no other platform in Boston, the African Baptist Church provided the meeting place. It was here in 1832 that the New England Anti-Slavery Society was formed. Throughout the antebellum period, temperance groups and fugitive slave–aid groups shared the church with social and cultural groups such as the African Society, a mutual aid society, the black Masons, and a va-riety of musical and drama groups.[29]

Often newcomers found that these groups offered opportunities to make friends and become part of community life. For those interested in music, there were various choral groups, such as the Baptist Singing So-ciety and the Attucks Glee Club. The Garrison Juvenile Choir was one of a number of musical groups in which children could learn to read music and meet others their age. Migrants not only joined these groups but often became their leaders. Francis Allen of New York was the di-rector of one of the juvenile choirs, and Nate Taylor of Virginia joined a drama group at the African Baptist Church and became one of its most impressive performers.[30]

Practice sessions and periodic concerts given in churches by small bands and orchestras provided opportunities for migrants who played instruments to meet other musicians. Walter Thomas, an unskilled worker, was new to Boston in the 1830s. At Sunday service he met some people who learned that he played the saxophone and was en-couraged to join a small band at the church. Thomas found enjoyment and companionship as a member of the band; he also met Peter Howard, a prominent barber, who provided him with employment.[31]

Once in Boston, black migrants found informal community insti-tutions that enabled them to make friends, find shelter and employment, and trace friends and relatives already in the city. In the nineteenth-century black community, as in the contemporary black community, local black-owned shops were important forums for discussion and the exchange of useful political and social information. Peter Howard's bar-bershop, for example, was a gathering place for all segments of black society. The conversations at Howard's shop were often the only form of political education available to barely literate members of the black community. J. J. Smith's barbershop was a frequent gathering place for antislavery forces. At Smith's, Charles Sumner, Massachusetts' ardent antislavery senator, was often found engaged in earnest debate with blacks. In these places, one could buy a ticket to community events, borrow money, or hear the latest gossip.[32] Henry Tillman, a seaman who migrated to Boston before the Civil War, remembered the "good" conversations he had in the boardinghouses and "colored shops." In these discussions he was convinced to join the Fifty-fourth Colored Infantry from Massachusetts.[33] One member of the Fifty-fourth recalled a celebration at one black barbershop after a group of the shop's regulars enlisted together then dropped by the shop to say goodbye. A few got haircuts, but most "just got drunk."[34] These shops and stores, like the church and the boardinghouse, were important centers that introduced the newcomer to the community.

Probably the most noteworthy aid to black migrants was provided for escaped slaves who made their way to Boston on the Underground Railroad. Often the aid was provided informally by individuals rather than formally by organized groups. Informal efforts were especially important before the 1830s. During these early years, individual blacks assumed responsibility for the protection of slaves in danger of being returned to the South. In 1827 John and Sophia Robinson were convicted of withholding a five-year-old slave, Elizabeth, from her white guardian, whom they feared would return her to slavery. The Robinsons, who were part of no organized antislavery organization, received a sentence of four months in jail. Other blacks came to the aid of this child, who was never recovered but "disappeared into the black community."[35]

Although individual action never ended, beginning in the 1830s, group action became important in the protection and aid of fugitives. When George Latimer, a fugitive from Virginia, was captured in Boston in 1842, the black response was more organized. One group tried unsuccessfully to rescue Latimer. Protest signs were printed denouncing the police as "human kidnappers," and other blacks joined white abolitionists' legal efforts to secure Latimer's freedom. Blacks called protest meetings in the African Baptist Church, participated in the printing of a protest journal, and joined in gathering 64,526 signatures on a 150-pound petition calling for Latimer's freedom. Finally blacks raised enough money to purchase Latimer's freedom. Black and white abolitionists then worked to pressure the Massachusetts legislature into passing the Personal Liberty Act of 1843, which forbade state officials or facilities from being used in the apprehension of fugitive slaves.[36]

In 1845 blacks formed the Freedom Association to protect and aid fugitives. Although fugitive rescues were the most exciting phase of its work, the group also provided food, clothing, shelter, and, for those fugitives who remained in the city, jobs. Whites joined blacks in 1846 to establish an interracial organization called the Boston Committee of Vigilance. This new group provided every conceivable form of aid and service to fugitives. White members usually provided the financial resources that the black community lacked; blacks generally provided goods and services. Black clothiers provided clothes; individual households provided food and shelter; John Rock, a black physician, provided medical services; and Robert Morris, a black attorney, provided legal aid.[37]

The job of protecting and aiding fugitives was one not limited to native blacks. Migrants, even relatively new migrants, shared in this exciting, sometimes dangerous work. Rock was a migrant from Philadelphia, and Lewis Hayden, militant abolitionist, was not only a migrant but an ex-slave. David Walker, Boston's most famous black abolitionist before 1830 and author of *David Walker's Appeal,* a militant call for slave uprising, had come to the city from North Carolina.

Southern migrants had conspicuously active roles in Boston abolitionist groups.[38] Many of them, such as the Reverend Leonard Grimes, minister of Boston's Twelfth Baptist Church, had seen slavery firsthand. Grimes, originally from Washington, D.C., had not been a slave but had observed slavery while employed by a slave trader in the South. Later, remembering this experience, Grimes opened the doors of his church to runaways. The Twelfth Baptist soon became known as the "fugitive slave church."[39]

Of course, many southern migrants had been slaves themselves. Because of them the abolitionist activism in Boston and the efforts to protect fugitives took on special personal meaning. Migrants, ex-slave or not, played important roles in all Underground Railroad activities. Just as they were often instrumental in the adjustment of fellow migrants to Boston, they were important in aiding fugitives.

Significantly, migrants were not only participants in the social activism of Boston's black community but also in many instances its leaders. This was true for abolitionist actions, civil rights protests, and integrationist activities. Unlike the pattern established during later migrations, the migrants to mid-nineteenth century Boston did not form their own political groups. They became part of ongoing community associations, or they established associations composed of natives and migrants alike. Social activism was an important channel through which newcomers moved rapidly into community life.

The aid to fugitives represented a more organized version of the informal aid to other black migrants. The black community of antebellum Boston often was able to aid newcomers until they became independent, although it was handicapped by its limited financial resources. Many black natives and migrants never became self-sustaining and left the city, some migrating to the surrounding mill towns. A few were found in the city's workhouses or jails.

Although the lot of a migrant is seldom easy, black newcomers to nineteenth-century Boston had several advantages over some European immigrants. Blacks could speak English, and many had experience in American urban environments. Because the number of black migrants to antebellum Boston was relatively small, the facilities of the native black community were not overwhelmed and the white community was not threatened.

The mechanisms enabling these newcomers to adjust to their surroundings shed much light on the structure, function, and importance of community support for free blacks in the antebellum period. Historians have begun to understand how slave communities shielded their members from the harsh physical and psychological surroundings of the plantation, but few understand the workings or key elements of the free black community of that period. For free blacks on the move, community meant safety, aid, and companionship. It also meant psychological sanctuary from a hostile world among persons whose experiences and values, and hence concerns, were similar. Boston's black community was never monolithic, but its members were, with few exceptions, committed to the aid and support of those in need who came among them.[40]

After the Civil War and in the first quarter of the twentieth century, black migration became a major national concern. In antebellum Boston it was hardly noticed. Yet the mechanisms that helped these early black migrants adapt to their new surroundings and the motivation that moved them northward were strikingly similar. During the twentieth century, the church, boarding, and informal community institutions remained important. Then as earlier, blacks migrated in search of jobs, better living conditions, new opportunities, and a more liberal racial climate. But there were also striking differences that highlight the unique world of antebellum free blacks.

During the Great Migration, conflict often developed between newcomers and long-term residents of urban black communities. This conflict arose because of educational and cultural differences between the two groups and because the great number of migrants overtaxed the facilities of the established community. Pre–Civil War black migrants to Boston were less educated than Massachusetts-born blacks, but, because many came from northern urban areas where some education was provided, the majority were literate, at least as classified by census takers. The regional cultural differences so important during the twentieth century were only minimally important in 1850, as most black migrants to Boston had experienced northern urban living, and the number of black migrants to antebellum Boston was small.

Unlike the experience of twentieth-century black migrants, the antebellum newcomers found a Boston black community united not only by common economic condition but also by a shared antislavery effort. The community expectation was that strangers often would come in need of substantial and immediate help. It also was expected that these migrants would be poor and perhaps fugitives from slavery. The peculiar institution touched the lives of all blacks, whether through personal experience or the experience of kin or friends. The menacing presence of slavery served as a constant reminder of the precariousness of black freedom. The strengthening of fugitive-slave laws in the 1850s made even free blacks vulnerable to slave catchers and kidnappers. A black person without some access to a secure black community was often endangered. With the abolition of slavery, one important reason for the rapid absorption of migrants may have disappeared. If this is so, it may be one more significant difference between antebellum and postbellum patterns.

Until recently historians have emphasized the differences of black life, North and South. Although the differences slavery created can never be breached, important connections between black life in the North and the South should not be overlooked. The study of migration and adaption in one northern city suggests some of these connections. Viewed from the perspective of a northern black community, the tradition of cooperation so strongly emphasized in the recent literature on slave life looks quite familiar.

Black abolitionists were among the founding members of the American Anti-Slavery Society, the first national organization of its kind. This emblem, produced as a cameo by Josiah Wedgwood in 1787, became the symbol of the abolitionist movement. It emphasized the basic humanity of the slaves. (Library of Congress)

Chapter 2

Generations of Protest

Black Families and Social Reform

Antebellum Boston was a center of social reform and antislavery activity. As the home of William Lloyd Garrison and his *Liberator* and such nationally prominent reformers as Wendell Phillips and Charles Sumner, Boston had a well-deserved reputation for being one of the most liberal cities in the country. Devotion to personal freedom and human rights had, by the nineteenth century, become traditional in many fine old Boston families. The reform impulse of Brahmin families atop Beacon Hill has been well illuminated, yet an equally strong tradition of social protest and community action burning on the lower slopes has been only dimly revealed.

In the shadow of the lordly mansions at the crest of the hill was the largest concentration of Boston's black community. In this area lived some of Boston's most distinguished black leaders. For many black Bostonians, social protest was also a family tradition. This black community took pride in its contributions to America's struggle for independence, and venerated its black revolutionary war heroes. Although the Revolution had settled the question of national liberty, the struggle for racial justice continued throughout the antebellum period. In this fight against local discrimination and national slavery, generations of Boston's blacks played important roles.

The tradition of leadership in community action, organization, and protest in Boston's black society can best be illustrated by examining the activism of a number of important black families. In the eighteenth century, free black artisans and domestic slaves of prominent white Boston families were leaders in the black community. After the Massachusetts Supreme Court found slavery unconstitutional in 1783, these groups formed the middle and upper classes of Boston's black society. They were the founders of the original black organizations, and their influence extended through most of the period prior to 1830.

Most prominent of these early leaders was Prince Hall, founder of the first black Masonic lodge. Prince Hall was born in Bridgetown, Barbados, British West Indies, on 12 September 1748, the son of a white English leather worker and a free woman of African and French descent. At the age of seventeen, Hall worked his way on a ship to Boston where he found employment as a leather worker. By the 1780s he had become a property owner and a qualified voter. He married at least three times, the first before he was twenty-one and the last after his fiftieth birthday.[1]

Prince Hall, only five feet three inches tall and of slight build, taught himself to read and write, developed a strong interest in religion, and became a lay minister. Although he was of mixed ancestry and light complexion, he was concerned that no class lines be drawn within the black community on the basis of color or occupational status. He was an evangelical crusader, urging his followers forward, whether in the drive for decent education for black children and to admit blacks to the ranks of George Washington's forces or in his protest against the injustice of slavery and the discrimination suffered by black Bostonians. For a time Hall was minister to an informal black church in Cambridge, a position of considerable influence that helped make possible his leadership in community affairs.[2]

In 1784 Prince Hall and fourteen other free blacks formed the Negro Masonic Order, a fraternal organization chartered by the English Masonic Order.[3] By 1809 the African Lodge (later known as the Prince Hall Lodge) had become an important part of black social and economic life, drawing members from various economic classes. Its education and community service programs complemented those of the African Church and the African Society, a mutual aid and relief society providing needed services to the black community, and its leadership interlocked with that of other black institutions.

The African Masonic Lodge was an early forum for the black community's condemnation of slavery and racial discrimination in the United States. Prince Hall was one of the first abolitionists in Boston's black community and a leader in the early movement for black educational institutions. His orations on the evils of slavery were well known among blacks as was his condemnation of the injustice and discrimination blacks faced daily. On 24 June 1797, he issued to the African Lodge a stinging attack on "the iron yoke of slavery . . . and the daily insults [met] in the streets of Boston" by the black citizens. He hailed the black revolution in Haiti, denouncing the oppression of blacks in his home city: "We may truly be said to carry our lives in our hands, and the arrows of death are flying about our heads. Helpless women have their clothes torn from their backs . . . by a mob or horde of shameless, low-lived, envious, spiteful persons . . . without provocation, twenty or thirty cowards have fallen upon one man. O, the patience of the blacks."[4]

Prince Hall was typical of early black leaders, who were affiliated with many black organizations, based in the church, and concerned less with the integration of blacks into white society, largely because this seemed impossible, than with the development of black institutions. His son Primus Hall was also actively involved in black community affairs.

As a boy at the time of the revolutionary war, Primus Hall was the body servant of Colonel Pickering of Massachusetts. In 1798 he assisted his father in organizing the African School, which met for a time in his home. Black children did not generally attend public schools in Boston at that time because of discrimination, mistreatment, and ridicule by white students and teachers. Blacks under the leadership of the Halls had petitioned the city in 1787 for the establishment of a separate black school. When their petition was denied, the African School was founded as a private institution sponsored by the black community. It was not financed by public funds until 1820.[5] Primus Hall was also one of the founders of the first black church in Boston, the African Baptist Church. He was an important member of this group of founders but not its leader. That role was filled by another black man whose descendants were active social reformers—Thomas Paul.

In 1789 Thomas Paul, then sixteen years old, joined an informal, nondenominational group of blacks worshipping in private homes. Soon he assumed the role of "exhorter," explaining Scripture passages to the congregation.[6] By 1804 Paul, then thirty-one, was preaching to a growing number of worshipers. He returned to his native New Hampshire on 1 May 1805 to be ordained a Baptist minister. Back in Boston, he set about organizing a formal church. In July, Paul and Scipio Dalton, then members of the predominantly white First Baptist Church of Boston, sent the customary letter to the First and Second Baptist churches asking their aid in establishing a new church. On 8 August 1805, with their white brethren represented, the African Baptist Church was officially organized. The following year a meetinghouse was built to accommodate the large congregation coming to hear the black minister. On 4 December 1806, the Reverend Thomas Paul was installed as pastor.[7]

With the building of the African Meeting House on Southac Court off Belknap (now Joy Street), the black community not only had a home for its church but also a place for the African School, which promptly began classes in the basement. This church and its successors were focal points of community activity. Their organizational structures served as the basis for other organizations, and many of their leaders became community leaders, helping to train others. The African Meeting House later served as an arena for antislavery discussion. Ten years later the church itself was active in the education of black children, establishing a Sunday school that taught reading and writing in addition to Bible lessons. An independent black church provided a community-controlled base for community action.

Largely through his church ministry, Thomas Paul became an important leader. He was instrumental in the establishment of separate black religious and educational institutions, not only in Boston but also in other cities. Although maintaining cordial relations with white Baptists, he left no doubt that his was a black church and that his services were reserved largely for the black community.

By 1819 the African Baptist Church was an established institution with 103 members. It had extended its aid and influence to black communities in other cities, sending its pastor in the summer of 1808 to New York City to establish what later became the Abyssinian Baptist Church, twentieth-century home of Adam Clayton Powell. Paul also conducted revival tours for the Baptist Missionary Society, including at least one successful trip to Haiti. Filling the pulpit during his absences were ministers from the Home Mission Society and two young men from the church who had been called to preach, Eli Ball and Nathaniel Paul, Thomas Paul's son.[8]

The Paul family was not only actively involved in the church but also in reform movements. Thomas Paul's brothers were ministers and antislavery activists. His younger brother, Nathaniel, traveled internationally as an antislavery speaker and later became an agent for Wilberforce, a Canadian settlement for fugitive slaves. His brother Benjamin, a Baptist Preacher in New York state, was an abolitionist and a member of the African Dorcas Association, which provided clothing to poor black children to enable them to attend school. His oldest son, Thomas Paul, Jr., became apprentice to William Lloyd Garrison, working on the *Liberator* and in the crusade against slavery and was the first black graduate of Dartmouth College. In the late 1840s and 1850s, he was schoolteacher and headmaster of the all-black Smith School, formerly the African School.[9]

Susan Paul, Thomas Paul's daughter, was one of the most distinguished female reformers in Boston in the antebellum period. Deeply involved in the antislavery movement as a life member of the Massachusetts Anti-Slavery Society, she was chosen in 1838 as one of the vice-presidents for the second annual Anti-Slavery Convention of American Women held in Philadelphia. Untiring in her efforts in the cause of abolition and social justice, she recruited a Garrison Junior Choir (a regular attraction at antislavery gatherings), served as secretary to Boston's all-black temperance organization, and was active in the regional black temperance group formed in 1835.[10] Her concern about injustices suffered by her race was extended to those suffered by her sex. Although she spoke in behalf of the women's rights movement, for her, as for many black women, the cause of racial justice won her first allegiance. She was quick to realize the connection between the existence of slavery and the persistence of racial discrimination toward free blacks. Writing to Garrison in 1834, she made clear her belief that the latter condition was inextricably bound to the former.[11]

This pattern of family involvement in community affairs over generations may be seen in many other black Boston families. Perhaps as active as Thomas Paul in early community organizations was Scipio Dalton, who was connected with virtually every early Boston black institution. He was one of the founders of the African Society, an organizer with Thomas Paul of the African Baptist Church, founder of the African School, and active in the African Masonic Lodge.[12]

Scipio Dalton's son, Thomas, also took part in community affairs. Thomas Dalton worked at various times as a bootblack, clothing-store owner, and waiter. His identification with black community action was just as varied. He was the first president of the Massachusetts General Colored Association, an all-black antislavery society that predated Garrison, and a leader of the movement resulting in its merger in 1833 with the New England Anti-Slavery Society. He served as treasurer of the Boston Mutual Lyceum, a black cultural and educational society. Joining the African Lodge in 1825, he became senior warden in 1827, was co-secretary with David Walker, author of *Walker's Appeal,* and remained an active member until at least 1876, when he was eighty-three years old.[13]

There were two distinct phases of black community organization and leadership in Boston during the antebellum period. The first was characterized by the establishment and development of institutions and organizations whose leaders were based almost entirely in the black community. But in the 1830s a new kind of black leadership arose. The appearance of William Lloyd Garrison and his antislavery society in the early 1830s profoundly affected the nature of black leadership. No longer did black leaders work solely with blacks; they often broadened their roles to include liaisons with the white community. It is significant that after 1830 black leaders placed greater emphasis on the integration of blacks into the city's total society. The commitment of white abolitionists to the cause of racial justice raised the hopes of black Bostonians. For the first time there were white abolitionist groups of consequence, and leadership positions in these groups were open to blacks.

Black antislavery leadership in the city welcomed the merger in 1833 of the Massachusetts General Colored Association and the New England Anti-Slavery Society. Because this merger did not involve white displacement of black leadership, those who had originated the all-black Massachusetts General Colored Association became active leaders in the New England Anti-Slavery Society.[14]

Sometimes this shift in emphasis from all-black to integrated organizations could be traced through two or more generations of black leadership. William G. Nell was a steward aboard the *General Gadsden,* sailing out of Charleston, South Carolina, during the War of 1812. He was captured with the ship's crew by British forces and spent time in a British brig as a prisoner. When he regained his freedom, Nell traveled to Boston. By 1817 he was working as a tailor and had become a member of the black community. He married Louisa, a black woman from Brookline, Massachusetts, and became active in the African Baptist Church and an associate of David Walker.[15] In 1826 Nell was one of the founders of the Massachusetts General Colored Association. He subsequently became vice-president, and was known in the black community as a "race leader." William Nell was active as a black leader mainly prior to 1830, and was chiefly concerned with separate black action and organization. By contrast his son, William Cooper Nell, assumed a leading role after 1830 and pursued integrationist ends and means.[16]

William Cooper Nell was born in 1817 on Beacon Hill. He attended the segregated Smith School in the basement of the African Meeting House. An excellent student, he stood with a number of white students as eligible to receive the Franklin Medal, awarded by the school committee for scholastic achievement. Because of his color he was denied the medal and was not invited to a special dinner honoring the medal winners. He was allowed to attend not as honored guest, but as a waiter. This humiliation profoundly affected Nell's decision to dedicate his life to the elimination of all racial barriers.[17]

Some measure of the psychological effect of this kind of discrimination is reflected in Nell's own comments. As a boy of fourteen in Lyman Beecher's church in 1831, he was asked by his Sunday school teacher about his plans for adulthood. Nell replied, "What is the use of my trying to be somebody? I can never be anything but a nigger anyway."[18] It would seem that a boy of Nell's family background and scholastic achievement might have had more hope and a better self-image. That he did not may indicate the extent to which prejudice had robbed him of self-esteem and the usual middle-class aspirations.

Despite his early doubts, William Cooper Nell grew up to be "somebody" in Boston's black community. At the age of sixteen he was secretary of the Juvenile Garrison Independent Society, a group of black youths organized for education, community service, and self-help. He showed exceptional ability as a speaker and writer. In October 1833 Nell's address at the second anniversary of the Juvenile Garrison Independent Society was so inspiring that it was printed in the *New England Telegraph*. In 1834 Nell was featured in an oratorical exhibition for the antislavery cause.[19]

Although Nell was modest and unassuming, Garrison recognized his talents when he worked as an errand boy for the *Liberator*. Against substantial opposition, Garrison made Nell an apprentice in the *Liberator* office when "no colored boy could be apprenticed to any trade in any shop where white men worked." The white community was sure that no "nigger could learn the art of printing and it was held to be evidence of [Garrison's] arrogant folly to try the experiment."[20]

William Cooper Nell, unlike his father, worked side by side with many dedicated whites, seeking equal opportunity for blacks. As a result of his experience, Nell became an ardent integrationist, leading the fight for the integration of Boston's public schools, urging the abolition of all-black organizations such as the Massachusetts General Colored Association, and going so far as to encourage the abolition of black churches. In 1843 he attended the National Negro Convention held in Buffalo, New York. Admitting that the organization had been of substantial value to blacks, he nevertheless believed that it should not remain an exclusively black organization. He asserted that racially separate groups had once been valuable but that time had passed. Nell urged blacks to abandon "all separate action" and become "part and parcel of the general community."[21]

Nell's emphasis upon integration, however, did not prevent his support of separate black organizations when they performed services for the black community that were neglected by integrated groups. When the Freedom Association, a black group, was founded in 1842 to protect fugitive slaves, Nell became an active member. The stated purpose of the Freedom Association was to provide fugitives with food, clothing, shelter, and other aid necessary to assure their freedom. The activities of the association were clearly illegal and at times violent, yet members saw the association as legitimate. Funds for the operation of the Freedom Association came from black contributions. The group sponsored juvenile music concerts, charging a small admission, and substantial funds were collected through black churches.[22] Nell remained a member of the Freedom Association until 1846 when the Committee of Vigilance, an integrated group, was organized for the same purpose.

Nell clearly placed the good of the black community ahead of his disapproval of separate black action. He favored integrated action because he believed it to be most effective and beneficial. There can be little doubt that one important source of his integrationist zeal stemmed from his close association with Garrison and other white abolitionists. He hoped that if blacks overcame legal and extralegal segregation, they would be able to share in American opportunities. He also believed that separate black organizations could only serve to perpetuate racial prejudice.

The pattern of family involvement over generations was widespread, not only among black leaders but more generally among black Bostonians. If one member of a family was involved in civil rights, antislavery, or general social reform, other family members were likely to take part.

John Bailey of Charlestown was owner of a gymnasium on Franklin Street in Boston and for a time was boxing master at Harvard University. He was active in the drive to integrate Boston's public schools and with the aid of Peter Randolph, also of Charlestown, organized the blacks of that area to support the struggle. He was one of a number of blacks who organized petition drives in Boston and the vicinity, which by 1855 had become instrumental in the integration of Boston schools.[23]

John Bailey's father was Peter Bailey, a founder of the African Society in 1796. He was one of Boston's earliest active black community members and a close associate of Prince Hall. In 1855 Bailey's daughter, Julia, was one of the black children who honored William Cooper Nell, leader of the fight for school integration, at a testimonial dinner. His wife was an active member of the Boston Female Anti-Slavery Society. For the Baileys community action and antislavery work was a family project.[24]

The Lewis family was another example of community involvement as a family heritage. Thomas Lewis had been one of the original officers of the African Society. He was a member of the First Baptist Church of Boston until 1805, when Thomas Paul and Scipio Dalton led him and a number of other blacks in the establishment of the African Baptist Church. Thomas Lewis was also a member of the African Masonic Lodge and a follower of Prince Hall in the campaign for improved education for black children. His son, Walker Lewis, was a prominent black abolitionist who in 1826 helped found the Massachusetts General Colored Association. Walker Lewis, a hairdresser, was a militant abolitionist and close associate of David Walker.[25]

Simpson H. Lewis, Walker's son, was born in Boston in 1814. He worked for a short time as a laborer before opening his own clothing shop in 1837. By 1846 he had married Caroline Butler from Rhode Island, a woman eight years his junior, and was the father of Frederick Lewis, born that year. The Lewises were active in various community projects, including attempts to obtain better jobs for blacks, the integration of Boston's public schools, and sheltering and aiding fugitive slaves in conjunction with the Boston Committee of Vigilance. They supported Garrison without sharing his ambivalence toward political action. They were willing to campaign, as a family, for the Liberty and Republican parties, and Simpson was a registered voter. The Lewis family was usually well represented at community functions. At the testimonial for

Nell, for example, Simpson was vice-president, Caroline was a committee member and sang the floral invocation, and Frederick, then nine years old, delivered an address praising Nell as a "champion of equal school rights."[26]

It is significant that later generations of black community leaders and activists often were much more militant in their approach to civil protest. Until late in the antebellum period, most protest was within the bounds of law and civility, using petitions to express grievances. Whereas early blacks were willing to issue protests and were generally concerned with the establishment of black community institutions and organizations, later generations, through their participation in the Freedom Association and the Boston Committee of Vigilance were willing to take more direct, often illegal, action to protest racial injustice or aid fugitive slaves. The Nell and the Lewis families serve as examples of this pattern. Even more striking were the activities of the Snowdens.

Samuel Snowden was a Methodist minister who became pastor of the African Methodist Episcopal Church on May Street in Boston in the 1830s. He was elected as a counselor to the New England Anti-Slavery Society and in 1831 was a member of the Boston committee attending the first annual Convention of Free People of Color, a national gathering of blacks urging united black action against slavery and discrimination. The Reverend Samuel Snowden, who was very active in the anti-slavery movement, was mainly involved in the more moderate aspects of the struggle characteristic of the movement before 1850.[27]

In the 1850s the growing militancy accelerated after the new fugitive slave law convinced blacks that they would not receive just consideration from the federal government. Boston's blacks of all classes joined to protect fugitive slaves, and among the younger reformers willing to violate the law were Samuel Snowden's daughters, Isabella and Holmes. Both women worked with the Committee of Vigilance, providing direct assistance to fugitive slaves in Boston.[28] Nor did Snowden's two sons confine themselves to moderate activity. In 1851, when they were arrested in Boston for carrying guns, they justified their action as a necessary defense against slave kidnappers operating under the fugitive slave law.[29]

During the antebellum period, Boston's black community had developed strong institutions that provided a base for community action. In keeping with the reform tradition of the city, many blacks played active roles in the struggle for both local and national rights and in the fight against slavery. Thus the tradition of reform in Boston was not limited to white Bostonians. Generations of blacks had been deeply involved in social protest. The character of their protests changed with differing circumstances and new opportunities. The possibility of interracial action caused a shift after 1830 toward movements for integration. By the 1850s frustration created by federal actions, the passage of the Fugitive Slave Law of 1850, the return of fugitives to slavery, and the Dred Scott decision heightened the growing militancy of the black community and its leaders.

The families presented here are representative of the reform tradition so important among antebellum black Bostonians. Boston's reputation as a center for social reform before the Civil War rested not only on the efforts of well-known white families on Beacon Hill but also on the traditional involvement of black families who lived, then and in the pages of history, in the shadow of Beacon Hill.

Chas T. Webber   The Underground Railroad

Escape from slavery was not easy, especially for family groups. The very young and the very old were less likely to be successful than young adults. Women found escape more difficult because they were often charged with the care of their children. (Library of Congress)

Chapter 3

Links to Bondage

Free Blacks and the Underground Railroad

The Underground Railroad was one of the most romanticized aspects of antebellum reform. Dramatic tales were perpetuated by the abolitionists themselves and, since the end of the nineteenth century, by historians such as Wilbur H. Siebert, who wrote about the adventures of the dedicated men and women who organized the extensive network for slave rescue. Eventually these stories were incorporated into American mythology, featuring selfless white heroes and some heroines who guided grateful but relatively passive fugitives to safety. Even today in many small eastern and midwestern towns, local history enthusiasts relate stories of the Underground Railroad and identify community buildings believed to have been stations in which fugitives were hidden.[1]

In the first half of the twentieth century, few historians acknowledged a significant role for African Americans in the Underground Railroad or abolitionist reform movement. They drew on the self-serving accounts of white abolitionists who often exaggerated and romanticized the role of formal antislavery organizations and their white leadership. Historians also were influenced by the views of the proslavery southern press, which refused to acknowledge the participation of blacks in the antislavery movement except as the dupes of unscrupulous white radicals. These accounts were generally accepted by a twentieth-century reading public disposed to seeing black people as historically passive.[2]

Carter G. Woodson, Charles Wesley, and other black historians were among the first twentieth-century scholars to acknowledge African

Americans as major actors in the Underground Railroad and antislavery reform. Their work during the first half of the century, that of Herbert Aptheker in 1941, and Leon Litwack's survey of northern free blacks in 1961 set the stage for a major reinterpretation of the Underground Railroad and a comprehensive study of blacks in the antislavery movement.[3]

In 1967 Larry Gara challenged conventional views of the Underground Railroad with his study *Liberty Line: The Legend of the Underground Railroad*. Gara asserted that the role of white abolitionists and formal antislavery organizations had been greatly exaggerated and mustered formidable evidence to show that fugitives themselves were largely responsible for planning and executing escapes, sometimes with the assistance of local blacks or friendly whites. Organized abolitionist groups came into contact with runaways mainly after they reached the relative safety of the North. The actions of these strong-minded and self-reliant runaways were documented in the records of William Still and other black abolitionists. The Underground Railroad, Gara argued, was not as organized as historians believed, and white reformers were far more marginal than had been assumed.[4]

Gara's treatment of black participation in the Underground Railroad provided the context for Benjamin Quarles's study of African Americans in antislavery reform. Quarles, in his classic study *Black Abolitionists,* detailed in vivid and dramatic passages the story of black abolitionists as movement leaders, as antislavery speakers, and as conductors on the Underground Railroad. In doing so he entered the names of countless black activists into the historical record. The contributions of secondary leaders such as James McCune Smith, Charles B. Ray, Charlotte Forten, and George T. Downing were set beside those of Frederick Douglass and Martin Delany. Always mindful of the grass-roots nature of the black commitment to antislavery, Quarles reiterated Gara's admonition that contrary to the myth, many abolitionist activities were carried out by people who were not themselves formal members of the movement, and that most of these nonaffiliated abolitionists were black.

Quarles and others made clear the African American contribution to the antislavery movement. Yet the relationships and the depth of feeling linking slaves in the South to free blacks of the North remain more obscure.[5] Several historians have doubted the significance of that feeling, arguing that free blacks often separated themselves from slaves and saw freedom as a badge of superior status. One scholar has even suggested that the free blacks of the North were so immersed in the struggle to improve their own lives that they had no time and little interest in underground abolitionist activity. "Why after all, should a Northern black be an active abolitionist?" historian Frederick Cooper asked. "Whatever feelings he had for his brethren in bonds, blacks in Northern cities still had to live their daily lives . . . The idea of self-help was of far more relevance to their lives than the crusade against slavery."[6]

Cooper was correct to see self-help as a central concern for free black people, but he drew too sharp a distinction between self-help and antislavery, assuming that commitment to one lessened involvement in the other. In doing so he failed to appreciate the bond between slaves and free blacks, a bond that illustrated the African American community's propensity for collective self-help. Although there were frictions within that community, which on occasion led to political and social fractures, there were also bonds of blood, of culture, of common experience, and of a common world view that recognized the injustice of American racial inequality. These provided a strong magnet that drew blacks toward one another for fellowship and safety. These bonds help to explain the central role that blacks played as participants and leaders in the underground railroad and the abolitionist movement.

This chapter explores the bonds of family and fellowship that connected ordinary black people on both sides of the Mason-Dixon line and that provided the foundation for grass-roots black abolition. It focuses especially on the interregional lines of communication and the individual and collective aid provided to fugitives by those without ties to abolitionist organizations. Although there were many influential black leaders who were important in organized efforts to free slaves and to protect fugitives, there were thousands more who were not well known but whose actions were significant to the struggle for freedom.

The fight against slavery was every black person's fight, a fact acknowledged among African Americans. In 1855 Frederick Douglass spoke of the responsibility of all free people of color to speak and act on their own behalf and on behalf of the slaves. African Americans must not depend upon others to win justice and freedom for them. "Our elevation as a race is almost wholly dependent upon our own exertions," he said.[7] Daniel A. Payne, bishop of the African Methodist Episcopal Church in the 1850s, agreed that the oppression of slaves weighed heavily on, "every man who has a drop of African blood in his veins."[8]

The actions of Thomas Watson, a black sailor, illustrate the role played by many who never held membership in a formal antislavery group nor spoke publicly on behalf of the movement but who served the cause of freedom for very personal reasons. He was a militant abolitionist who believed that any delay in freedom was intolerable. For Watson slavery was no abstract evil, he had been a slave for almost thirty years in Virginia before he escaped in 1835, leaving behind a wife and three children. For Watson their freedom was the very essence of the abolitionist cause.[9]

Although he had much in common with other abolitionists who believed in immediate emancipation, Watson's motivation was very different from that of William Lloyd Garrison, Lewis Tappan, or Theodore Dwight Weld. These men came to abolition out of principle and philanthropic commitment. For them the antislavery cause was a benevolent and evangelical mission bound to an array of religious concerns. They opposed a broad range of sins—slavery, violence of any kind, gambling, and the drinking of alcohol. For them slavery was the worst example of a general evil that robbed humans of their free will.[10]

Black abolitionists also saw slavery as the manifestation of a far-reaching evil. Bishop Payne opposed the institution "not because it enslaves the black man, but because it enslaves man." Others supported abolition not only because it "was designed for the liberation of the slave" but also because it served to stimulate the principles of democracy and to ensure "the preservation of American liberty itself."[11] Many blacks, however, expressed their opposition to slavery in less cosmic terms. For Watson the issue was more straightforward. Although he vehemently hated slavery, he did not associate its evil with the broad moral concerns of more genteel reformers. Watson drank, he gambled, and he was not known for his commitment to pacifism. African Americans were committed to the abstract principles of liberty and freedom, but for them the fight against slavery also took on a more personal significance.

On the eve of the Civil War there were more than four million slaves in the United States and fewer than half a million free blacks. By midcentury almost all America's slaves were held in the South. The institution had existed in all colonies before the Revolution and nationwide during the first years of independence, but it was less economically powerful in the North. Northern slaveholders could not resist the reforms of the early nineteenth century, which abolished slavery outright or set it on the road to evolutionary extinction. Still, throughout most of the antebellum period there were a few slaves in the northern states. In New York and New Jersey, for example, where emancipation came gradually during the antebellum period, the last slaves were formally set free under the Thirteenth Amendment in 1865. After 1830, however, there were very few northern slaves. By that time slavery was an institution peculiar to the South.[12]

Despite slavery's early demise above the Mason-Dixon line, most northern blacks knew slavery either directly or indirectly. Many who had not lived in the South were tied to slavery through the experiences of parents who had been enslaved in the North before slavery was abolished there. Albert Cozzens of Providence never knew slavery personally. He was born free in a state that had abolished the institution a generation before his birth. Yet Albert felt a personal link to slavery through the experience of his father, Richard Cozzens, and his mother, Julia, both of whom had been slaves in Rhode Island in the late eighteenth century.[13]

Other northern blacks were southern migrants. Many, like Watson, had fled slavery, leaving friends and family behind. In midwestern cities such as Cincinnati and Detroit, well over half the black population was southern born by the mid-nineteenth century. Even in New England cities such as Boston, more distant from the South with far smaller southern-born black populations, at least one-fifth to one-quarter of the blacks were southern by birth by the time of the Civil War.[14]

Fugitives who escaped the South were never safe from recapture no matter how long they remained free. Some fugitives remained free only a few months; others lived in the North for years, established families, and settled themselves into communities before being taken back into slavery. George Washington McQuerry escaped from Kentucky crossing the Ohio River in 1849. He met and married a free black woman and settled in a small community in Miami County, Ohio. There he and his family lived for four years before his master, who had learned of his whereabouts, had him arrested by the federal marshal. Despite the attempts of Ohio blacks and abolitionist forces to prevent it, McQuerry was finally returned to slavery in Kentucky.[15]

Nor were fugitives in larger cities secure. George Garnet and his family escaped from Maryland and settled in New York City where George found work as a shoemaker. The Garnets enrolled their son Henry in the African Free School, made white and black friends in the community, and lived in comparative comfort for five years before they were tracked down by slave catchers and forced into hiding. Their story was not unusual. After the passage of a stronger fugitive slave law in 1850, many blacks fled to Canada from cities such as Boston and Cincinnati, where some had lived for decades.[16]

No African American was safe from slavery. Slavery reached out from the South to threaten all black people, not only fugitives. Even legally free blacks were in danger from kidnappers selling them into slavery. Some reports indicate that the majority of blacks captured as fugitives during the 1850s were apprehended without the aid of legal authority, and thus without due process of law. One historian surveying fugitive slave captures between 1850 and 1860 estimated that in more than two of every five cases captured blacks were given no opportunity for a defense.[17]

Free African Americans were thus almost as vulnerable as fugitives. This vulnerability encouraged hundreds of rumors, making fear of being kidnapped a widespread and legitimate concern. This concern turned to anger after the Fugitive Slave Law of 1850 made the legal defense against kidnappers more difficult by denying suspected fugitives the right to a jury trial or the right to testify in their own behalf. The perceived danger was so great that several black leaders suggested that blacks carry weapons for self-defense. Members of one Boston group arrested for carrying guns on the Boston Common explained their actions by citing the need to protect themselves and other blacks from slave catchers. In New York black abolitionists such as Henry Highland Garnet and Samuel Ringold Ward armed themselves, and others advised those threatened by slave catchers to act "as they would to rid themselves of any wild beast."[18]

Reflecting the concerns of their constituents, northern black leaders and institutions regularly addressed the slavery issue. The earliest groups, such as the African Union Society begun in 1780 in Newport, Rhode Island, or the African Society formed in 1796 in Boston, were mutual-benefit societies for free blacks of the North. They provided for widows and orphans, saw to proper burials, and administered the wills of their members. They also linked the maintenance of a free society to abolition and the welfare of free blacks to that of slaves, attacking the inconsistency of slavery tolerated by a "freedom loving nation." In an "Essay on Freedom," one member of the African Society of Boston attacked slavery and the hypocrisy of a people who "love freedom themselves . . . [but who] prevent [others] from its enjoyment . . ." Whatever else the focus of these associations, they became devoted to the abolition of slavery.[19]

Even African American children were enlisted in the antislavery cause. In youth associations in several northern cities, boys and girls debated issues of racial justice and slavery and raised money for abolitionist activities. The Juvenile Garrison Independent Society, formed in Boston in the early 1830s, provided service to the local community and sponsored antislavery rallies and lectures.[20] In New York a similar youth group included in their organizational constitution a promise to work toward "the downfall of prejudice, slavery, and oppression . . ." At the New York African Free School, a group of grammar school boys resolved not to celebrate the Fourth of July until slavery was abolished. Years later Alexander Crummell, who had been part of the group, recalled that "for years our society met on that day [the Fourth of July], and the time was devoted to planning schemes for the freeing and upbuilding the race." The boys pledged that after their education they would "go South, start an insurrection and free our brethren in bondage."[21]

Young people in these groups grew up to become some of the leading black abolitionists of the 1840s and 1850s. For William Cooper Nell, Henry Highland Garnet, William H. Day, David Ruggles, and other antebellum black leaders, these groups were their training grounds for social protest. They were generally encouraged by their parents, their teachers, and other adults active in the cause. Charles C. Andrews of the New York African Free School, for example, was also a founder of the New York Society for the Manumission of Slaves. Along with the strong academic program at the school, he also taught his students about the importance of freedom.[22]

There were similar concerns among black children elsewhere. When students in Cincinnati's black schools were asked to write an essay on the question What do you think most about?, many made clear the impact of slavery on their young lives. One seven year old wrote of his hope that "we get a man to get the poor slaves from bondage." A twelve year old claimed to speak for the children and explained that "what we are studying for is to get the yoke of slavery broke and the chains parted asunder and slaveholding cease for ever."[23]

Like their elders, many of these young people spoke from experience and out of concern for friends and relatives held in bondage. A ten year old wrote, "I have two cousins in slavery who are entitled to their freedom." He was deeply concerned, because "they [slaveholders] talk of selling them down the river . . ." He asked, "If this is the case what would you do?" Another child wrote of his experiences in slavery and explained that he, his mother, and stepfather had all known bondage. Clearly, to these children slavery was no abstract evil. It was personal and was associated with the misery of loved ones. Like their parents, young blacks wondered aloud "how the Americans can call this a land of freedom where so much slavery is."[24]

The response of free blacks to the program of the American Colonization Society reflected their ties to those in slavery. Founded in 1816, the society hoped to secure private and government funding to establish a colony in West Africa and to encourage the emigration of free blacks and those slaves who might be freed. In 1822 colonizationists, with federal assistance, founded the West African colony of Liberia. Many of the early settlers were African Americans, but the vast majority of free black Americans refused to endorse the colonization plan. They especially objected to the program's failure to recognize the black commitment to remain in the United States and continue the struggle for racial justice. As one black Bostonian put it, "This being our country we have made up our minds to remain in it, and to try to make it worth living in." Free blacks believed colonization would remove the strongest advocates of abolition from the country. Additionally, the plan would allow masters to eliminate troublesome slaves by selectively transporting them to Africa, securing the institution from internal disruption.[25]

The rise of the Colored Convention movement, begun in the 1830s, was a direct response to the widely held notion among blacks that colonization posed a threat not only to the rights and progress of free blacks but also to the abolition movement. At the national level, these conventions called for continued antislavery agitation and stressed the responsibility of blacks who enjoyed the "privilege" of freedom to take a stand against slavery at every public opportunity.[26] African Americans also held state conventions at which these issues, along with state and regional concerns, were debated. In resolutions passed at the 1843 Michigan convention held in Detroit, free blacks left no doubt as to their loyalties: "Resolved, that we, the colored citizens of Michigan, be united in sentiment and action and never to consent to emigrate or be colonized from this, our native soil, while there exists one drop of African blood in bondage in the United States."[27]

There were sharp differences over the question of emigration among Ohio blacks who met in Columbus in 1849. Smarting under the racial hostility encountered by African Americans in his home city of Cincinnati, former slave John Mercer Langston expressed a willingness to "go wherever I can be free." Aware of violent attacks on blacks in cities such as Cincinnati, which in 1829, 1831, and 1841, reached major and deadly proportions, Langston believed America to be "a land which will not protect me" and argued that blacks must have a nationality "before we can become anybody."[28]

Despite his belief that blacks would achieve only limited progress in America, Langston was ready to support the majority position that colonization should not be considered "while a vestige of [American] slavery lasts . . ." Should slavery be abolished, however, he was "willing, it being optional, to draw out from the American government, and form a separate and independent one, enacting our own laws and regulations . . ." Clearly Langston's decision, and that of many others who agreed to support the majority position, was greatly influenced by their concern for the well-being of the slaves.[29]

On the local level, too, African Americans made clear their intention to work for freedom and justice for themselves and those in bondage. In cities such as New York, Philadelphia, and Boston, free blacks regularly called protest meetings to communicate their outrage and to plot strategy to deal with the evils of racial injustice. Conducted in the manner of town meetings, these gatherings were important forums for the interchange of ideas and provided a training ground for local black leadership. Black newspapers were filled with notices of community meetings called to discuss abolition, civil rights, educational issues, and general concerns of social and political reform. Even in Cincinnati, where black public protest was more restricted than it was in cities farther north or east, local community meetings were important vehicles for reinforcing the resolve and commitment of the grass-roots community that the slave must never be forgotten and the fugitive must always be protected.[30]

The information presented here supports some of the earlier analysis of the Underground Railroad. Gara was correct to see it as an informal, loosely knit activity in which organized abolitionist groups played an important but not a dominant role. As he suggested, it was staffed informally by people of good will, often black but sometimes white, most of whom had a personal connection to those enslaved.

Quarles's picture of black leadership at all levels of the formal and the informal underground is also confirmed. Cooper's notion of free blacks as remote from the lives and problems of slaves is not sustained, however. There were exceptions, but there is strong evidence that free blacks were extremely concerned about the problems of slaves, personally involved in a variety of underground efforts, and enthusiastically supportive of abolition. Yet nagging questions remain. Given the distance that separated free blacks from slave relatives and friends, how were personal relations sustained?

An answer to this question is suggested by that fact that northern free blacks were never completely insulated from slavery. Fugitives were most likely to plan and execute the initial phase of their escape on their own or with the aid of associates in the South, but for those lucky enough to reach the free states, local black communities became critical to maintaining freedom. Fugitives generally found free blacks, even strangers, willing to help. James Curry, a runaway from Person County, North Carolina, found a "colored family, with whom [he] rested for eight days" in Washington, D.C., before he pushed northward. Further along in his journey, Curry "entered a colored person's house . . . where they gave me breakfast and treated me very kindly."[31]

There was no formal declaration of involvement necessary for free blacks to become an integral part of underground activity. Sometimes participation was a matter of circumstances, being in the right place at the right time. The Fitzgeralds, for instance, were a family of free blacks living in Chester County, Pennsylvania, in the 1850s. Situated at the edge of freedom near the boundary of a slave state, Chester County had more than its share of fugitive-slave traffic, and the Fitzgerald farm became a popular stopping place for those on the run. A Fitzgerald descendent wrote, "Great-Grandfather Thomas noticed that his barn began to attract a lot of strangers." When black travelers asked to be lodged overnight in the Fitzgerald barn, Thomas always offered them a room in the house, but they never accepted. Nor did they remain for the morning breakfast that he always offered. Although the travelers never accepted the food, it was reported that often after their departure "Great-Grandfather Thomas thought one of his cows gave a quart less milk than usual."[32]

These were not organized or planned incidents but individual acts of humanity that more than any other illustrate the links between slaves and free black people. The black family in Washington, D.C., who sheltered Curry were not known to be abolitionists. Of the Fitzgeralds it was said, "They were not joiners of reform movements but they were stubborn in what they believed to be right." They believed slavery to be wrong, and like so many other scarcely known blacks "without fanfare . . . met the issue squarely when it confronted them."[33]

News about fugitives circulated in the free black communities throughout the North. There were constant rumors of their presence or stories of their travels, which kept free African Americans aware of and in touch with the plight of slaves. Kidnapping was an ever-present danger, and all blacks knew it. Thus even for those without immediate and personal concerns for specific slaves, the threat of slavery was always close at hand. The contention of one black leader in the mid-1850s that "every colored man is an abolitionist" may have been an exaggeration, but the special relations between slaves and free blacks helped to make most African Americans foot soldiers in the antislavery cause. Ultimately, African Americans agreed that "the fight against slavery is a black man's fight."[34]

White assistance was significant and usually gratefully accepted. Partly because fugitives were less likely to trust whites or to seek their help, however, such assistance was uncommon. Even the most prominent white abolitionists were not often known to fugitives by sight. The testimony of another black person was frequently required to verify their trustworthiness. When fugitive Anthony Burns was jailed in Boston in 1854, he was visited by white abolitionist lawyer Richard Henry Dana. Burns did not know Dana and gave the lawyer the impression that he was willing to return to slavery. After this first meeting, Dana described Burns as simple and "child-like." Subsequently the fugitive was visited by several members of the black community who assured him of Dana's trustworthiness. After their next meeting, Dana described Burns, quite differently, as "self-possessed, intelligent and with considerable force of mind and body." The remarkable change in Burns's demeanor was no doubt attributable to the change in Dana's status from suspicious white stranger to verified ally.[35]

Fugitive distrust of unknown white people was understandable and was sometimes well founded. There were numerous examples of betrayal at the hands of those unwilling or unable to defy federal provisions requiring the return of a runaway and promising severe punishment to those who aided fugitives. Some profited from the capture of runaways. In New York City the notorious Blackbirds, a gang of poor whites, many of them recent immigrants, earned money by delivering fugitives and sometimes even free blacks, into slavery.

Black abolitionist Henry Highland Garnet was well acquainted with the work of the Blackbirds. He was at sea when the gang, accompanied by a relative of his family's former master, broke into the family home. Henry's father escaped by jumping from a second story window into the adjacent yard. His mother also escaped and was hidden by a white grocer, a family friend. His sister, Eliza, was not so lucky, however. She was taken by the gang to be delivered back into slavery. Only through the efforts of local abolitionists who worked through a friendly court system was her identity as a New York resident established and her freedom secured.[36]

Most captured runaways were not so fortunate. Fugitives, and free blacks, lived in constant danger of being taken by bounty hunters paid by southern slaveholders. One fugitive who escaped to Cincinnati sent word to her children, planning their escape in North Carolina, to beware of young white men who acted too friendly, for they might be "kidnappers."[37] Fugitives generally felt safe among other blacks. "We did not dare ask [for food], except when we found a slave's or free colored person's house remote from any other, and then we were never refused, if they had food to give."[38] A wise runaway, however, regarded all strangers with suspicion. Stories circulated about blacks who would take advantage of their fellows for money, to escape punishment, or to improve their own position by currying favor with influential whites. Cato, a slave in revolutionary Philadelphia, tricked another black man into suffering punishment meant for him. Cato's master, seeking to discipline his slave, gave him a letter to be delivered to the local jail. Suspecting his master's intentions, Cato asked an unfortunate illiterate fellow to deliver a letter for him. Sure enough the bearer of the letter was administered a dozen lashes.[39]

This was not an isolated case. There were always a few blacks willing to profit at the expense of their fellows. Some were willing to take advantage of fugitives or to turn them in for the often sizable rewards offered for their capture. One African American from Illinois traded the fugitive he had consented to help to the authorities for the one-hundred-dollar reward. In Kentucky a free black man teamed up with a white to entice slaves to run away, the pair then returning the fugitives and collecting the reward posted for their capture.[40] When one runaway passed through Boston, a black stranger sold him a slip of paper represented to be a train ticket. The fugitive was told to place the "ticket" in the band of his hat when entering the train, which he did. Fortunately a sympathetic white conductor removed the paper from the fugitive's hat before anyone could read its message: "I am a fugitive slave."[41]

Sometimes such betrayals reflected the natural interpersonal conflict between human beings engaged in very human relationships. In 1848 Judson Diggs, a black Washington hack driver, foiled the escape of more than seventy fugitives attempting to make their way north aboard the sailing vessel *Pearl*. His reasons were more personal than financial. There were stories that Diggs, who had driven many of the runaways to the ship, was angered at the small tip he received. It was more likely that it was the rejection of his affections by one of the women in the fugitive party that really prompted his treachery. Whatever was true, Diggs's relations with the fugitives was important in explaining his motivation.[42]

Diggs's actions drew strong disapproval from Washington blacks, for it was an example of what they and other African Americans feared—betrayal from within. Calls for "Negro unity" echoed from many corners of black society. Perhaps David Ruggles exaggerated when he wrote that "while every hand is against us, our every hand is against each other." There was, however, a general concern about those who could not be trusted and considerable pressure to turn every African American toward "the hallowed cause of reform."[43]

All other things being equal, however, runaways were better advised to trust an unknown African American than a white stranger. Some whites—the Quakers, who were known to be sympathetic to the plight of black people, for example—were all but exempt from suspicion. Quakers had fought to outlaw slavery, first among their membership and then generally, since the mid-eighteenth century. Their reputation as opponents of slavery was legendary among blacks. That is why Curry sought out a group of Pennsylvania Quakers during his escape. He spoke for many blacks when he explained that the members of the Society of Friends were those "whom I never fail to trust . . ."[44]

Quakers were the exception, however. Among free blacks or runaway slaves, most whites were regarded with suspicion. One member of a largely black underground society reported that although the group admitted whites, "We were always suspicious of the white man, and so those admitted we put to severe tests, and we had one ritual for them alone . . ." Under these circumstances African Americans were most likely to find themselves called upon by black strangers in need, and the record is persuasive that aid was generally given.[45]

Even though strangers helped and chance frequently determined a fugitive's fate, escape would have been almost impossible without the intricate communication networks linking slaves to the northern free black community. Slaveholders sought to isolate their slaves from the outside world, especially from the subversive influence of free blacks and abolitionists, but total insulation was impossible. Throughout the antebellum period, there was a steady stream of communication passing along the underground connection linking those in and out of bondage. Communication was maintained by black and white interregional travelers. Many would not have thought of themselves as part of an underground at all. In many instances this communication was as simple as "telling of thems at the home place"—spreading news or gossip about familiar people and places.

African Americans expected newcomers to share their knowledge about friends and acquaintances. Fugitives told of conditions in the South and brought news of friends and family. They carried with them valuable details that not only satisfied a personal curiosity but also could aid in the planning of future rescues. William Still, Philadelphia's premier Underground Railroad conductor, often interviewed fugitives at length to gather useful intelligence. In interviewing one young man, Still discovered that he was speaking to a brother he had never known.[46]

Black travelers, especially those from the South, were closely questioned. In antebellum Cincinnati local blacks knew that the Dumas Hotel was a place to gather information on people and conditions in the South. Visiting slaveholders often quartered their personal servants at the Dumas. While masters pursued their business in the city, their slaves sought the company of Cincinnati blacks. Information was regularly exchanged, and many northern blacks maintained contact with loved ones in the South through this link.[47] For thirty years Willie Lee Mathis of Cincinnati kept in touch with her mother, enslaved in Virginia, by using visiting southern blacks as messengers. Another Cincinnati woman used this communication service to smuggle letters to her children bound in North Carolina. During the antebellum decades, the Dumas became a kind of underground post office.[48]

There were other examples of southern message carriers who helped maintain the contact between blacks kept apart by slavery. James

King was a slave in Lexington, Kentucky, who was permitted by his master to pastor a black church across the river in Cincinnati. He was one of the founders of Allen Temple, a church King led to the African Methodist Episcopal denomination in 1823. King traveled regularly between Lexington and Cincinnati and was a major link between the blacks of each area. Because large numbers of Kentucky-born blacks lived in Cincinnati throughout the antebellum period, this information route was a popular one, linking them with slaves across the Ohio River.[49]

The information that flowed South was put to good use. Runaways often followed the lines of communication, moving North to areas that they had heard about. A fugitive might acquire the names of those who could be trusted or places of shelter once in the North. Fugitive escape routes were a part of the pattern of black chain migration apparent in the cities of the antebellum North. Midwestern cities such as Cincinnati and Chicago drew greater numbers of southern migrants from western Virginia, Kentucky, and the western South, whereas eastern cities such as Boston, New York, and Philadelphia tended to attract smaller numbers of southern-born blacks from eastern Virginia, Maryland, and the Carolinas. Southern blacks traveling north, fugitives and nonfugitives alike, were most likely to settle in areas where friends and relatives had gone before. Thus blacks from adjacent areas migrated to Cincinnati, swelling its southern-born black population. A similar pattern is evidenced in Philadelphia, which attracted significant numbers of southern-born blacks. This in turn ensured that more southern-born migrants would seek these cities where they were more likely to have personal contacts.

In Boston, much farther north and thus less likely to attract southern-born blacks, there were fewer contacts to encourage large numbers of southern black migrants. Yet many came despite the distance, for southern blacks were not ignorant of the possibilities for freedom in Boston. Peter Randolph was born a slave in Virginia. After he secured his freedom he and sixty-six others traveled to Boston, led there by the underground communication that passed the word to southern blacks. "The name Boston," Randolph explained, "always had a musical and joyous sound to the colored people of the South." Although several southern whites attempted to convince Randolph and his party that the North generally and Boston in particular was a dangerous place, southern blacks knew better. They understood, as one said, that "this city is foremost in advocating the Negro's cause and vouchsafing to him the immunities of citizenship."[50]

Masters were ever vigilant, continually attempting to isolate their slaves from "northern information," but generally they were not successful. African American institutions in southern cities, always suspect as centers of subversion, were closely watched. Slave religious meetings were often attended by whites, as one slave reported, who took note of the subjects discussed. Black churches were sometimes ministered to by white preachers who, it was hoped, would maintain control over their black congregation. Despite the slaveholders' best efforts, however, the institutional and noninstitutional southern black church was an integral part of the interregional underground.[51]

Even though Richmond's First African Baptist Church had a white minister, its members kept in touch with those gone North through a clandestine mailing system based in the church. As one contemporary explained, "Several servants escaped to the North from their masters . . . they wrote back to Richmond to their former comrades . . . detailing the manner of their escape and proposing to them facilities and information for the same experiment." Messages and letters were brought to the church and distributed to slaves and free blacks in the city. The system was shut down in the mid-1850s, after it was discovered by local slaveholders.[52]

Black seamen and boatmen were especially important message carriers. The tradition of African Americans in water transport dates from colonial times when blacks manned whaling ships and ocean-trade vessels as well as riverboats. As river transport became more important in the nineteenth century, black boatmen were included as crew members. In seaport and river port cities such as Boston and Cincinnati, the water routes offered an important source of income to black workers.[53]

These seamen traveled frequently and were well versed in what one historian referred to as *travel craft,* that is, the ability to seek out the keepers of information vital to the survival of a black traveler in strange and probably hostile places. Despite the efforts of authorities, many free black sailors from the northern states, the West Indies, and England put ashore and spent time between voyages among the black communities in southern ports. Some slaves were also used as part of the crews on riverboats or coastal vessels. Associations between free blacks and slaves were relatively easy, despite southern fears that such contact was dangerous. Seamen were pivotal to the interregional communication system.[54]

Yet for blacks attempting to cope with the complications imposed by slavery, communication with southern kin was sometimes critically important. Henry Williams escaped from slavery in Louisiana in the 1830s and traveled to Cincinnati, where he was able to secure work and maintain his freedom for a number of years. While living in Cincinnati, Henry met and married a women from a neighboring town. This enraged his fellow members at Cincinnati's Union Baptist Church, because they knew that Henry was already married and that his wife, still a slave, was living in New Orleans. The church congregation charged Henry with bigamy. Despite the special problems involved, he was said to have "deserted" his wife in slavery, and the church demanded a signed release from her before it would sanction a new marriage. Henry faced a grave problem. How could a fugitive in Cincinnati safely contact a slave in New Orleans to secure a signed document? The answer was found in the underground communication link. Henry was able to contact his first wife through a boatman who regularly traveled to New Orleans and several other southern port cities. Her X and her enthusiastic support in dissolving the marriage was obtained, and the church recognized Henry's new marriage.[55]

Seamen were routinely depended on to bring information of family and friends whenever they returned from the South, and they carried similar news to southern blacks. One Cincinnati woman kept in touch with her mother for more than three decades through messages smuggled by black boatmen. During these years she consulted her mother about her choice of a husband and informed her of the birth of children. Thus in 1843 the news of her grandchild's enrollment at Oberlin Collegiate Institute found the proud grandmother in a Mississippi slave hut, bound in body, she reported, but free in spirit.[56]

Seagoing blacks were also important conductors on the Underground Railroad, which stretched into the South. The literature is replete with stories of fugitives being aided by black sailors and boatmen. These blacks had access to a means of transportation to freedom, and they were likely to have contacts in the North with the black underground.

Southern officials believed that black seamen posed a danger to the stability of the slave system, especially in waterfront communities, and acted to isolate them from local blacks. Some charged that ships' crews in general and black mariners in particular were heavily influenced by northern abolitionists and took every opportunity to indoctrinate slaves. One southern newspaper asserted that sailors actually kidnapped slaves who might otherwise be unwilling to leave the South.[57]

After uncovering Denmark Vesey's plot for slave rebellion in 1822, the city of Charleston, South Carolina, sought to control the flow of information to local blacks from outside by holding blacks sailors in jail for the duration of their time in port. Although this practice was declared unconstitutional by the Supreme Court in 1824, city officials felt so strongly about the matter that they were willing to disobey the court ruling in the interest of "maintaining order."[58]

Southern authorities in port cities had good reason for their claims. The earliest copies of *Walker's Appeal,* a highly incendiary pamphlet calling for slave insurrection, were brought into Savannah, Georgia, by a ship's steward from a Boston-based vessel. The steward delivered sixty copies of the pamphlet to Henry Cunningham, a local black minister. Cunningham, who had lived for two years in the North, was a free man, though he had been born a slave. Although the seaman claimed ignorance of the contents of the package and the minister turned it over to the local authorities, the delivery created great excitement among the city's whites. Many demanded regulations that would shield the community from such dangerous literature. In response the Georgia legislature drew up measures, similar to those in South Carolina, that restricted the movements of black seamen while in Georgia ports.[59]

This practice spread to other southern ports. New Orleans also jailed many boatmen during the 1840s for similar reasons. The incarceration of black seamen while in port might have consequences greater than a temporary loss of freedom. One boatman, jailed in New Orleans, smuggled communication to friends in Boston that his freedom papers had been confiscated and that he feared that he would be sold into slavery. Only after significant political action and the intercession of the governor of Massachusetts was he freed.[60]

Despite southern efforts the communications underground continued and black sailors continued to play an important role. Even for those black seamen who did not visit southern towns, aiding fugitives became an important task. William Wells Brown was a runaway who eventually acquired a job on a lake boat on Lake Erie. He was instrumental in the transportation of many fugitives across the lake to Canada. "In the year 1842," Brown reported, "I conveyed from the first of May to the first of December, sixty-nine fugitives over Lake Erie to Canada."[61]

Sometimes these seamen became formally attached to the abolition movement, but often they did not. Many remained important in the underground simply because they were willing to befriend a fellow black in trouble. Shortly after his arrival in New York City, fugitive Frederick Douglass was aided by a seamen who warned him of the dangers of recapture and put him in touch with the Underground Railroad in the city. Although the seaman was not directly connected to the underground, he apparently understood its function and was acquainted with some of its conductors.[62]

The presence of slavery and its hold over every black person, either directly through personal experience or indirectly through concern for the welfare of family and friends, bound most African Americans together. The communication links discussed here were extremely important factors in the continuing commitment of the free to the unfree. The importance of these links is illustrated by the diminished commitment to abolition exhibited by blacks beyond the reach of these communications networks. Blacks in California, for example, seemed less passionately devoted to the cause of abolition and expressed concern for those in slavery less frequently than blacks in eastern and midwestern cities. There is little evidence that local abolitionist groups were formed in the California Territory during the 1840s or in the state after 1850. Further, blacks who were radical firebrands in the East—men such as Philip A. Bell and J. Holland Townsend, both abolitionist editors from New York—become strangely silent on the subject once they settled into the San Francisco community.[63]

Black San Franciscans did not ignore racial injustice. In the mid-1850s they organized and spoke out against inferior education for black children, the inability of African Americans to vote or to gain equal access to the courts, and the general lack of civil rights accorded California blacks. Yet there was a dearth of antislavery rhetoric. In the state conventions there was none of the fiery condemnation of slavery routinely found in the East and Midwest. These gatherings did not sanction the antislavery resolutions passed by the national convention. In the 1855 California state convention there was an attempt to read a series of resolutions passed by the national meeting in Philadelphia. William H. Yates, the convention president, interrupted, saying, "No extreme subject should be brought forward to disturb the harmony of [the] proceedings." The chair was sustained by acclamation. Later a motion to send an account of the state convention to the *Liberator* and to *Frederick Douglass' Paper* for publication was voted down. Significantly, Yates was a former slave who had been extremely active in the Underground Railroad when he lived in the East.[64]

When in 1856 one member of the state convention brought up the question of slavery and asked the membership to take a stand on it, he was declared out-of-order. He was charged with wasting the time of the convention with "much useless discussion" that was "retarding the proper business of the convention"—that is, the improvement of the condition of California blacks. One member explained that "with the question of slavery, and union, we have nothing to say. This is not the time or place for the introduction of such inflammable and discordant subjects."[65] Apparently many black San Franciscans agreed. In 1856 the *Mirror of the Time,* the city's first black newspaper, pledged itself to antislavery only as a secondary issue. Peter Anderson, black editor of the *Pacific Appeal,* wrote in 1859, "We must let the slave sit for a while as being too heavy a load for us to carry at present." In striking contrast to black newspapers published in the East or the Midwest, which were filled with information about slavery and provided a constant voice for abolition, California black newspapers played down such issues in favor of local issues apparently of greater concern to West Coast African Americans.[66]

The evidence suggests that although they favored abolition, California blacks were less likely to publicly condemn slavery except when it became a local issue. When confronted with a fugitive in need, they were quick to provide aid. Starting in March of 1851 and continuing throughout the 1850s, they organized to assist those about to be returned to the South and raised money for the legal defense of runaways. They held mass protest and strategy meetings, and on several occasions they resorted to violent confrontation with authorities in their attempt to shelter slaves from slaveholders and from the proslavery actions of the California legal system. Although their efforts were hampered by restrictions against black court testimony and by the additional limitations placed on fugitives and their allies by the California Fugitive Slave Act of 1852, black San Franciscans acted locally. This made their quiescence on broader abolitionist issues all the more curious.[67]

Frederick Cooper's analysis of the concerns of antebellum free blacks failed to describe eastern and midwestern communities, but it seems relevant to California. There, apparent black preoccupation with state and local racial limitations may be partly explained by the relative isolation from the masses of African Americans. Although San Francisco was a major seaport city, less than 18 percent of its employed black men worked as mariners by 1860. This proportion was smaller than that for black men in Boston or Cincinnati. Black San Franciscans may have had proportionately less access to southern communication links, perhaps making it easier to subordinate concern for the slaves to concern about local matters, which included efforts by powerful forces to eliminate blacks from California. Perhaps blacks feared that the alarming oppressiveness of their immediate circumstance would grow worse if they took too strong a stance against slavery. These conditions may have magnified the impact of geographical isolation.[68]

The evidence strongly suggests the importance of the underground communication network, which provided regular contact between eastern and midwestern blacks and the slaves of the South. This communication ensured that every black person within its reach remained aware of the conditions slaves were forced to endure and of their responsibilities to work for the overthrow of the South's evil institution. In addition, variations observed here highlight the importance of recognizing how critical local circumstances are in shaping the concerns and actions of individual black communities. Again, communication was important, for it linked local black communities to the resources and support of the wider black community. Without that reassurance it was easy to feel both alone and vulnerable.

The communication of common concerns helped to define the organization and structure of the black communities that addressed these issues. The community institutions and those seen as community leaders were charged with responding to the particular interests of community people. Although it is not yet clear what impact the peculiarly local concerns of black San Franciscans had on their societal structure, it is reasonable to assume that there were differences between that community and those of the East and Midwest. An in-depth exploration of the nature of those differences is beyond the scope of this book, but it is certainly a topic worth study as an illustration of the importance of regional variation among black communities.

Most striking is the breadth and depth of the identification among free northern blacks with the struggle of those in slavery and the willingness to aid fugitives even when those in need were strangers. There were a few conspicuous exceptions, but those who betrayed others of their race were subject to harsh criticism, even ostracism or violence. The bond between the free and the unfree, although generally not based entirely on race, was certainly one in which race was recognized as an important element. A common concern with matters of antislavery and racial injustice helped to bind antebellum free blacks in a community of shared disadvantage. Interregional contacts and lines of communication were the important threads that bound all African Americans, free and unfree.

2

Multiple Identities

Gender, Color, and Nationality

The following chapters examine the three most significant defining characteristics in antebellum northern black communities: gender role, skin color, and national identity. Within African American communities, the issue of race manifests itself in more subtle hues than black and white, and the middle-class ideal of gender in the nineteenth century was at once less practical and simpler than the variety of real life "roles" demanded of black men and women. Race also complicated the African American national identity, leading to intense internal debate over protest strategy. How these potentially divisive issues played themselves out in different regions of the country and in different life circumstances is integral to the story of the nineteenth-century black community.

Chapter 4, "Violence, Protest, and Identity: Black Manhood in Antebellum America," examines the struggle to overcome slavery's attempt to deny black manhood. This struggle was a community effort, for the term *manhood* implied more than gender and was often used to apply to the race in general. Manhood rights, then, became not only the rights of black males but those of black people. There were important gender implications here, but racial issues disrupted nineteenth-century gender expectations for black people. Slavery sought to create dependency and obedience among its captives, and racism attempted to reinforce these objectives through social, political, and economic restrictions limiting black achievement and perverting gender roles within free black society. Denied access to jobs that would allow him to play the masculine role of provider, generally unable to exercise the political power that by the mid-nineteenth century had become synonymous with manhood in America, struggling with white attitudes that denied him respect and endangered his ability to protect his family, the black man faced a unique challenge. Under these circumstances the debate regarding violent means in the name of abolition and civil rights took on particular relevance to both gender and community.

But racial restrictions contradicted gender preconceptions not just for black men but for black women as well. As can be seen in Chapter 5, "Freedom's Yoke: Gender Conventions among Free Blacks," in the private sphere the traditional ideal of male and female roles coexisted with both traditional and nontraditional behavior. This could make life especially burdensome for black women, for whom racial solidarity often meant, of necessity, concession to male authority in the name of preserving black manhood. The issue of gender in black community was a potentially divisive one, sometimes so volatile that it was removed from public view as one of the most private of interior issues.

Equally private, and perhaps potentially even more volatile, was the question of color among African Americans. Chapter 6, "Shades of Color: The Mulatto in Three Antebellum Northern Communities," shows how African Americans of "mixed blood" in certain times and places occupied a privileged middling position between whites and darker blacks—in both the consciousness of whites and the socioeconomic order. Regional variation was evident as patterns of color stratification in the South differed from those in the North, affecting relationships within the black communities and between blacks and whites. This study of three northern cities finds southern and northern economic and social patterns that illustrate the importance of these regional variations.

These issues of gender and color illustrate the diversity of opinion and historical experience within the African American community. Diversity did not, however, imply that the black man and black woman could choose from a wide menu of life options. In fact, their choices were severely limited by social and economic strictures. The conflict between expectation and achievement created tremendous pressures, and often anger, which fueled internal debate over national and racial identity.

Chapter 7, "Double Consciousness: African American Identity in the Nineteenth Century," examines discussions among blacks over their dual heritage—African and American. These discussions, which were heated at times, were given urgency by various programs to colonize free blacks in West Africa. In response to these programs and to the rising tide of racial restrictions in the Civil War era, African Americans struggled to agree on a racial and national identity that would recognize their contributions to and continuing support of the ideals of the American Revolution while maintaining racial solidarity and pride in the face of strong differences of opinion. An exploration of these tensions within the community is central to this section.

Years after his encounter with Covey, the slave breaker, Douglass became an important symbol of black manhood as the most celebrated antislavery speaker in America and Europe. (Courtesy of The New-York Historical Society, New York City)

Chapter 4

Violence, Protest, and Identity

Black Manhood in Antebellum America

JAMES OLIVER HORTON AND LOIS E. HORTON

In his autobiography, Frederick Douglass recalled his confrontation with the slave breaker Covey as the first step on his escape to freedom. After regular beatings from Covey, to whom he had been hired, he had run away, and then returned to face certain and severe punishment. This time, though, the adolescent slave resisted, and the two became locked in a two-hour struggle that left both exhausted. Young Frederick was not subdued, and Covey never beat him again. This successful resistance changed the slave: "My dear reader this battle with Mr. Covey . . . was the turning point in my life as a slave . . . I was nothing before; I was a man now."[1] It was natural for Douglass to express his new-found power in terms of manhood, as power, independence, and freedom were often thought of as traits reserved for men in nineteenth-century America. To be a man was to be free and powerful.

Although the American man in the nineteenth century could choose from a variety of gender ideals, virtually all the combinations of characteristics, values, and actions constituting each ideal included self-assertion and aggression as key elements. Aggression, and sometimes sanctioned violence, was a common thread in American ideals of manhood. Charles Rosenberg believes that two masculine ideals exemplified the choices open to nineteenth-century men, the *Masculine Achiever* and *Christian Gentleman*. The Masculine Achiever ideal was closely associated with the rapid economic growth of the nineteenth century. As the rise of the market economy disrupted local relationships and tied formerly isolated communities to distant economic affiliations, this ideal provided American men with a dynamic model of behavior. The man of action was unencumbered by sentiment and totally focused on advancement, the quintessential individualist and the self-styled ruthless competitor. He was the rugged individual succeeding in the world of commercial capitalism.

The Christian Gentleman ideal arose in reaction to the Masculine Achiever and threats to traditional values and relationships. Eschewing self-seeking behavior and heartless competition in the commercial world, this gentler ideal stressed communal values, religious principles, and more humanitarian action. It was a natural outgrowth of the religious revival that blossomed under the Second Great Awakening of the early nineteenth century and stressed self-restraint and Christian morality. Christian Gentlemen were not expected to be passive. Dynamic and aggressive action was assumed, but in the name of moral values and self-sacrifice, not personal greed.[2]

E. Anthony Rotundo argues that an additional ideal emerged among northern males in the nineteenth century—the *Masculine Primitive*. This ideal stressed dominance and conquest through harnessing the energy of primitive male instincts and savagery lurking beneath the thin veneer of civilization. This was a more physically aggressive ideal, based on the natural impulses of man's most primitive state, and violence was its confirming feature.[3] Although Rotundo sees this ideal as influential among northern men by the middle of the nineteenth century, southern historians have found a strikingly similar ideal in the South throughout the eighteenth and nineteenth centuries. Bertram Wyatt-Brown and Grady McWhiney describe the violence in defense of honor sanctioned by even the most genteel southerners. Elizabeth Fox-Genovese notes the simultaneous existence of gentility and savagery: "Southern conventions of masculinity never abandoned the element of force or even brutality . . . This toleration of male violence responded to the perceived exigencies of governing a troublesome people . . ." The behaviors believed necessary for managing the slave system were incorporated into the gender ideals for all southern white men.[4]

Black men growing up as slaves in southern society had an especially complex gender socialization. The gender ideals of white southern society overlaid the foundations of African cultural expectations and the intentional socialization imposed on slaves. The dual and contradictory genteel and savage images applied to southern white manhood paralleled characteristics whites imagined black men possessed. The happy, contented Sambo stereotype slaveholders wanted to believe existed was placed alongside the brute, savage Negro they feared. Slaveholders tried to cultivate a slave approximation of the Christian Gentlemen ideal, typified by Harriet Beecher Stowe's Uncle Tom, all the while dreading the emergence of the barbaric Masculine Primitive. Thomas R. Dew argued in 1832 that Africans were by nature savage and that it was only the civilizing influence of slavery that restrained their brutish nature. According to William Drayton, another nineteenth-century apologist for slavery, only slavery checked the "wild frenzy of revenge, and the savage lust for blood" natural to the African and dramatically apparent in the Haitian Revolution. In 1858 Thomas R. R. Cobb alleged that once removed from the domesticating influence of slavery, Haitian blacks "relapsed into barbarism."[5]

Ever watchful for any outward signs of rebellion, white southerners went to great lengths to suppress black aggression and assertiveness. As one former slave recalled, "Every man [was] called boy till he [was] very old, then the more respectable slaveholder call[ed] him uncle." Actions expected of white men were condemned in black men. No black man could defend his family from a white attacker, "let him be ever so drunk or crazy," without fear of drastic reprisal. Yet a black man under the orders of white authority could legitimately use his strength against a white person. A slave directed by his overseer could strike a white man for "beating said overseer's pig."[6]

"A slave can't be a man," proclaimed former slave Lewis Clarke.[7] Slavery was designed to make it impossible for a man to freely express his opinions and make his own decisions. Yet many slave men asserted aspects of manhood even under the most difficult circumstances. William Davis refused to be whipped by his overseer. When the white man realized he could not administer the beating alone, he ordered three "athletic fellows" to assist him, but Davis served notice that he would not be taken easily. "Boys, I am only a poor boy and you are grown men, but if either of you touch me, I'll kill one of you . . . ," he warned. Davis was not whipped.[8]

Slave men found many ways to assert themselves. Even the threat of self-assertion could be effective. One man reported that he avoided being sold at auction by meeting the gaze of prospective buyers directly as they inspected him, an obvious sign of a hard-to-handle slave. Another stopped his master from beating slave children by standing beside them, glaring at the master as he began punishment. Among the slaves, men who refused to submit to the master's authority were accorded respect. Those who submitted too easily to the master's authority lost respect. "Them as won't fight," reported Lewis Clarke, "is called Poke-easy."[9] How could a man be both manly and a slave? A central theme in the abolitionists' attacks on slavery was that it robbed men of their manhood. The widely used antislavery emblem was a manacled slave kneeling in the supplication, "Am I not a man and brother?"[10]

David Walker, a free black North Carolinian who migrated to Boston, gained national attention and raised southern fears by urging slaves to prove their manhood, to rise up and take their freedom by force if necessary. His call to arms was issued in partial answer to Thomas Jefferson's suggestions that African Americans were an inferior species and could not be granted freedom. Walker asserted that the African American could not be domesticated like an animal and could never be held in slavery against his will. He goaded black men to action by rhetorically wondering how so many could be enslaved: "Are we Men!! How we could be so submissive to a gang of men, whom we cannot tell whether they are as good as ourselves or not, I never could conceive." Blacks, he wrote, must not wait for either God or slaveholders to end slavery. "The man who would not fight . . . to be delivered from the most wretched, abject and servile slavery, that ever a people was afflicted with since the foundation of the world . . . ought to be kept with all his children or family, in slavery or in chains to be butchered by his cruel enemies."[11]

In his *Appeal* David Walker called upon the memory of the successful Haitian Revolution in 1804 as proof of the power of unity and manliness. "One thing which gives me joy," he wrote of the Haitians, "is, that they are men who would be cut off to a man before they would yield to the combined forces of the whole world." Black men demonstrated in Haiti, Walker contended, that "a groveling, servile and abject submission to the lash of tyrants" is not the African man's natural state. Walker believed that slaves could transform themselves into men through aggressive action. "If ever we become men," he said, "we must assert ourselves to the full."[12]

In his call to action, Walker claimed the physical superiority of black men. "I do declare," he wrote, "that one good black can put to death six white men." The assertion that slaves were stronger and better in combat than their masters was not new. It became part of the racial folklore of the period and was often cited in conjunction with rumors of slave uprisings. Yet this declaration posed problems for African Americans. The use of violence to assert manhood tended to reinforce white stereotypes of the "brutish African nature" only restrained by slavery.[13]

Despite David Walker's mysterious death in 1831, his advocacy of the use of violence as an acceptable tactic for the acquisition of freedom and equality, what were increasingly referred to as *manhood rights,* remained an important position among blacks throughout the antebellum period. At the time that Walker wrote his *Appeal,* the American imagination was captured by Greek revolutionaries seeking independence from Turkey, by rising Polish discontent with their Russian masters, and the revolutions in Latin America that, in 1826, brought the abolition of slavery to the former Spanish colonies. Thus he drew on more than the distant models of the American Revolution and the revolt in Haiti. He was undoubtedly aware that freedom was being sought through violence abroad and that revolutionary armies in Latin America included black soldiers bearing arms supplied by the Haitian government.[14]

Walker was not alone in using international illustrations to attack slavery or in considering the prospect of slave revolt. In 1825 in his commencement address at Bowdoin College, John Russwurm, one of the first African Americans to graduate from an American college, assailed the institution, taking as his paradigm the establishment of Haitian independence.[15] Later, as coeditor of *Freedom's Journal,* Russwurm speculated that if the federal government would stop providing protection for slaveholders, slaves might very well settle the question of slavery themselves. Ohio judge Benjamin Tappan shocked an acquaintance by inquiring rhetorically "whether the slave has not a resort to the most violent measures, if necessary, in order to maintain his liberty? And if he has the least chance of success, are we not, as rational and consistent men, bound to justify him?" Historian Merton Dillon asserts that most antislavery proponents of the time accepted the right of slaves to strike for their liberty.[16]

The 1830s brought a new, more forceful critique of violent means in the fight against slavery as William Lloyd Garrison began publishing his newspaper, the *Liberator,* in Boston. His commitment to immediate emancipation for slaves and civil rights for free blacks was popular among African Americans who had worked toward these ends for decades with only marginal assistance from white reformers. Garrison was a nonresister—a pacifist opposed to cooperating with any government built on slavery and compromise with slaveholders. His pacifism led him to oppose government that forced citizens to participate directly or indirectly in violence, through, for example, war, imprisonment, or capital punishment. He opposed voting or participating in politics, and condemned the use of violence even to achieve freedom. The route to manhood, he believed, was through strength of character and principled action. In the pages of the *Liberator* he rejected Walker's call for slave revolt, and although he praised Walker personally, Garrison made clear that "we do not preach rebellion—no, but submission and peace." His stand on the use of violence by slaves was complex. He considered slaves "more than any people on the face of the earth" justified in the use of force and compared slave revolt to the American Revolution in the justice of its cause, but a just cause, Garrison believed, was no justification for violence.[17]

Garrison's strong commitment to nonviolence and his philosophy of nonresistance entered the continuing debate within black society over violent and nonviolent means for the abolition of slavery. African Americans had been influenced by arguments for nonviolence early in the colonial era. Quakers, some of their first allies, were pacifists. Blacks who became Friends often wrestled with the question of the practicality of nonviolence for a people violently deprived of their rights. Yet blacks were obliged to "become convinced of [Quaker] principles" in order to be accepted into the society. During the War of 1812, black Quaker David Mapps of Little Egg Harbor, New Jersey, demonstrated his pacifist principles and refused to transport cannon balls aboard his schooner, explaining, "I cannot carry thy devil's pills that were made to kill people."[18]

Although black Quakers were strongly committed to nonviolence, most African Americans expressed a great deal more ambivalence on this issue. At the opposite extreme from the Quakers, many continued to agree with David Walker that violence was the surest route to freedom and manhood. Some opposed the use of violence on practical grounds, others wrestled with moral issues and searched for alternative ways to assert themselves and to achieve dignity without the use of force. Garrison and his philosophy had become the center of this debate by the 1830s, but the debate was over means, not ends. All blacks agreed that freedom and equality were the goals, and most continued to equate these with manhood.

Speaking to a gathering of black Bostonians in 1831, black activist

Maria W. Stewart echoed Walker's call to black men to assert their manhood: "O ye fearful ones, throw off your fearfulness . . . If you are men, convince [whites] that you possess the spirit of men." Yet hers was not a call to violence. She called forth the "sons of Africa" to show their bravery, their intelligence, and their commitment to serving their community. "But give the man of color an equal opportunity . . . from the cradle to manhood, and from manhood to grave, and you would discover a dignified statesman, the man of science, and the philosopher."[19]

Maria Stewart urged a version of the Masculine Achiever ideal of manhood that incorporated achievement, autonomy, and "intensive competition for success in the marketplace."[20] Her ideal, however, was not completely individualistic. The object of success in the masculine competition was to prove black men the equals of other men. It was also important, according to Stewart, that successful men become assets to the black community and contribute to the struggle of black people. Even though Stewart was a friend and co-worker of Garrison, her appeal was not incontrovertibly nonviolent. The heroes she called upon to inspire black men to the competition included the black soldiers of the American Revolution and the War of 1812—and David Walker.

Garrison agreed that bondage and discrimination denied human dignity and pledged his efforts to combat these destructive forces. He was a pacifist, but his philosophy and style was neither passive nor apologetic. As he began the *Liberator*, Garrison promised to speak clearly and forcefully in words that could not be misunderstood. He was unequivocal in his opposition to slavery, but he also believed he had a responsibility to free blacks in the North. He dedicated himself and his paper to work for their "moral and intellectual elevation, the advancement of [their] rights, and the defense of [their] character." Less than two months after beginning publication, Garrison felt his venture had already met with success. He reported: "Upon the colored population in the free states, it has operated like a trumpet call. They have risen in their hopes and feelings to the perfect stature of men . . ."[21]

Garrison's conception of manhood, characterized by intellectual achievement, personal dignity, and moral responsibility, was shared by many abolitionists, whose underlying antislavery motivation was religious. It had particular appeal for black abolitionists, who felt they carried the added burden of disproving the claims of black inferiority advanced by Jefferson and the proslavery interests. Yet even among black Garrisonians there was some ambivalence regarding total reliance on the pacific means of moral suasion. A widely circulated poem composed by the intellectual black abolitionist Charles L. Reason illustrates this ambivalence. Reason's poem, entitled "The Spirit Voice: or Liberty Calls to the Disfranchised," is filled with martial images but comes to a decidedly nonviolent conclusion. He wrote:

> Come! rouse ye brothers, rouse! a peal now breaks,
> From lowest island to our gallant lakes,
> 'Tis summoning you, who long in bonds have lain,
> To stand up manful on the battle plain,
> Each as a warrior, with his armor bright,
> Prepared to battle in a bloodless fight.[22]

Respect for Garrison and his work kept many black abolitionists from openly questioning reliance on moral suasion, even when they harbored doubts about its effectiveness. Some Garrisonians, of course, were committed to nonviolence on principle; others saw it as a practical strategy. Throughout the 1830s and early 1840s, the small band of antislavery crusaders was continually under attack. Mobs broke up their meetings, attacked them in the streets, and occasionally set fire to their lecture halls and homes. Slaveholders posted rewards for the most notorious abolitionists, dead or alive. In the face of such opposition, taking the principled stance of moral suasion had the additional practical benefit of attracting adherents while avoiding inflaming even more violent reactions.

Yet some continued to proclaim the right of slaves to take their freedom "like men." One of the most radical and elaborate schemes for the forcible abolition of slavery came from a white sixty-year-old politician, Jabez Delano Hammond, a jurist and former U.S. congressman from Cherry Valley, New York. In 1839 Hammond proposed that abolitionists sponsor military academies in Canada and Mexico that would train blacks in military arts and sabotage. The trainees would then be set loose in the South to commit terrorist acts and to encourage and lead slave rebellions. Referring to these infiltrators as potentially "the most successful Southern missionaries," Hammond explained that such steps were necessary because "the only way in which slavery at the South can be abolished is by force."[23]

Many black reformers were also growing impatient with moral suasion as the primary weapon against slavery and moral elevation as the surest route to progress for free blacks. Peter Paul Simons spoke for a growing minority in 1839 when he challenged the efficacy of moral reform. Instead of lessening the hold of slavery and prejudice on blacks, he believed, it had encouraged timidity and self-doubt. African Americans do not suffer from lack of moral elevation, he argued. "There is no nation of people under the canopy of heaven, who are given more to good morals and piety than we are." He contended that blacks suffered from a lack of direct "physical and political" action. They lacked confidence in one another, he said, and were thus likely to depend on the leadership of whites, a not-so-subtle reference to the willingness of many blacks to follow Garrison's lead. His argument continued, charging that black children learned passive acceptance not manly action and leadership from parental examples. Action must be the watchword: "This we must physically practice, and we will be in truth an independent people."[24]

Although Simons stopped short of endorsing a David Walker–style call for violence in this pursuit of self-confident independence, his statements did signal the move toward a more aggressive posture. He was not alone. Many who worked most closely with fugitive slaves or on behalf of free blacks kidnapped into slavery were among those least able to accept the doctrine of nonviolence. Black abolitionist David Ruggles, an officer of the New York Committee of Vigilance, had never been totally committed to nonresistance. As early as 1836 he wrote that in dealing with slave hunters and kidnappers, "Self-defense is the first law of nature."[25] Gradually Ruggles grew more impatient with the slow pace of antislavery and civil rights progress. In the summer of 1841, he addressed a meeting of the American Reform Board of Disfranchised Commissioners, a New York protest group of which he was a founding member. In strident tones he rallied the group to action and explained that "in our cause" words alone would not suffice. "Rise brethren rise!" he urged the distant slaves. "Strike for freedom or die slaves!"[26]

Two years later at the Buffalo meeting of the National Negro Convention, twenty-seven-year-old black abolitionist minister Henry Highland Garnet echoed David Walker's exhortation, urging black men to act like men. Addressing himself to the slaves, he used provocative and incendiary language. "It is sinful in the extreme," he admonished, "for you to make voluntary submission." As Walker had accepted the necessity for a man to use violence in the assertion of his manhood, so Garnet concluded that "there is not much hope of Redemption without the

shedding of blood." Black men must not shrink from bloody confrontation—there was no escape. A mass exodus was not an option for
African Americans, he argued. The solution must be found in America,
and it might well be violent. "If you must bleed, let it come at once,
rather, die freemen than live to be slaves." Garnet did not urge a revolution. "Your numbers are too small," he observed. But all slaves should
immediately "cease to labor for tyrants who will not remunerate you."
He assumed, however, that violence would be the inevitable result of
this tactic. And when it came, he instructed, "Remember that you are
THREE MILLIONS."[27]

As Maria Stewart had done a decade earlier, Garnet used black heroes as a standard for manhood, and he found contemporary black men
wanting. Questioning the commitment of his fellows to the assertion of
manhood, Garnet cut to the heart of masculine pride. "You act as
though your daughters were born to pamper the lusts of your masters
and overseers," he charged. Garnet continued forcefully: "And worst of
all, you timidly submit while your lords tear your wives from your em-
braces and defile them before your eyes. In the name of God, we ask,
are you men? Where is the blood of your fathers? Has it all run out of
your veins?"[28] Here Garnet drew upon one of the most powerful
justifications for the link between physical prowess and masculinity in
American gender ideals—the responsibility of men to protect their families. This responsibility was an important part of all male ideals in the
society. Even those most committed to the Christian Gentleman ideal,
even the most fervent black nonresisters had great difficulty arguing
that nonviolence was the only recourse when one's family was in physical danger. Garnet's charge to the slaves forcefully affected the black
and white abolitionists and observers in his audience as he evoked the
universal images of manhood.

Garnet's speech split the convention; debate was heated. Ardent
Garrisonians Frederick Douglass and Charles Lenox Remond spoke
against endorsing his sentiments. They pointed to the bloody retribution
slaves and free blacks, especially those in the border states, might suffer
should the convention support such a radical call to violence. Although
there was substantial support for Garnet's message, by a narrow margin
the convention refused to endorse his words. For the time being the
black Garrisonians remained convinced and had successfully blocked
the open embrace of violent means.[29]

A commitment to nonviolence and a sense of the dangers the relatively powerless slaves faced continued to prevent most blacks from urging slaves to gain their freedom through physical force. Many black abolitionists had been slaves and were intimately familiar with the dangers involved. Even Frederick Douglass, who recounted the story of attaining his manhood through physical confrontation, was aware of the risks and continued to be reluctant to sanction calls for slave rebellion. A news story he printed in his paper in the late 1840s illustrated the horrors of slavery and made the point that resistance could be deadly:

> Wm. A. Andrews, an overseer of J. W. Perkins, Mississippi attempted to chastise one of the negro boys who seized a stick and prepared to do battle. The overseer told the boy to lay the stick down or he would shoot him; he refused, and the overseer then fired his pistol, and shot the boy in the face, killing him instantly. The jury of inquest found the verdict, "that the said Wm. A. Andrews committed the killing in self-defense."[30]

In the 1840s Garrisonian nonresistance came under fire from many quarters. There was a split in the abolition movement at the start of the decade, and many of those committed to political antislavery cast their lot with the newly formed Liberty party. Among white abolitionists there was also growing intolerance of what some saw as Garrison's unreasoned radicalism, not only attacking slavery but also condemning the Constitution, the entire federal government, and the national political system. Further, some criticized his support of women's rights as an unnecessary complication that made abolition even less palatable to the general public and threatened to blunt the central thrust of the movement. This fear was reinforced when feminist Abby Kelley was elected to be the first female member of the business committee of the Garrisonian-dominated American Anti-Slavery Society. Opposition groups sprang up to challenge this and other Garrisonian organizations.[31]

This debate between those who favored political participation and those who opposed it split the black abolitionist ranks. Despite their ambivalence, most black Bostonians remained personally loyal to Garrison. New York's *Colored American* attempted to remain neutral, but many black New Yorkers sided with the political abolitionists. Blacks in several northern states faced the curtailment or loss of their voting rights. The vote was an instrument of males' political power, and blacks viewed disenfranchisement as symbolic emasculation. Garrison himself conceded that where rights were in jeopardy, black voters should vote in self-defense.[32]

The debate was short lived among blacks, and even Boston blacks openly took part in electoral politics by the mid-1840s. There were Liberty party announcements inserted in the pages of the *Liberator,* and by 1848 the paper reported on meetings at which African Americans in Boston discussed the formation of an auxiliary to the Liberty party. William Cooper Nell, one of the most loyal of the black Garrisonians, allowed his name to be put into nomination as Free-Soil party candidate for the 1850 Massachusetts legislature.[33]

By the mid-nineteenth century, Garrisonians were also reassessing their stand on nonviolence. Among African Americans almost all reservations about the appropriateness of violence in the struggle against slavery were wiped away by the passage of the federal Fugitive Slave Law of 1850. This measure, which made it easier for fugitives to be captured and for free blacks to be kidnapped into slavery, was seen as a direct blow against all African Americans. It generated a strongly militant reaction even among those who had favored nonviolence. Charles Lenox Remond, who had opposed Garnet's call to arms in the early 1840s, a decade later demanded defiance of the law, protection of all fugitives, and the withholding of federal troops should the southern slaves rise against their masters.[34]

Douglass, who had joined Remond in voting against Garnet, published a novella in 1853 in which slaves killed the captain of a slave ship and a slave owner. In an editorial entitled "Is It Right and Wise to Kill a Kidnapper?" published in *Frederick Douglass' Paper* a year later, he was even more forthright. Violence, even deadly violence, was justifiable when used to protect oneself, one's family, or one's community.[35] At a community meeting in Boston, Nell cautioned African Americans to be watchful for kidnappers. If confronted, he urged them to defend themselves.

The defection from nonviolence was not limited to African Americans. Boston journalist Benjamin Drew suggested that when the government supported oppression, violence against the state might be reasonable.[36] Pacifist minister Samuel J. May and five fugitive slaves stood before an antislavery convention in Syracuse. In surprising tones for the longtime Garrisonian, May asked, "Will you defend [these fugitives] with your lives?" The audience threw back the answer: "Yes!"[37]

Most plans of action were far less offensive. New vigilance committees were formed to protect the safety of fugitives, and already established committees redoubled their efforts, publicly vowing that no slave would be taken. This was a manly pursuit it was said, for every "slave-hunter who meets a bloody death in his infernal business, is an argument in favor of the manhood of our race."[38] Yet not all blacks viewed violent confrontation with slave catchers as the route to manliness. Former slave Philip Younger, who sought refuge in Canada in the 1850s, wrote that even more than in the free states, Canada offered a black man self-respect and dignity. "It was a hardship at first," he reported, "but I feel better here—more like a man—I know I am—than in the States."[39]

Some reformers, such as New York's Gerrit Smith, were critical of men who protected themselves and their families by escaping to Canada, viewing this as a cowardly act. Black abolitionist William Whipper took offense when Smith published such criticism, considering it a slur on the bravery of all black men. Whipper offered a combative reply, saying that he could not understand Smith's attack, considering that African Americans were leaving "a country whose crushing influence . . . aims at the extinction of [their] manhood."[40] Reactions to the Fugitive Slave Law of 1850 ranged from flight to confrontation—different, but each an assertion of personal dignity.

The rising anger at the attack by the "slave power" through its influence over the federal government went beyond militancy to an interest in military preparedness. The Negro Convention in Rochester in 1853 called for the removal of all restrictions on black enlistment in state militia. Sixty-five Massachusetts blacks petitioned their state legislature, demanding that a black military company be chartered. The right to bear arms for their state, they contended, was part of their "rights as men." Their petition was rejected, but a black military company called the Massasoit Guard was formed in Boston in 1854. The unit took its name, their second choice, from a powerful seventeenth-century Indian chief. Most would have preferred the name Attucks, in honor of the black revolutionary hero Crispus Attucks, but the name had already been taken by two other black military companies, the Attucks Guards of New York and the Attucks Blues of Cincinnati. Before the decade ended, there were several black military units in northern cities. Binghamton, New York, named its company after black abolitionist Jermain Loguen, an associate of John Brown, and Harrisburg, Pennsylvania, formed the Henry Highland Garnet Guards. Thus during the 1850s, black men armed themselves, poised to strike against slavery and to reaffirm their manhood through military action.[41]

The opinion in the Dred Scott decision in 1857, which declared that African Americans were not citizens of the United States, further inflamed antigovernment sentiment, as it placed African Americans in an even more perilous position. Increasing militancy and the continuing formation of black military companies led white abolitionist John Brown to believe that substantial numbers of northern free blacks might join a military attack on slavery. He was wrong; in 1859 only five blacks and sixteen whites (three of whom were Brown's sons) joined his attack on the federal arsenal at Harpers Ferry, Virginia. Despite the depth of their antislavery feeling, anger, and frustration, African Americans were not ready to join a private venture that seemed doomed to failure.

Within two years Brown's private war assumed national proportions. Although Lincoln firmly proclaimed preservation of the Union as his sole Civil War aim, northern blacks were convinced that abolition would be its outcome. Their immediate offer of service was refused, even though more than eighty-five hundred men had joined black militia units by the fall of 1861. Two years later, however, with U.S. casualties mounting and the nation bogged down in a protracted war, the government reversed itself and began active recruitment of African American troops. Black abolitionists became energetic recruiters. Jermain Loguen, William Wells Brown, Martin R. Delany, Garnet, and Douglass were among those who encouraged black men to provide their services to the forces of the United States. Victories in the abolition and civil rights struggles during the antebellum period had enhanced their self-image, and most viewed the war as another opportunity to prove themselves to a skeptical white populace. "The eyes of the whole world are upon you, civilized man everywhere waits to see if you will prove yourselves . . . Will you vindicate your manhood?" challenged the *Weekly Anglo-African* in 1863. African Americans hoped that the war would do more than end slavery. Dignity awaited the black man who would "get an eagle on his button, a musket on his shoulder, and the star-spangled banner over his head."[42] Black men marched off to win freedom for slaves and respect and equality for those already free. War was the culmination of the aggressiveness emphasized in much of the resistance to slavery. It celebrated the instincts necessary for survival and reinforced the violence of the Masculine Primitive ideal.

Given the realities of life for African Americans under slavery or in freedom during the antebellum period, the irony of using the term *manhood* to apply to the assertion of dignity or the acquisition of freedom is striking. All black people were aware that such action respected no lines of gender. Yet both black men and women used the term. Maria Stewart, David Walker, and Henry Highland Garnet used appeals to manhood to incite blacks to action, but it was not clear whether black women were included. Did calls for slave resistance include women? Were they expected to be "manly"?

Black women's resistance to slavery paralleled black men's, running the gamut from trickery and feigning illness to escape and physical confrontation.[43] Women's physical prowess was acknowledged and often admired within the slave community. Silvia Dubois was proud of the strength that enabled her to run a ferryboat better than any man on the Susquehanna River. As a child she endured her mistress' brutality, but when grown to five feet ten inches tall and weighing more than two hundred pounds, Silvia finally exacted her retribution by severely beating her mistress. After intimidating white spectators who might have subdued her, she picked up her child and made her escape from slavery.[44]

Woman's rights advocate and abolitionist Sojourner Truth often spoke with pride of her ability while a slave to do the work of any man. She did not find her strength or her six-foot frame incompatible with being a woman. Nor did Frederick Douglass question the appropriateness of one slave woman's refusal to be beaten and her physical ability to stand her ground against any disbelieving master. When Douglass was resisting Covey, a slave woman named Caroline was ordered to help restrain him. Had she done so, Douglass believed her intervention would have been decisive, because "she was a powerful woman and could have mastered me easily . . ." Thus only because a women defied her master was Douglass able to assert his manhood.[45]

For black women no less than black men, freedom and dignity were tied to assertiveness, even to the point of violence. Slavery blurred distinctions between the gender expectations in black society and reinforced the broader economic and political roles provided to black women by their African heritage. Slavery attempted to dehumanize the slave without regard to gender. Both men and women resisted in concert with others and through the force of their individual personalities; dignity and respect could be achieved by remarkable individuals of both sexes. In freedom, black women protected themselves and their families from slave catchers and kidnappers. They were also aggressive wage earners, providing substantial portions of their household income. Scholars have described the independence and economic autonomy of women in precolonial West and Central Africa. As women's spheres and traits became increasingly differentiated from men's in nineteenth-century America, the experience and traditions of black women led them to depart from American gender expectations.[46]

There was no ideal in American society encompassing the experience or honoring the heritage of black women.[47] Perhaps the closest was the notion identified by Ronald W. Hogeland as *Radical Womanhood*, which allowed women a public role. But even this most extreme norm was not sufficient. It accepted the separation of feminine and masculine capabilities, granting moral superiority to women but reserving intellectual and physical power to men.

Accepting masculine traits as the opposite of feminine traits was one of many ways black men sought to establish and define themselves as men in the face of assaults by slavery and racial discrimination. Gender comparisons in Western society were carefully controlled to favor men, limiting women's sphere. Here black people participated in the ongoing effort in nineteenth-century America to construct gender roles in what Hogeland argued was a male-initiated attempt "not conceived of essentially to improve the lot of women, but [implemented] for the betterment of men." The argument set forth by black minister J. W. C. Pennington in opposition to the ordination of women into the African Methodist Episcopal Church illustrates this point. Pennington contended that women were unsuited for "all the learned professions, where mighty thought and laborious investigation are needed," because as "the weaker sex" they were "incapacitated for [them] both physically and mentally."[48]

The force of prevailing gender conventions outside the black community led some to promote gender expectations totally inappropriate for black women's lives. In the face of solid evidence to the contrary, several blacks, such as abolitionist Charles B. Ray, argued that the proper place for women was in the home, as "daughters are destined to be wives and mothers—they should, therefore, be taught to . . . manage a house, and govern and instruct children."[49] Even Douglass, who spoke at the Seneca Falls Convention in 1848 in favor of women's right to vote, asserted in that same year that "a knowledge of domestic affairs, in all their relations is desirable—nay, essential, to the complete education of every female . . . A well regulated household, in every station of society, is one of woman's brightest ornaments—a source of happiness to her and to those who are dependent upon her labors of love for the attractions of home and its endearments."[50] Although this may have been an appropriate ideal for many white middle- and upper-class women of the time, it was unrealistic for white working women, and even more unrealistic for black women. Most black women did become wives and mothers, but for many their knowledge of domestic affairs was necessarily applied in someone else's home in exchange for wages to help support their families.

Of all the techniques for bolstering black manhood, this was the most internally destructive. It demanded that women affirm their own inferiority in order to uphold the superiority of their men. Not that every African American accepted these gender images, many did not, but they nevertheless became touchstones for gender conventions within black society. Moreover, women faced sanctions for disregarding them, for to do so was viewed as furthering the aims and continuing the effects of slavery, depriving black men of their manhood.[51]

There were women who recognized the dangerous consequences of counterpoising male and female traits, but only the boldest voices were raised in opposition. One of those voices was Sojourner Truth's. In the aftermath of the Civil War, when Congress debated the Fifteenth Amendment and related legislation providing the franchise to black men but not to women, she warned of the dangers inherent in such a move: "I feel that I have a right to have just as much as a man. . . . if colored men get their rights and not colored women theirs, the colored men will be masters over the women, and it will be just a bad as before."[52]

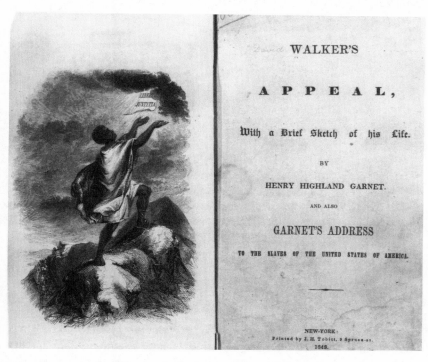

Walker's Appeal became the pivotal statement of black militancy during the antebellum period. In 1848 Henry Highland Garnet published *Appeal* and included a short biography of Walker and his own 1843 call for slave revolt. (Library of Congress)

Freedom's Yoke

Gender Conventions among Free Blacks

> Honey, de white man is de ruler of everything as fur as Ah been able
> tuh find out. Maybe its some place way off in the ocean where de
> black man is in power, but we don't know nothin' but what we see.
> So de white man throw down the load and tell de nigger to pick it up.
> He pick it up because he have to, but he don't tote it. He hand it to
> his womenfolks. De nigger woman is de mule of the world so fur as
> Ah can see.
>
> Zora Neale Hurston

Thus the reality of race and gender in early twentieth century Florida
was passed on to Janie Sparks by her grandmother in Zora Neale
Hurston's 1937 novel, *Their Eyes Were Watching God*.[1] The folk wisdom of this old black woman presented a major theme in black history,
as black women and men lived out their lives and worked out their relationships in the face of limitations imposed by American society and
Western culture. The gender role expectations of antebellum society
were extreme and did not conform to the realities of life for most
women and men of the period. For black people the twin burden of race
and sex widened the discrepancy between the real and the ideal. Attempts to approximate the gender conventions of the day in the harsh
presence of racial reality strained the fabric of black personal and communal relationships.

This chapter will investigate gender conventions among free
blacks in the antebellum North. It will seek to compare the stated ideals

of the general American society to those of the free black society of the time. These ideals will then be measured against the realities of antebellum black life in the Free States. Of central concern is the impact of race on the relationships of black women and men. The data for this study were drawn from the most influential black newspapers of the period, the *Colored American, Freedom's Journal,* the *North Star,* the *Weekly Advocate,* and the *Aliened American.* Other information was taken from the letters, speeches, and the military and probate records of northern blacks. Important data also were gathered from the U.S. censuses of 1850 and 1860. Because of the nature of the data used in this study, any conclusions presented here are weighted toward the urban black experience. The difficulty in this situation is partly offset by the fact that antebellum northern blacks were disproportionately urban. They were, in fact, the most urban group in America at that time.[2]

Freedom came to northern blacks in the wake of the Revolution in response to abolitionist pressure and to the legal and extralegal agitation of slaves who appealed to the rhetorical ideals of the American cause. The limited economic importance of northern slavery and its powerful moral opposition overwhelmed proslavery forces in the region. By 1800 the institution was abolished or set on the road to abolition in every northern state. As America struggled to establish a national identity during the first decades of the nineteenth century, northern blacks set about establishing communities, building institutions, and adjusting family relationships to their new "freedom."[3]

The gender conventions dictating the roles of these newly freed black women and men descended from African American traditions developed during colonial times, influenced by African, European, and American Indian cultures and by the realities of eighteenth-century slavery in the northern colonies. The small and scattered slave holdings of the colonial North had complicated black family life. Often husband and wife belonged to separate masters and could be together only during periods when one or both were allowed to be away from their duties. Visitation was governed not only by a slave's limited free time, but also by the considerable travel it might require. Usually the husband journeyed to the wife's home, as masters were more likely to permit men to travel. Women were limited in their travel by child-care responsibilities as their masters generally retained ownership of the children of slave marriages.[4]

The slave experience in the North, as in the South, reinforced the

African traditions that assigned child care to women. Because slave children were generally considered the property of their mother's master, the economic value of female slaves was increased. This also reinforced many of the gender role assumptions of white Americans. It did not limit the sphere of the slave woman to child care and other domestic duties, however. As Jacqueline Jones suggested for the plantations of the antebellum South, the role of slave women on eighteenth-century northern farms was largely determined by the production needs of the master. This was especially true on the larger estates of the Hudson Valley region of New York or the plantations of Narragansett in Rhode Island. There, traditional Western views of acceptable roles for women did not prevent slave women from being used in heavy field work as well as in domestic duties. For them the ideals of feminine delicacy proved no shelter from the punishing lash or the lustful whims of slave masters. They were never too pregnant or too young or too frail to be subject to the harsh demands of an insensitive owner. They shouldered the work load of their race, unable to draw upon the protection generally accorded their sex.[5]

Slavery also affected gender roles for black men. Most of these men did "man's work," heavy physical labor. They were valued for their strength and their skill. Yet slavery demanded that black men forego the intellectual, emotional, and temperamental traits of manhood. The ideal slave recognized his inability to control his life. Theoretically the male slave's masculinity was, like his person, the property of his master. Thus the black man could offer little protection to his loved ones, especially when they were threatened by the slave master. As slavery forced black women into masculine work roles that affronted femininity, so black men were forced to accept limitations generally imposed only on women. Only within the bounds of the slave community were black men allowed to publicly display those traditional qualities of masculine aggressive power assumed by both European and West African culture. Within the family black women were not totally without power, but their power was limited by the need to not reinforce the goals of slavery, that is, to strip black men of that manhood that was surely a threat to masters and to the institution itself.

In the political life of northern blacks during the eighteenth century, women played important but not dominant roles. One of the most significant political public events among northern blacks in the colonial period was the annual "governor elections." Held in the spring or early summer, these were festive occasions allowed by masters who saw them as offering a controlled outlet for their bondpeople. To the slaves these festivals were far more. They were community times when families could share more than a few hours together, especially important to those separated by distance and the vicissitudes of temperamental masters.

The festival, which might last a week or more, included competitive games, food and drink, singing and dancing, and involved the election of a "governor," or "king," of the slaves. Although this was largely a ceremonial position, on occasion masters invested real power in the "king" and his appointed council. They often acted as an alternative legal system, settling disputes among blacks and doling out punishment to those whom it determined to be culpable. Among blacks these were positions of substantial power to which only men were elected. Moreover, those who voted for the officeholders and those who competed in the sports competition during festival days were men. Women prepared the food and catered the feasts.[6]

Men also dominated the political actions by slaves that helped bring abolition to the North at the end of the eighteenth century, although some action included both men and women. Individual court suits were brought by women such as Jenny Slew, a Massachusetts mulatto, who in 1765 charged that her master, John Whipple of Ipswich, held her in bondage unlawfully for three years. She demanded not only her freedom but also damages in the amount of twenty-five pounds. Although Jenny Slew lost her case initially, a year later on appeal she was awarded four pounds and court expenses. The vast majority of cases in the colonies were, however, brought by men.[7]

The pattern was the same for the petitions presented by northern slaves to colonial governments and to those of the new nation demanding freedom and other benefits of the Revolution. Although a few, such as one presented in 1779 by eight Salem, Connecticut, slaves to the Connecticut General Assembly included the names of women, most were brought by black men alone.[8] One of the earliest of these presented before the colonial legislature in Boston in 1773 complained, "We have no Wives! No Children! We have no City! No Country!" Women helped plan collective actions of protest aimed at the acquisition of freedom and civil rights and liberties, but where white authority was publicly addressed, the presentation was most often by black men. Thus as northern slaves emerged into freedom in the nineteenth century, a pattern of male political visibility had already been established.[9]

During the first quarter of the nineteenth century, as black institutions were established in the cities and towns in the North, men dominated their leadership but women played key roles. Before the African Meeting House became the home of the African Church of Boston, black Baptists of that city met in private homes. Women took part in the initiation of services and helped raise the funds that financed the building of a permanent church home in 1806. They also filled minor leadership roles in the church, although no woman was selected minister.[10]

In Philadelphia and New York the pattern was similar. Although a few black women acted as itinerant ministers, and a few others filled church pulpits on a temporary basis, generally they participated in, but did not lead, formal religious services. Black men played out their roles as leaders and protectors of their women where they could. The mutual aid groups and fraternal organizations were specifically dedicated to the care of widows and orphans in the absence of husbands and fathers. Clearly there was the hope, even the expectation, among some black men that with freedom would come the possibility that black people could form their lives to approximate gender conventions of American society at large. Indeed, for black men the ability to support and protect their women became synonymous with manhood, and manhood became synonymous with freedom. Manhood and freedom were tied to personal power. After offering resistance to his master for the first time, Frederick Douglass recalled feeling that where as before "I was nothing . . . I was now a man." The role played by black men within their families and within their communities had an important bearing on their perception of manhood, the possession of which slavery had sought to rob them.[11]

Gender ideals of black society were heavily influenced by middle-class black males through the pages of black newspapers, in the bylaws of black organizations, and from the pulpits of black churches. The message was not unlike that conveyed to the American population at large, but there were differences that were both liberating and burdensome for black people. Women were told that they were the gentler sex, naturally more moral, more loving, more caring than men. In 1839 one article in the *Colored American* laid out the differences between men and women in clear and comparative terms:

Man is strong—Woman is beautiful
Man is daring and confident—Woman is deferent and unassuming

Man is great in action—Woman in suffering
Man shines abroad—Woman at home
Man talks to convince—Woman to persuade and please
Man has a rugged heart—Woman a soft and tender one
Man prevents misery—Woman relieves it
Man has science—Woman taste
Man has judgement—Woman sensibility
Man is a being of justice—Woman an angel of mercy[12]

This was the message given not only to black women, but to all women. Black newspapers were clear in their support of the place reserved for the female sex in American society. In their pages were countless stories of the dire consequences that awaited those who did not accept and conform to the pattern, within the limits of their ability. One anecdote that appeared in an 1827 issue of *Freedom's Journal* related the plight of a woman doomed to a life without a man because she violated one cardinal role of female behavior, she "could not keep her mouth shut." Black women were told that they must provide a subtle guidance for their husbands and all black men. Care must be taken, however, that guidance did not become nagging annoyance. The story of the woman who allowed her perfectionist ideals to lead to the frustration and degeneration of the health of a boarder in her home was used as an object lesson lest the limits of reason be crossed. She "drove him crazy" with her admonitions to sit properly in his seat and exhibit correct table manners. She did not let him disturb his place setting during dinner and even went so far as to chastise him for using the wrong peg on the household hat rack.[13]

Similarly, these newspapers instructed black men, in terms not unlike those applied to other American males, in the ways of manhood. The *Aliened American* stressed the virtues of the True Gentleman, but other newspapers advised that black men must do more than "bow and tip their hats." A man must be strong enough to protect his woman and children. There was heavy emphasis on independence, for as one editor put it in 1839, "Men are made to be their own masters" both in the household and in the business and politics of society.[14] Black men also were admonished to work hard and to be enterprising. In true republican fashion, there was great value placed on black men becoming entrepreneurs, and acquiring skills was seen as one of the best routes to business success. Frederick Douglass was among those who urged black men to learn and practice trades. He was one of the authors of an address delivered at the 1848 National Convention of Colored Citizens held in Cleveland that encouraged that skills be acquired in order that menial employment would not continue to be the mainstay of black economic survival. It was not only a man's duty to himself and his family to learn a skill, it was his duty to the race. Trade skills passed on to the sons of the coming generations would help ensure racial progress.[15]

This charge to individuals to act for the good of the race permeated all aspects of gender conventions in antebellum black society, and it placed additional pressure on those already struggling with weighty economic problems. There were several aspects to this responsibility of race. First, there was the need to pass on to coming generations the practical tools of progress, that is, education and skills, knowledge and property. Parents were reminded that the children were not only their posterity but also the future of the race. The young must be taught the value of hard work and imbued with a sense of responsibility. They should be impressed with the importance of fulfilling contracts and paying debts. Although personal strength and self-reliance were seen as important virtues, there was great value placed on sensitivity to the feelings of others. Parents were told that children must be taught to exhibit tenderness and kindness toward others, regardless of their circumstance.[16]

Mothers were to play the dominant role in this aspect of the child's education. For this reason the black woman was urged to spend significant amounts of time with her children and to improve her mind so that she might pass on her knowledge to her young. Education for children was a top priority, and parents were strongly advised to get their children into school and to be sure that they arrived on time each day. Here again the mother had particular responsibility. There was special mention of the importance of cultivating the minds of daughters so that one day they might play an important role in "the domestic and social relations of life."[17]

Fathers were to teach more by example than by conversation, although it was thought important that they converse frequently with their sons, especially on work-related matters. The teaching of sobriety and hard work was stressed. It was recommended that fathers tell their sons the story of the squirrel that anticipated winter, laying out a supply of nuts, and the bird who did not prepare for the future. Of course winter taught the bird a hard lesson, which black boys should learn as well.[18]

Black newspapers also carried the message that each black person must become a living refutation of the racial stereotypes held by white society. Men must never be ill-mannered, improperly dressed, or drunk in public. Children must always be neat and clean and display proper respect for their elders, lest it reflect badly on the race. Women were told to be especially careful of any public display of sexuality. Every "sensible woman," it was said, realized the wisdom of delicacy, discretion, and simplicity in dress. She understood that as the "more beautiful sex" she had no need of ornamentation, for her wish was not to "seduce by her appearance, but only to please." It was the foolish woman who was "led astray by fashion and splendor," whereas those responsible to their "community duties" looked to religious examples of moderation.[19]

This concern that black women not flaunt their sexuality was intended as partial protection from the unwanted attentions of white men. As physical beauty might be a curse to a female slave, so too protection was important for the nearly 50 percent of black women in the cities of the antebellum North who labored as servants in the homes of white families. All women who worked under the control of males were of course vulnerable in this regard. Sexual mythology was often used by men who took advantage of women over whom they held power to justify and excuse their immoral acts. Lower-class women, especially black women, were often charged with inviting the lust of morally suspect men. Class stereotypes, combined with stereotypes about African American sexual appetite and aggressiveness and the relative lack of legal protection afforded to blacks, assured that black women suffered special problems of sexual harassment.[20]

Black men were seldom in a position to protect their women. Racism helped create economic conditions that made it impossible for black men to support their families without the supplementary incomes of their wives and contributed to the numbers of black women, without men, called upon to support families on their own. Sexism limited the types of employment available to women, increased their liability to the demands of white male authority, and forced almost all women to rely on the protection of some man. Under these circumstances, black women dared not display overt sexuality.

As the popular media demanded of all women, black women were expected to maintain the highest moral standards themselves and to be responsible for the morality of their men. They were instructed to resist all men who indulged in drinking and gambling and through their "smiles and economical conduct in [their] domestic pursuits . . . provoke the indolent and improvident husband to active industry and frugality."[21]

Gender conventions among free blacks carried the added burden of the struggle to counteract the distortion of slavery and other racial injustices. Slavery sought to reduce black people to dependent, passive, childlike characters. It especially tried to make black men irrelevant as far as their women and children were concerned. Male slaves, it was supposed, could neither provide for nor protect their families and so took little interest in them. As one historian wrote: "According to the slaveholders, slave men had little sense of responsibility toward their families and abused them so mercilessly that Ole Massa constantly had to intervene and protect the women and children." Effort was made to emasculate male slaves, making them less terrifying and making the master more manly by comparison, at least in the white imagination. The punishment of slave men in the presence of their wives and children and the abuse of family members in the presence of husbands and fathers served to make the master's point; slave men could not play the complete masculine role.[22]

Historians have argued convincingly that this attempted emasculation was less than successful not only because many black men refused to be broken but also because their families—especially their women—refused to blind themselves to the limitations of their situation. Women knew what was and what was not possible and respected their men within the context of the realities of black life. In fact, that respect itself became an act of resistance. In freedom, too, black people moved within the limits of the practical constraints of racism, which insured that the vast majority of African Americans would be poor.[23]

Throughout the antebellum North, black men found steady employment at reasonable wages difficult or impossible to secure. Even a trained black worker was generally not allowed to use his skill. Frederick Douglass was a skilled caulker who should have found ample opportunities to ply his trade on the docks of New Bedford, Massachusetts. When he went to the wharfs in search of work, he was told that "every white man would leave the ship, in her unfinished condition, if I struck a blow at my trade." Douglass was forced to take work as a common laborer, for which he received one-half of what he earned as a caulker.[24]

Black men who sought to go into business for themselves found similar problems. Black cartmen in New York City were denied licenses to sell their wares because of the objections of their white competitors.[25] Equally frustrating barriers existed in Philadelphia, Cincinnati, and Boston; in fact, anywhere black workers sought work they were likely to confront the resistance of white competitors. Blacks were almost always the losers in such competition, so it was improbably that a family could be supported on one salary. The domestic work open to black women was often steady employment, unlike the seasonal nature of much of the work available to black men. One attractive feature offered by domestic work in the homes of others, or by "taking in" washing or sewing at one's own home, was that such an arrangement allowed for the care of children at the workplace. Under these circumstances it was unreasonable to expect that black women could at the same time be model housewives, yet that was exactly what they were urged to do in the pages of black newspapers.

Unrealistic or not, these black women were also expected to be "true women." It was far too much to demand, as one black editor did, that a woman keep her house neat and clean, insure that her family always had clean clothing to wear, be sensitive to the unspoken problems of her children, and take time to plan nutritional and tasty meals—if at the same time that woman was expected to devote eight to twelve hours a day as a wage earner. Yet black women were to do all this and more. A woman should rise early, one article said, so that she might prepare breakfast for her husband, allowing time to listen to his conversation, express interest in his work, and provide sympathy for his problems. Another article suggested that the black woman always attempt to cook her husband's favorite food, never gossip about him, keep his secrets, and "always receive him with a smile."[26] Obviously this combination of tasks was impossible.

Yet some women actually performed all or most of these jobs with great skill. Sarah Watson of Westerly, Rhode Island, lived with her husband and five children. Thomas Watson, a revolutionary war veteran, worked as a laborer for most of his life, and Sarah was a domestic servant. When Thomas was taken with rheumatism, his work became even more sporadic than before. The Watsons took in boarders to make ends meet. Although Thomas was at home much of the time with his illness, Sarah performed all the work to serve the boarders. One of the Watson's neighbors explained that "of course this kept Sarah plenty busy between working outside, keeping the children and the men [male boarders], especially with him [Thomas] always in the way." Interestingly, there was no expectation that a black man aid in the household duties.[27]

The story of Chloe Spear provides a more complex picture of woman's role in the black family. Born in 1750 in Africa and held in slavery in Boston until the late eighteenth century, Chloe married Cesar Spear, also a slave. After the family was freed, the Spears operated a boardinghouse in the city. In addition Chloe did domestic work for a prominent Boston family. While she was at work Cesar saw to the cooking and other duties associated with the boardinghouse, but when she returned in the evening he turned the operation over to her while he "was taking his rest." After working all day, Chloe cooked dinner for her family and the boarders and cleaned the house. In order to make extra money she took in washing, which she did at night, setting up lines in her room for drying the clothes. She slept a few hours while the clothes dried, then ironed them and prepared breakfast for the household before going off to work for the day.[28]

The unbelievable work schedule of women like Chloe Spears might easily lead to the conclusion that black women were cruelly exploited by their husbands, but the situation was not so simple. Chloe did not routinely hand over her wages to her husband as was usual for white working women of the period. She controlled her own money. At one point she decided to purchase an unfurnished house. Because the law would not allow a married woman to buy a house in her name, Chloe was forced to approach her husband to make the purchase for her. His reaction is instructive. On learning that the house cost seven hundred dollars, Cesar determined that he could not afford it. "I got money," Chloe announced, after which Cesar agreed to make the purchase.[29]

Obviously Chloe was not simply putting away the "egg money," the traditional wife's secret treasury. She earned money and was not required to account to her husband for her earnings. Most interesting here is the fact that Chloe was limited not by her husband's demands but by the law, which limited all women in American society. Studies of the black family have long noted the increased independence and even authority black women exercised within the household because of their important role in the family economy. Chloe is an excellent example of the way black women asserted that role.[30]

The arduous domestic duties black women were exhorted to undertake by the press, and required to undertake because of economic realities, were performed for the good of the family. There was yet other work to be done for the good of the race. The *Weekly Advocate* began the new year of 1837 with a series of articles instructing black women to use their time and their influence for the elevation of their race.[31] Another newspaper article suggested that if a woman were truly well organized she could complete her responsibilities early enough to attend night classes and abolitionist meetings in the evening. An education might provide a woman with one way out of domestic employment, which, despite its advantages, increased her vulnerability to the advances of white men. Education was also a service all black people were encouraged to provide to the community. It was believed that education would not only counteract racial prejudice but also better prepare blacks to understand and to participate in the ongoing struggle for racial justice.[32]

Black women were encouraged to take on reform activities that departed from the gender expectations in the wider society, and black men were generally supportive of these reform efforts. White female reformers, on the other hand, often encountered severe opposition from white men when they attempted to publicly address mixed (female and male) audiences. Many black women were recruited by men as antislavery speakers. One of the most popular female voices of protest was that Sojourner Truth. Truth was the first woman to join the antislavery lecture circuit and as such was often the target of considerable abuse. At one point in 1858 she was willing to break the rules of female propriety, publicly baring her breast in response to the charge of a hostile crowd of white men that she was not a woman. No black man ever attacked her in this manner.[33]

Maria W. Stewart, inspired by the Bible and *Walker's Appeal*, spoke out against racial injustice of all kinds. On 21 September 1832, she became the first American woman to deliver a public address when she lectured to a mixed audience at Boston's Franklin Hall. Her effort was welcomed by the black men of Boston and regarded as a triumph for the race. Yet these men were far less complimentary when, at a lecture before the African Masonic Lodge in the city one year later, she took black men to task for not doing all they could for the race. "Have the sons of Africa no souls? Feel they have no ambitious desires? ... There may be a few such men among us, but they are rare." Her remarks caused such outrage in her listeners that she was forced to leave Boston. Black women who spoke on behalf of abolition and civil rights were applauded by their men. There were limits, however, to the public chastisement that these men were willing to endure, especially from a woman who questioned their manhood, even one whom they admired in other respects.[34]

Other black women who did not attack black men so directly were encouraged. Women such as Francis Ellen Watkins, whose "soft and musical voice" was said to "take a deep hold on the human heart," was a favorite in Pennsylvania and New Jersey.[35] Sarah Parker Remond often toured with her brother Charles and other abolitionist speakers and became well respected for her presence and speaking ability. So popular was she that she was invited to lecture in England, an invitation she accepted despite the fact that young ladies of the day did not generally go abroad alone.[36]

Black women were also included in Underground Railroad efforts and in the call by several black state conventions for business education for blacks.[37] Further, black women were charged with raising money for the various community activist causes, and they were expected to help provide medical care for fugitives who passed through the underground. These things were done not just by those few black women who did not work outside their homes, for their numbers were far too small for the enormity of the task. The female foot soldiers in the war on poverty and slavery included black washerwomen and domestic-service workers. They were women such as Hannah Austin from Hartford County, Connecticut, who although illiterate managed to raise four children, care for an invalid husband, take in washing, participate in church activities, and raise funds for the local antislavery society.[38]

Clearly black women were expected to shoulder the responsibilities of their sex and of their race. These responsibilities taken together expanded "black women's work" to herculean proportions. They were driven by the demands of slavery to take on "slave's work" in the fields or in the master's house, then to perform "women's work" in the slave quarters for their families; similarly, the economics and the politics of freedom demanded that these women work at multiple occupations and fill multiple roles. Yet the limitations of race and sex ensured that they could never quite live up to societal expectations for any of the roles they filled. The limitations under which all blacks labored brought a poverty that made it impossible for black women to be "true women" in the full nineteenth-century sense of that term, and the limitations imposed on women combined with those on blacks to all but foreclose the possibility of an enterprising woman becoming a true economic success. The black woman was then trapped by pressures from her community, from the wider society, and from the economic reality of her times.

In freedom the black man also faced obstacles to living the gender ideal. Men may have been made to be their own masters, as one black newspaper advised, but black men knew better.[39] Their reaction to this contradiction was varied and complex. Before he became successful as a writer and a political leader, William Cooper Nell was deeply depressed about his chances in a society of restricted black opportunity. Nell's spirits were lifted and his self-image improved through his involvement with other blacks and a few white allies in the activism that sought to deal with the racial problems of Boston and the national problem of slavery. Black men often addressed the questions of manhood in close association with fellow black males. Sometimes these were formally organized associations, such as the black Masonic Order, which began in Boston and spread throughout the North before the Civil War. There were groups associated with a particular occupation, such as those formed by black seamen, and more general associations such as the American League of Colored Laborers, formed in New York City in 1850. There were also informal social and political groups formed around popular business establishments such as Smith's Barber Shop in Boston or the Dumas Hotel in Cincinnati. These establishments housed groups that provided emotional and psychological support for their male members.

These black male groups validated their members' humanity and manhood. The governor elections, which continued well into the middle of the nineteenth century, offered occasions for sporting competitions in which men displayed their physical prowess and skill. Celebrations in the Masonic lodges included conveying titles and offices, fancy-dress parades, and speechmaking in which only men participated. The informal groups generally built their activities around card playing, drinking, and storytelling—all-male activities that created a bond. When Fletcher got married, his male friends lamented his transformation from flashy dressing, hard-drinking comrade to teetotaling family man. It was said that Fletcher moved away from his old friends in Boston's North End to settle in the more family-oriented black residential area of Beacon Hill. Although his friends were much amused by these changes, they were also saddened when Fletcher "got married, got religion, and moved to the hill." Their amusement thinly masked their feeling of loss.[40]

Black women, no less than their men, had separate groups. They formed literary societies in Boston, New York, and Philadelphia, and temperance organizations in most major northern cities. There were women's groups to improve the education of black children and to provide for those in need of charity, and women's clubs specifically designed to address the issue of abolition. As was true for men, women who participated in formally organized groups were most likely to be the most economically secure, although women from all economic levels took part. Informal groups received the day-to-day attention of most working-class black women. Black men were likely to meet outside the home, on the street, in the barbershop, or in some other business establishment in the community, but black women were apt to gather informally at home, often in conjunction with work being done there. The chief exception to this was the association that went on during trips to and from market or church.[41]

The practice of taking in boarders, so popular among antebellum urban blacks in the North, sometimes provided black women with a live-in support group, particularly because those who boarded in black households were most likely to be young females. They usually paid for their room and board with services and became an important factor in the ability of the women in the host families to take employment outside the home. Thus insofar as black women were able to meet the obligations imposed by the demands of their race and their sex, they often did so with the assistance of other black women.[42]

The separation of black male from black female groups served to underscore gender divisions common in nineteenth-century America. The reaction of Fletcher's male friends to his "settling down" betrayed a tension between women and men symbolized by a male ambivalence toward marriage. Also, the reaction of Fletcher's comrades can be understood, in part, as that of young working-class men to the institution of marriage. For middle-class black men, marriage was more expected, and although there may have been a similar notion of the limitations imposed by the institution, it is doubtful that most would have reacted as Fletcher's friends did.

In most instances, marriage did not limit the professional activity of black men, because their wives were quite capable of handling family responsibilities, including providing the needed family income. Anna

Murray Douglass not only raised five children and conducted all the household affairs but also worked as a shoe binder to help support the family while her husband, Frederick, was busy making an international reputation as an antislavery speaker, author, and newspaper editor. Throughout their marriage of forty-four years, Frederick's speaking duties took him away from the family for extended periods (he spent almost two years lecturing in England in the mid-1840s), during which Anna managed alone. Rosetta Douglass remembered her mother's willingness to manage the house, to take pride in the knowledge that "when he [Frederick] stood up before an audience that his linen was immaculate and that she had made it so." "Father was mother's honored guest," Rosetta explained. "He was from home so often that his home comings were events that she thought worthy of extra notice. Everything was done to add to his comfort."[43]

Some marriages did not survive the rigors of the abolitionist's life. Elizabeth Brown, wife of reformer William Wells Brown, could not adjust to her husband's long absences. Her extramarital involvements eventually led to the couple's separation and forced William to call on black friends to care for his children while he continued his antislavery duties.[44]

Marriage was more likely to impose limitations on women's public and professional lives. Elleanor Eldridge was advised by her aunt never to marry because it was a "waste of time." She believed that marriage imposed economic hardships on a woman and restricted her professional life. Elleanor apparently took the advice with some profit, becoming a successful businesswoman and the owner of considerable property.[45] Many black women remained single or postponed marriage while they pursued a career in business or reform. Paul Cuffe, a wealthy black businessman from Westport, Massachusetts, who gained national attention by transporting several black families to Liberia in the early nineteenth century, sold many of the African goods he imported through the New York business owned by his unmarried sister Freelove Slocum. Freelove had invested in his business and helped to finance his African trip and hoped to encourage interest in African trade by making products available to her New York customers. She also gave Paul and their brother John business investment advice, a practice highly unusual for women in nineteenth-century America. Significantly, Freelove could not have held her property in her name if she had been married.[46]

In the few cases where married women pursued a politically active

career, juggling the roles of wife and mother was difficult and often depended on services provided by other women. Mary Shadd continued
her activities as teacher, traveling lecturer, newspaper business manager,
and editor after her marriage to Thomas Cary, a Toronto businessman.
The marriage was not a conventional one. Thomas, a widower twelve
years older than Mary with three children, continued his barbering and
bathhouse business in Toronto while Mary traveled. Within a week of
their wedding, she was off on a midwestern speaking tour, and thereafter she maintained residence in Chatham, about two hundred miles
west of Toronto, where she edited her newspaper, *Provincial Freedman*,
started in 1853. The children lived with Mary, cared for by her younger
sister in her absence. In this way Mary Shadd Cary continued her work,
which included the care of fugitive slaves who sought shelter in Canada,
the promotion of Canada as a safe haven and a land of opportunity for
American blacks, and the management of her newspaper. These activities paused but briefly when her daughter Sarah was born in 1857 and
again at the birth of her son Linton in 1860.[47]

Mary Shadd Cary was remarkable. Most could not manage such a
complex life or were not willing to maintain such a separate existence
from their husbands and families. Thomas Cary was also unusual;
many men would have objected to such a marital arrangement. Other
black women handled activism and marriage in different ways. Sarah
Mapps Douglass put off marriage until late in life so that she might
teach black students in New York and, later, operate her own school in
Philadelphia. She was an active and outspoken proponent of civil rights
and antislavery all her life. When, in her late forties, she finally did wed
William Douglass, the marriage was difficult. In letters to Sarah
Grimké, a white abolitionist, she shared the problems of marriage for
the activist woman, referring to them as "grievous trials" and "painful
results." For the woman who chose duty to race over duty to sex there
was ambivalence and personal tension. Sarah had difficulty curbing her
severe dedication to race and was uncomfortable with her husband's
less active stance toward abolition.[48]

The decision not to marry was unconventional, but it offered one
means of reconciling the conflicting responsibilities placed on black
women. Many women prepared themselves for the possibility of life
without a man as a realistic response to the gender imbalance among
urban free blacks. Black men had a higher death rate than women, and
they were more likely to leave the city in conjunction with or in search

of work. Even in middle-class black families, it made sense that young girls be readied for self-sufficiency. Unmarried black women were not common, but neither were they unique. Accordingly, when black women elected to prolong their "bachelorhood" in the cause of political activism, their decision was not generally condemned. Perhaps they might take on their community responsibilities and their family duties serially.

A number of black couples worked as abolitionist teams, sometimes traveling together and even sharing the lectern. William and Ellen Craft, two fugitive slaves, were a popular pair on the antislavery circuit. Robert and Harriet Purvis of Philadelphia were well known in reformist circles for their work in abolition and in the movement to gain the right to vote for black men and all women. Such partnerships tended to narrow the distance between the sexual spheres among the couples involved.[49]

Even though there were many instances of intergender cooperation among African Americans, racial oppression and sexual oppression made it difficult for black women and men to work together as equals. No nineteenth-century Americans were able to totally escape the gender dictates of the wider society. Black men were generally supportive of the political action of black women, but they were not always willing to accept these women into male-dominated organizations. Black women did not allow their exclusion or subordination to pass without stern comment. One striking example of intraracial gender disagreement was the controversy that arose over the question of the role black women should play in the black state and local conventions of the antebellum period. These conventions were held periodically to address the concerns of black people and to select representatives to national conventions. Women were not selected to represent local black groups at state gatherings, and, although they were sometimes invited to the conventions as observers, they were normally not allowed to take part in the discussions. Rather, they provided the food and the musical entertainment during the social segments of the meetings.

At the 1858 meetings held in Troy to discuss the question of black suffrage in New York state, the women did not participate in the debate. They did, however, arrange "a table loaded with the most palatable refreshments, which were eaten during the recess, with a relish." At other state gatherings throughout the North, black women were appointed to committees to raise money. This conformed to the "helpmate" role expected of nineteenth-century women and was consistent with the admonitions of the black press, but often black women refused to comply. These women were important to the economic and political life of the black community, and on occasion they attempted to exert pressure on their men for a voice in community affairs.[50]

At the 1849 Ohio state meeting, the black "ladies" threatened to walk out of the convention and never return if they were not allowed to take part in the discussion. After much debate among the men, it was decided that the women could participate as full members in the meetings. A year later at the Cazenovia convention in New York state, three women were appointed to the five-member business committee. In 1855 Mary Shadd Cary was elected corresponding member to the National Convention of Colored Citizens meeting in Philadelphia. She addressed the largely male gathering on the subject of Canadian emigration. Although their full participation continued to be problematic and black women continued to provide the food and music for the gatherings, clearly they could assert power within their community unparalleled among white women of the time. Just as clearly, black women were not accorded full and equal partnership.[51]

Women's political and economic importance expanded their role, but it did not eliminate traditional gender ideals. Protests like that at the Ohio convention were not common, but it is important that they occurred. Because most discontented people do not protest publicly, those who do take on special significance. Yet there was surely a range of opinion among black women. Those who pressed for their inclusion at conventions spoke for countless other women, but there were women satisfied to cater the meetings, allowing the men to handle convention matters.

During the nineteenth century, as now, black liberation was often defined in terms of the ability of black women and men to become full participants in American life. Ironically, this not only meant the acquisition of citizenship rights, almost all of which were applied only to men, but also entailed an obligation to live out the gender ideals of American patriarchal society. There were surely greater potential advantages in this brand of liberation for black men than for black women.

All women were expected to defer to men, but for black women deference was a racial imperative. Slavery and racism intended to emasculate black men; black people sought to counter the effects of such an intention. Part of the responsibility of black men was to "act like a man," and part of the responsibility of black women was to "encourage and support the manhood of our men." A woman should "never intimidate him [the black man] with her knowledge or common sense, let him feel stable and dominant."[52] It was seen as a black woman's duty to the race to allow black men to feel "tough and protective" even if the realities placed severe qualifications on the man's ability to exhibit these characteristics.[53] Whereas all women faced sanctions for not living out the demands of the American patriarchy, and many working-class white women worked outside their homes as black women did, the commitment to racial liberation that black women felt was an extra burden with which they had to deal.

Nevertheless, it would be a great oversimplification to assume that black women and men simply accepted the nineteenth-century male view of female inferiority. At a time when white women were condemned and punished by white men for public speaking and other "unladylike" activities, the contributions of black women to abolition and civil rights were encouraged by black men. Maria Stewart's "assault" on the black Masons in Boston in 1833 was an exception. Many, if not most, black men supported women's rights. Historians have long noted the actions and statements of black men such as Frederick Douglass, for example, who not only supported equal rights for women but also was the only male to speak in favor of women's suffrage at the Seneca Falls Convention in 1848. Douglass was instrumental as well in the election of Mary Shadd Cary to the 1855 Philadelphia convention.[54]

Many other black men agreed with Douglass and said so publicly. Martin Delany was a strong supporter of women's rights and especially of women's right to a liberal education. "The potency and respectability of a nation or people," he wrote, "depends entirely upon the position of their women; therefore, it is essential to our elevation that the female portion of our children be instructed in all the arts and sciences pertaining to the highest civilization." For these men the elevation of black women was a part of the struggle. Delany went further. When the Emigration Convention met in Cleveland in 1854 to consider the possibilities of African American emigration to Africa, Delany, who had been a prime mover in the convention, supported the presence of six female delegates, one of whom was his wife, Catherine Delany.[55]

Although black men supported women's rights, they accepted many conventional notions about women's sphere. Delany, for example, believed in the "equality of the sexes" but also believed that the place of the married woman was at home as long as the economics of the family permitted it. As one historian has written: "Although critical of the female who worked just to be able to purchase luxuries, Delany had 'nothing to say against those whom necessity compels to do these things, those who can do no better.'" Delany had strong words for black women "who voluntarily leave their home and become chambermaids and stewardesses." He theorized that they only did so to obtain meaningless luxuries and charged them as "symbolic of the degradation of the black race." Even the most liberal black men saw the woman's natural place as in the home.[56]

As we have seen, Frederick Douglass's wife, Anna, bore the burden of the family nurturer and partial provider while Frederick moved in the world of men. Robert and Harriet Purvis may have worked together in the struggle for reform and they may have both supported women's rights, but Harriet was still expected to perform her "domestic responsibilities." Small wonder some black women preferred to participate in the public world as an alternative, not a complement, to marriage.[57]

A few black women were outspoken in the condemnation of the burdens placed on them by sex and race. Sojourner Truth demanded the equality of women as well as the equality of blacks. She called attention to the plight of black women specifically in her famous speech in Akron, Ohio, in 1852 with the words that have become symbols of the coalescence of race and sex as major stigmas in American society: "Ain't I a woman?" By the end of the nineteenth century, other black women, such as Mary Church Terrell and Anna Cooper, took up the symbol in their struggle as blacks and as women, but during the antebellum years few spoke publicly in opposition to the subordinate position they were urged to assume in black society. At an 1838 meeting held in Philadelphia, black women urged that their sisters "patronize and encourage" the *Colored American* as a great voice of black people. No matter the unrealistic demands made on women by this newspaper, racial loyalty demanded that they be steadfast in its support.[58]

There was only one newspaper edited by a black woman in the antebellum period, Mary Shadd Cary's *Provincial Freedman* in Chatham, Canada. Despite her reputation as "a notorious mischief maker," despite her political militancy (she once said that if she had been a man she would have stood with John Brown at Harpers Ferry), and despite her own unconventional marriage, Cary did not publicly address the special problems of black women in their relationships with black men. She was not timid in her criticism of black men on other issues—her feud with black abolitionist Henry Bibb was notorious—but most of her comments on gender were "in strict keeping with the popular notions of the 'sphere of women.'" She even attempted for a time to hide the fact that a woman edited the newspaper, writing under the name M. A. Shadd. Although after the Civil War she was an outspoken advocate of women's rights, with the exception of an article entitled "Man's Sphere" in which she encouraged the independence of women and the cooperation of white and black women, she never directly tackled gender roles within African American society.[59]

Black people were handicapped, then, by racism that prevented most black men from economically fulfilling their part of the gender ideal and demanded that black women take on important economic roles. Economic influence and independence accrued to these women because of their expanded role, but the need to aid the race and to counter assaults on black manhood by a racist American society diminished these benefits. Sexism was also a handicap because it further curtailed black women's earning power beyond that already limited by racism. This made total independence for black women all but impossible, even as limited economic opportunities for black men made wifely dependence impractical. Political activism was another contribution to the race that expanded black women's role, but it too extracted a price. Part of this contribution was female deference to black manhood. The ideology of gender required that black men be made to feel the "king of their castle" no matter how humble the castle and no matter the hardships extracted from women who should have been treated as fully contributing partners in the family economy. As long as black liberation meant the creation of a black patriarchy, black women could not themselves be liberated.

In a challenging book on the subject, Bell Hooks argues that black women must overcome the narrow view that defines racial liberation in masculine terms. She writes: "Today masses of black women in the U.S. refuse to acknowledge that they have much to gain by feminist struggle. They are afraid of feminism. They have stood in place so long that they are afraid to move. . . . They are afraid to openly confront white feminists with their racism or black men with their sexism, not to mention confronting white men with their racism and sexism." One might add that many black men continue to fall prey to the masculine ideal that restricts their relationships with their families and obligates them to be part of the system maintaining the oppression of their women. This situation creates and exacerbates stress within African American society, making relationships difficult. At a time when the black family faces economic and social assaults unrivaled for generations, black people can ill afford these traditional tensions.[60]

Investigating the history of this contemporary situation is painful; it threatens to lay bare the rough inner sores of a world long protected by a façade of racial unity. It calls into question the judgement of those who, through antebellum black newspapers, preached the gospel of continued gender oppression even as they supported the struggle for racial freedom. If no black person can be free until all black people are free, then that freedom must know no limitation of gender. Only then will African Americans have thrown off the historic burden of race and sex and moved all Americans closer to genuine human equality.

The charm of the mulatto woman was legendary in black society, idealized and romanticized in poetry and song. "The Yellow Rose of Texas" was a song celebrating the "high yellow" complexion of the light-skinned beauty. (Library of Congress)

Chapter 6

Shades of Color

The Mulatto in Three Antebellum Northern Communities

> The gods bestow on me
> A life of hate.
> The white man's gift to see
> A nigger's fate.
>
> Seymour Gordden Link,
> "The Mulatto addresses his Savior on Christmas Morning."

The tragic mulatto has for the past three centuries been a familiar image in the literature of American race relations. The merging of the races supposedly created one who exhibited many of the "superior" intellectual and emotional characteristics of Caucasian heritage while suffering under the disadvantages of black "inferiority." The tragic mulatto was one torn in identity, yearning toward the elevation that genetically and socially was beyond the grasp, forced to settle for a lower place in the social order. Like the near-white characters in Harriet Beecher Stowe's *Uncle Tom's Cabin,* who were rebellious by "nature" and were driven to seek freedom as fugitives from slavery, the image was one of tortuous dissatisfaction with the role prescribed by man and nature.[1]

This view of the impact of interracial heritage is of course an oversimplification of a complex situation. No doubt the lives of some mulattoes were tragic for reasons that may or may not have had to do with their light skin. There is substantial evidence, however, that mulattoes enjoyed important advantages over darker blacks because many whites believed that the infusion of "white blood" increased their ability and civility. The social position of light-skinned blacks differed over time and space, making comparative study important to an understanding of the meaning of mulatto status. Segregationist law, established during the late nineteenth and early twentieth centuries, did not generally recognize *mulatto* as a racial designation but demanded that all African Americans be treated equally under the inequitable system of Jim Crow.[2]

Gradually the practical significance of racial hereditary status among blacks based on shade of color waned. In the twentieth century the *M* designation, used earlier in the federal census to connote mulatto, was dropped. Recent study has shown, however, that before the last decade of the nineteenth century, mulattoes were often favored by whites and sometimes separated themselves from darker blacks. Among African Americans, too, light skin frequently assumed an advantage, but attitudes toward mulattoes were complex and the pressure of race created significant ambivalence.

In 1918 sociologist Edward Reuter reported that mulattoes outdistanced darker blacks economically and socially because of what he saw as their greater ability and industry. His analysis was influenced by the notion that lighter skin suggests higher intelligence and greater innate ability. In the next generation, black sociologist E. Franklin Frazier agreed that mulattoes had certain advantages but attributed these to historical circumstances that had provided lighter blacks with a head start over others of their race. Other scholars studying African Americans during the 1930s and 1940s also found mulattoes holding an advantage among blacks as a result of their standing among whites.[3]

One of the most important historical treatments of mulattoes in America was a 1971 comparative study of American and Brazilian race relations by Carl Degler. Degler concluded that in the United States *mulatto* was a descriptive term, having no significance for social status. Obviously greatly influenced by the striking differences in the racial systems of the two countries, he overstated his case. "There are only two qualities in the United States racial pattern," he told the reader, "white or black. A person is one or the other, there is no intermediate position."[4] Degler's statement should be qualified to make clear its strongly comparative nature. Several subsequent studies made such qualification necessary.

Robert Toplin, studying the status of the mulatto in the antebellum South, found that status significant indeed. In 1979 he wrote in the *Journal of Southern History*, "Many southern whites preferred mulattoes to darker Negroes and provided them with better opportunities in slavery and freedom." This pro-mulatto bias among southern whites, especially slaveholders, was convincingly documented in the same year in a study by Leonard R. Lempel. Using runaway slave advertisements, Lempel illustrated white assumptions of mulatto superiority in intellect and physical appearance. What emerges from this data is an assumption based on the notion of white supremacy, a picture reminiscent of the stereotypical tragic mulatto, genetically superior to other blacks, chafing under the constraints of their racial status and, thus, always suspect.[5]

In 1980 Joel Williamson published the first full-length study of mulattoes to appear since Reuter's 1918 work. Covering the span of U.S. history, Williamson treated the complex status of light-skinned blacks in detail. Most important, he saw mulatto status as dynamic over time and space. Not only did whites treat lighter blacks differently in the upper and lower South, but that treatment was changing by 1860, evolving toward the "one drop rule," which would later in the century bring on race relations approximating those Degler saw in the United States. Although several historians have noted the change in mulatto status over time, few have recognized the regional variations Williamson outlined. In the upper South, where mulattoes were likely to have resulted from unions between blacks and nonelite whites, their status was lower than that of mulattoes in the lower South, where they were generally the product of unions between slaves and the planter aristocracy.[6]

These variations are important, not only because they provide insight into the relations between the races but also because they allow us a window into the structure of black society. That structure differs depending on the relationships of blacks to one another within their community, and those relationships in turn depend greatly on the role and status of mulattoes among other African Americans. This chapter deals with the question of color as it functioned within black society in three northern antebellum cities—Boston, Buffalo, and Cincinnati. The role of the mulatto differed from one region to another in the North just as it did in the South. Because it depended on local conditions, generalizations necessarily misrepresent the place of mulattoes in black social structure.[7]

Presently historians understand far more about antebellum southern blacks than about those in the North. Important studies of southern blacks before emancipation have analyzed the slave and free black communities of that region. Although many of these studies differ on other issues, they generally agree that blacks with lighter skin, straighter hair, and Caucasian-like features were often favored on the plantation as slaves and in the southern towns as free people. Most important, mulattoes were granted freedom more often than blacks of darker hues.[8]

In the afterglow of the American Revolution, hundreds of southern slaveholders emancipated their slaves. Their actions were spurred, in part, by guilt generated by the glaring inconsistency of slaveholding by those who proclaimed freedom as a natural right of humankind. Mulattoes were the slaves most likely to be freed. The tendency to manumit mulattoes in disproportionate numbers continued in the nineteenth century. By 1850, for example, mulattoes constituted 65 percent of Virginia's free black population but only 22 percent of the state's slaves.[9]

There was an even greater disparity in the states of the deep South where there had been no widespread emancipation after the Revolution. Slaves freed in the lower and western South were generally set free because of some specific relationship they had with masters and were more likely to be favored slaves, individually rewarded with freedom. A significant proportion of slaves freed under these circumstances were no doubt the children of slave masters and their slave concubines. This was responsible for the fact that by 1860 mulattoes in the lower South accounted for only about 9 percent of the slave population but for three-quarters of the free blacks.[10] In Alabama, Louisiana, Mississippi, Texas, and South Carolina, the mulatto proportion among free blacks was even higher. In the South as a whole, mulattoes were a 400 percent higher proportion of the free black community than of the slave community.[11]

Not only were mulattoes far more likely to be freed, but they were generally better equipped to exploit their freedom. They were more likely than darker blacks to be skilled workers, more likely to be literate, and more likely to be considered intelligent by whites. In many southern cities, especially the port cities of the lower South, lighter skin was a mark of upper-class status among blacks. Although Ira Berlin in his study of free blacks in the antebellum South cautioned that all mulattoes were by no means wealthy, the existence of the Brown Fellowship Society in Charleston and other color-exclusive clubs, catering solely to lighter-skinned propertied blacks, in southern cities such as New Orleans supports the notion that mulattoes were disproportionately

Table 1
Mulattoes as Percentage of African American Population, 1860

	Free (%)	Slave (%)
United States	36	NA
North	31	NA
South	41	10
Upper South	35	13
Lower South	75	9

Source: Bureau of the Census, Negro Population of the United States, 1790–1915.

financially secure. Many sought, through their associations, to distinguish and separate themselves from the dark mass of black society.[12]

In order to test the extent to which a pattern of color stratification also existed in the northern cities, the U.S. census data for Boston, Buffalo, and Cincinnati for 1850 and 1860 were analyzed. Indicators of stratification selected for this analysis were property holding, occupation, residential patterns, literacy, and marriage patterns. As might be expected, mulattoes held an advantage over darker blacks in every category in each city. Most interestingly, the degrees of difference between cities seemed to form definite patterns.[13]

An analysis of the black community drawn from the census must be regarded with care. This is especially true for a census involving such a subjective variable as mulatto status. Census marshals were given few instructions to help them assign racial designation. In 1850 they were told simply to record blacks with a *B* placed in the column indicating race and to enter an *M* for mulattoes. Whites were to be recorded by simply leaving the column blank. Under these circumstances the census can not be said to have recorded racial heritage. Instead, it actually recorded apparent skin color. Each census taker was likely to record the race of a person in accordance with his perception of the person's racial group. Given the subjective decision to be made in distinguishing between blacks and mulattoes, some check of the census marshal's judgment on this question is needed.

Theodore Hershberg and Henry Williams, in their 1981 study of mulattoes in nineteenth-century Philadelphia, attempted to test census reliability on the question of race by linking successive census reports from 1850 to 1880 and tracing the racial designation applied to individuals over that thirty-year period. They found that one-third of African Americans in their study were assigned different color designations from one census year to another, and that the change was likely to move mulattoes to the black designation. This shift of mulattoes to the darker classification was also highly correlated with occupational status changes. As job status fell, color designation in the census was likely to darken. There appeared to be some evidence that upward mobility and the accumulation of wealth tended to "lighten," but the evidence on this phenomenon was not conclusive. Hershberg and Williams remain convinced, however, that the census is useful for analysis of mulatto status within the black community, but they caution that such analysis must be viewed with an understanding of its data-imposed limitations.[14]

In an effort to refine our understanding of these limitations, the census data used in this study were put to two reliability tests. First, an individual linkage check was performed using the Hershberg and Williams method for the 1850 and 1860 census years. Adult males were used for this linkage. This operation was less than satisfactory, because the low persistence rate (the percentage of people who remain in the same city from one census year to the next) for black adult males severely restricted the number of records that could be linked. It was surprising to find how few adults could be linked in any of the cities. Only 5 to 8 percent of the African American men listed in the 1850 census could be traced to the 1860 census. It was not clear if such a low persistence rate was real or ostensible. Although beyond the immediate scope of this study, if actual, such dramatic movement in the population would surely have significant and far-reaching implications. Given the low persistence rate, the findings of this test are of minimal value, but they do show a difference between the cities. Of those who could be traced, 60 percent in Boston, 65 percent in Buffalo, and 70 percent in Cincinnati were reported with the same color designation in both census years. In Boston and Buffalo those whose reported color designation changed most often (30 and 37 percent, respectively, of the total linked) were those listed as "black" in 1850 but listed as "mulatto" in 1860. In Cincinnati those color designation listed as "mulatto" in 1850 were most likely to be changed to "black" (19 percent of the total linked) in 1860. Although it may be significant that the greatest percentage of those whose listings changed were different in the three cities, it is not possible to analyze the difference because the percentage linked was so small.

Because the first test was not satisfactory, a second test attempting to link the records of the war department with census records was performed. Regimental descriptive books for the Civil War listed specific skin color as recorded by the company clerk. Color designations ranged from "black" through "copper" and "light brown" to "yellow" and "light." If race, as recorded in the census, was in fact a matter of perception by the census taker, it is reasonable that those racial designations should closely follow the more color specific descriptions provided in the descriptive books. One hundred and forty men were linked between the military records and the census records for the three cities; ninety-three from Boston, twenty from Buffalo, and twenty-seven from Cincinnati. Sixty-six of the Boston men were listed in the census as "black," and twenty-seven were listed as "mulatto." Sixteen Buffalonians were designated "black" in the census, and four were listed as "mulatto." In the Cincinnati census, the count was eight listed as "black" and nineteen listed as "mulatto." All but six blacks in Boston, four in Buffalo, and one in Cincinnati appeared to be properly listed when compared to the color specific listings of the military records. Mulattoes were listed correctly except for four in Boston, one in Buffalo, and six in Cincinnati. Thus only 16 percent of those listed in the census appeared to have been inconsistently listed in 1850 and 1860. This is hardly conclusive evidence that the color designations used in the census are reliable, but it is the strongest evidence to date on that score.[15]

This study is predicated on the theory that regional differences in the antebellum North were reflected in structural variations in African American community life. The significance of color within black society is so basic that it provides a reliable window through which to view important community patterns and thus aid an understanding of the development of African American social structure. These two perceptions form the bases for this effort to examine the impact of region on the role of color among northern free blacks.

Cincinnati, Buffalo, and Boston were selected for analysis because they were very different in their demographic characteristics, their economic and social orientations, and their geographic locations. Cincinnati, the northern city with clearly southern economic and social orientations, was tied to the plantations served by southern ports along the Mississippi River. As early as 1805, barges rigged with sails transported goods from the city to be traded in Mississippi River ports. The coming of steam helped to make Cincinnati one the most important river ports

Table 2
Mulattoes and African Americans as Percentage of Population, 1850 and 1860

City	Mulatto % of African Americans		African American % Total Population	
	1850	1860	1850	1860
Cincinnati	60.1	53.7	2.8	2.3
Buffalo	23.0	27.8	1.6	0.99
Boston	21.1	37.4	1.5	1.3

Source: Bureau of the Census, U.S. Census, 1850 and 1860.

in the Midwest.[16] The city's large southern born population and the substantial number of southern visitors and business dealers set the tone for much of the social and political life. Cincinnati's black population was also largely southern born, growing from eleven hundred in 1830 to more than three thousand by midcentury and to more than thirty-seven hundred by 1860.[17]

The actual number of blacks rose during these decades, but the white population, especially immigrants, grew even more rapidly. The percentage of blacks in the city thus fell by half to slightly more than 2 percent on the eve of the Civil War. During this period, however, the percentage of mulattoes grew, so that by 1850 they accounted for 60 percent of all Cincinnati blacks. Although this percentage dropped to a little more than half of the black population by 1860, this high proportion of light-skinned blacks was far in excess of the regional average for the North (31 percent) or even among free blacks in the upper South (35 percent). Only in the lower South was the percentage of mulattoes in free African American society higher (76 percent). Significantly, southern port cities had much higher percentages of mulattoes in their free black populations, as much as 90 percent in some cases. Thus, Cincinnati, although not comparable to the port cities of the deep South, did have a large percentage of mulattoes in its black population. This was just one of the city's many southern characteristics.[18]

The pattern was quite different in both Buffalo and Boston. Economically and socially, Buffalo faced eastward. Even before the completion of the Erie Canal in 1825, Buffalo was linked to New York City by wagon route, over which its grain and flour was carried to eastern markets. The canal revolutionized the city's economy. By the 1850s the transportation costs to New York City had fallen from 1817 levels of twenty cents a ton-mile to under one cent a ton-mile. The city's grain receipts rose from less than 500,000 bushels a year in 1836 to more than 3.5 million bushels by 1860, making Buffalo "Queen City of the Lakes."[19]

Buffalo also drew most of its population from eastern New York state and New England. Black Buffalonians, like their white counterparts, were generally northern born. By the mid-nineteenth century, more than half of the blacks in Buffalo had been born in the North, whereas only one-third had been born in the South. Reflecting the northern character of the city, the proportion of mulattoes in Buffalo's black community was low, only 23 percent by 1850 and slightly higher by 1860. Antebellum Buffalo was northern in almost every respect that Cincinnati was southern.

Boston was a commercial city in the mid-nineteenth century. Most of its capital resources went to finance the industrial development of the city's hinterland, composed of a system of satellite mill towns. Although Boston was tied indirectly to the southern cotton that supplied the raw material for the mills, the Yankee traditions of the city were far too strong to succumb to "southernism." Boston's population was as Yankee as its traditions until after 1845 when the potato rot in Ireland forced poor Irish farmers into the city's North End by the tens of thousands.[20]

Black Bostonians, like blacks in Buffalo and in contrast to those in Cincinnati, were primarily northerners. About 60 percent had been born in northern states, most of them in New England. The southern-born black population ranged between 17 and 24 percent in the decades before the Civil War. Compared to Cincinnati, mulattoes were far less numerous among Boston blacks, accounting for no more than 37 percent of the community by 1860. This percentage was slightly higher than that for the proportion of mulattoes in the African American population of Philadelphia (31 percent) but about average for the New England and Middle Atlantic region.[21]

Differences in the significance of color is suggested by variations in the residential patterns within the black communities of the three cities. In black Cincinnati there appeared to be substantial clustering by color, which grew in the decades before the Civil War. In 1850 the four wards with the largest African American population (69 percent of the total) were the First (434), Fourth (573), Sixth (409), and Ninth (821). The

Table 3
Most Populous Black Wards—Cincinnati, 1850 and 1860

Ward	African Americans	Mulattoes	Darker blacks
	1850		
First	434	58	42
Fourth	573	42	58
Sixth	409	68	32
Ninth	821	70	30
	1860		
First	314	40	60
Fourth	804	30	69
Sixth	291	60	40
Thirteenth	974	63	37
Fourteenth	257	85	15

Source: Bureau of the Census, U.S. Census, 1850 and 1860.

proportion of mulattoes and darker blacks in these wards illustrate this color clustering. Mulattoes, 60 percent of the African American population in 1850, were overrepresented in two of these wards, the Sixth (68 percent) and the Ninth (70 percent). They were substantially underrepresented in the Fourth Ward (42 percent) and proportionately represented in the First Ward (58 percent).

By 1860 the residential separation between mulattoes and darker blacks had increased. A combination of population shift and the redrawing of ward lines meant that the largest black wards in the city (with 72 percent of the black population) changed in size. They were the First Ward (314), Fourth Ward (804), Sixth Ward (291), Thirteenth Ward (974), and Fourteenth Ward (257). Mulattoes, who accounted for more than 50 percent of the city's blacks in 1860, were underrepresented in the First (40 percent) and Fourth wards (30 percent). They were slightly overrepresented in the Sixth Ward (60 percent) and significantly overrepresented in the Thirteenth (63 percent) and Fourteenth wards (85 percent).

Darker blacks constituted 60 and 70 percent, respectively, of the African American population in two adjacent wards, the First and Fourth, concentrating most heavily in "Bucktown," a poor, undesirable, and less-than-healthful area of the city. Mulattoes accounted for only 30 percent of Bucktown but were more than 80 percent of the African

Table 4
Most Populous Black Wards—Boston, 1850 and 1860

Ward	African Americans	Mulattoes	Darker blacks
	1850		
Fifth	221	48	52
Sixth	1210	14	86
	1860		
Fifth	275	73	27
Sixth	1397	36	64

Source: Bureau of the Census, U.S. Census, 1850 and 1860.

Americans in western wards (the Fifteenth and Fourteenth), a substantial distance from the worst areas of black poverty. Indeed, the index of dissimilarity of 34.8 computed for darker blacks' and mulattoes' residence in Cincinnati for 1860 shows just how separate these two groups were. It shows that there was as much residential separation between darker blacks and mulattoes in Cincinnati as there was between blacks and whites in Brooklyn (35.5) or San Francisco (34.6).[22]

As in Cincinnati, blacks in Boston lived in residential groupings, not totally segregated from whites in the city but clustered in definable black neighborhoods. Lighter blacks and darker blacks were less likely to be separated in Boston than in Cincinnati, and although such separation was growing in the latter city, it was declining in the former. Mulattoes, 21 percent of Boston's African Americans in 1850, were underrepresented (14 percent) in the city's largest black ward, the Sixth, "Nigger Hill." They tended to live in more affluent black areas, sharing residence with middle-class, darker blacks rather than with whites. In the adjoining Fifth Ward, the second largest black area, mulattoes were greatly overrepresented (48 percent).

A decade later, all blacks in Boston found housing outside the Fifth and Sixth wards difficult to obtain. Although nineteenth century Boston did not manifest the solid pattern of residential segregation associated with twentieth-century patterns of the urban ghetto, lines of discrimination in housing were undeniable. When Robert Morris, a prominent black lawyer, attempted to purchase a home outside of the traditional black community, whites hostility proved prohibitive. On another occasion white neighbors threatened to destroy a house rather than allow a black family to move into it.[23]

As Boston became more residentially segregated by race in the decades of the mid-nineteenth century, the residential separation of mulattoes from darker blacks declined. By 1860 lighter African Americans, then 37 percent of the black population of the city, were less likely to live apart from darker blacks. Mulattoes continued to be substantially more likely to live in the Fifth Ward than in the disproportionately dark Sixth Ward, but by then the distinction between the two wards was somewhat artificial, because they were adjacent. African Americans tended to live clustered on either side of the ward line, so that the area was considered one large neighborhood, all part of Nigger Hill.[24]

The increasing racial segregation of Boston's residential areas is another indication of the regional characteristics of these cities. In terms of residential patterns, northern cities were almost always more racially segregated than southern cities. Cincinnati was more segregated than most southern cities but less segregated than Boston. More important for this study, Cincinnati was less segregated by race than Boston, but within its black community there was more separation by color. This also was a southernlike pattern, although less extreme in than in most southern cities. As in other characteristics, here too Cincinnati occupied a middle ground.[25]

The residential pattern among Buffalo blacks was far less clear. In 1850, 96 percent of the city's mulattoes lived in the Fourth Ward, the largest and most affluent black ward in the city. Mulattoes were underrepresented or completely absent from wards containing poor blacks. It is likely that within the Fourth Ward there was clustering along economic lines. City directory data confirmed this, indicating that darker blacks and mulattoes of comparable occupations lived adjacent to one another within the ward.

The index of dissimilarity computed for Buffalo's African American population adds some confusion to this picture, however. At 32.5 in 1850 it was extremely high for a northern city, almost as high as Cincinnati's index in 1860, indicating greater residential separation between darker blacks and mulattoes than evidence drawn from the city directories suggested. Moreover, the level of intercolor separation among Buffalo blacks was growing. During the last decade of the antebellum period, the city's index of 38.8 by 1860 surpassed that of Cincinnati. The rise in the index may be due, at least in part, to the growth in the number of wards in the city during the period. In 1860 the census listed more than twice as many wards in Buffalo as it had ten

Table 5
Most Populous Black Wards—Buffalo, 1850 and 1860

Ward	African Americans	Mulattoes	Darker blacks
	1850		
Second	125	3	97
Fourth	418	36	64
	1860		
Fourth	138	12	88
Fifth	181	17	83
Sixth	140	8	92

Source: Bureau of the Census, U.S. Census, 1850 and 1860

years earlier. On the eve of the Civil War, mulattoes were more likely than darker blacks to be more evenly distributed through the new wards of the city. Because the addition of new wards meant a redrawing of ward boundaries the demographic shift is more apparent than real. Also, city directory data, although incomplete and difficult to compare for the three cities, indicate that the index, computed on a ward level, may exaggerate the degree of intercolor separation in Buffalo. In the absence of a more accurate measure, definitive conclusions on residential patterns among black Buffalonians remain suspect. Surely this phenomenon is worthy of further study.[26]

In all three cities mulattoes were occupationally better off than darker blacks, but the gap was narrower between these groups in Buffalo and Boston. Although there was a slight overrepresentation of Buffalo and Boston mulattoes in occupations above the unskilled level, mulattoes in Cincinnati enjoyed a far greater occupational advantage over darker blacks. Although in Buffalo and Boston mulattoes were more highly skilled than darker blacks, the local social and economic conditions made it almost impossible for them to find skilled jobs. In most of the urban North, blacks faced stiff competition from immigrant workers who generally refused to tolerate blacks as skilled co-workers. In Boston the situation was complicated by an economy offering comparatively few skilled jobs.[27]

Buffalo's economy was expanding during the antebellum period, except for brief slowdowns during the depressions of 1837 and 1857. Its manufacturers needed skilled workers, but the growing immigrant population and the exceedingly small number of black workers, fewer than 160 by 1860, did not encourage the employment of blacks in favored positions.

Cincinnati's booming economy, especially after 1840, and its larger pool of skilled mulatto workers combined with southern traditions that allowed for the employment of skilled African American labor. There were a number of examples of skilled blacks denied skilled employment in Cincinnati, but pressure, generally from competitive immigrant workers, was not sufficient to freeze blacks out of the skilled labor market as it did almost completely in Boston and Buffalo. In this respect employment conditions in Cincinnati approximated those in cities farther south where free African Americans, mainly mulattoes, did a considerable amount of the skilled work.[28]

It is significant that in all three cities barbering and hairdressing accounted for a substantial proportion of mulatto employment. Immigrant workers were generally tolerant of blacks holding these service jobs. A few African Americans, mostly mulatto, also became storekeepers and small-business owners, drawing large numbers of customers from the black community. Cincinnati's sizable African American population offered not only middle-level jobs in the general economy but also greater employment opportunities for blacks serving their own community. It was hardly surprising then that from among these predominately southern-born blacks, already advantaged mulattoes stepped forward to run the local businesses.

Mulattoes were more financially prepared for their role in business than darker blacks in all cities studied, but whereas the differential in Buffalo and Boston was extremely slight, in Cincinnati it was significant indeed. Buffalo mulattoes held a proportion of the black wealth less than 1 percentage point higher than their proportion of the city's African American population. In Boston they were overrepresented by less than 6 percentage points, with less than 45 percent of the city's black wealth. By contrast mulattoes held 75 percent of Cincinnati's black wealth, in 1860 more than 15 percentage points above their proportion of that city's black population. In this regard the economic position of Cincinnati mulattoes among the city's African Americans was much like that of mulattoes in port cities of the South, where they were the vast majority of black property holders with a disproportionate share of the wealth of the black community. One significant example was New Orleans in 1850, where mulattoes held 90 percent of the black wealth.[29]

Not only were mulattoes financially better situated than darker blacks to take advantage of business opportunities, they also were more likely to be better educated. In each city the rate of illiteracy was higher for darker blacks. There were no substantial differences between cities, although southern-born blacks, whether dark or light, were more likely to be illiterate than the northern born. The relatively high illiteracy in Cincinnati was no doubt due to the high proportion of southern born among its blacks. Data from this study help to confirm earlier speculation that Boston's black community was one of the most literate in the nation.

One interesting pattern directly related to rates of literacy emerged. Formal education was available in Boston earlier than in Cincinnati or Buffalo, but by the 1840s each city was supporting public and private schools for blacks. In Boston private schools began in the late eighteenth century, meeting first in homes and later in the African Baptist Church. There were private schools for blacks in Buffalo, and a few blacks, especially those "regarded as especially bright, or [whose] color was almost white" were allowed to attend white schools. Private education was provided to Cincinnati blacks in private facilities such as the Gilmore School until 1849, when a new law allowed for the establishment of a black public school system and the election of a black school board.[30]

Attendance rose in the decades following the appointment of mulatto educator Peter H. Clark as director of Cincinnati's black public school system. Yet the proportion of African American children between the ages of five and fifteen attending school remained lower in Cincinnati than in Boston. Significantly, the African American school in Cincinnati had a disproportionately high number of mulatto students in both 1850 and 1860. This is suggestive of the importance of color as a predictor of school attendance. In Cincinnati color was in fact a more important predictor of school attendance than region of birth. Even though southern-born African American children were generally less likely to attend school than the northern born, mulattoes, a disproportionately southern-born group, were more likely to attend school than darker Cincinnati blacks. In Boston and Buffalo, region of birth was more important than color in predicting school attendance. There darker black children, apt to be northerners by birth, were more likely to attend school than mulattoes, because mulattoes were disproportionately southern born. Thus mulattoes in Cincinnati held advantages not shared by their counterparts farther north, suggesting important regional variations.[31]

Perhaps the most significant of the indicators studied here for evaluating the self-consciousness of mulattoes in these northern cities was their choice of marriage partners. The strong patterns that emerge generalize to northern and southern cities. Mulatto men were likely to marry mulatto women. The rates were so high that it is extremely unlikely that this was less than a conscious choice. Cincinnati had the highest percentage of intracolor marriages. An overwhelming 92 percent of Cincinnati mulatto men married mulatto women, whereas only 7 percent married darker black women.

Lightness of color could have positive consequences for African American women. A mulatto woman had a much better chance of marrying a man with property and skilled or managerial employment than her darker sister. The desirability of the "high yellow" African American woman has been celebrated in black literature and art throughout the nineteenth and twentieth centuries. Songs such as "The Yellow Rose of Texas" have become part of American folklore, even though most are unaware of its reference to a mulatto woman. When black sailors sang "Shallo Brown," a song that announced a black seaman's intention to leave his darker women because "my [new] girl's a bright mulatto, she hails from Cincinnati," they gave expression to the phenomenon suggested in the census figures. There was status associated with the acquisition of the affections of a mulatto woman. Dark men might possibly marry lighter women if they (the men) were well situated financially and/or occupationally. Fully 90 percent of the darker men in Cincinnati who married mulatto women fit this description.[32]

The situation was similar in Buffalo and Boston, but the percentages were lower. Seventy-three percent of the mulatto men in Buffalo and 72 percent of the mulatto men in Boston married mulatto women, whereas only 7 and 4 percent, respectively, married darker women. These lower figures for Buffalo and Boston indicate only a variation in degree from the Cincinnati pattern; the phenomenon was exactly the same. Yet this variation is significant, for as this study contends, the northern pattern was not one that ignored shades of color, nor one that offered no advantage to lighter skin tone. It was one that diminished this distinction relative to border or southern cities.[33]

There were therefore important differences in the significance of color within black communities, depending on where these communities were located. The regional variations within the North appear to underscore those that Williamson and Berlin found for the South. It is unwise, then, to generalize from patterns found in one black community to those found in another, especially if there is a significant regional variation in the locations of these communities. One of the only studies that concentrates on a nineteenth-century northern city with respect to this question is the Hershberg and Williams Philadelphia study. Their findings parallel those for mulattoes in Buffalo and Boston. Philadelphia had a relatively high proportion of southern blacks but only a 19 percent mulatto component.[34]

Because Hershberg and Williams use "grid units" as a more accurate measure of geographical residence than the ward units used in this study, it is difficult to compare such data directly. It does appear, however, that Philadelphia most nearly fits the northern city model on this issue. Their findings on marriage patterns are compatible with those of this study, with percentages of intracolor marriages falling between those for Cincinnati and Boston. On the question of literacy, Philadelphia blacks had a level comparable to that of Boston, 80 percent literacy for darker blacks and 90 percent for mulattoes. This was substantially higher than literacy rates for Cincinnati. As for all the mulattoes studied here, Philadelphia mulattoes generally found higher levels of employment and were more affluent than other blacks.[35]

The data developed for Philadelphia seems to place that city in the northern city category by most measures. Yet Philadelphia, situated as it was in the southern part of Pennsylvania (a state bordering Maryland and Virginia), exhibited many southern characteristics as well. As Thomas Jefferson observed in 1785, Pennsylvania blended the temperaments and atmospheres of the North and the South. The state also attracted large numbers of southern-born blacks. Like other Pennsylvania cities, Pittsburgh for example, Philadelphia had a larger southern-born African American population than most other northern cities, but its relatively low proportion of light-skinned blacks no doubt helps to account for its northern characteristics on the mulatto issue.[36]

There remains the central question of why these patterns emerged where they did and, perhaps more basically, why mulattoes should have held such socioeconomic advantages. This latter question was partially addressed at the opening of this chapter. Mulattoes were most likely to be favored slaves. Often kin to the master, they were sometimes educated, allowed to learn skills, even freed and, on occasion, endowed from the master's estate. Lempel's study has shown that mulatto slaves were often seen by slaveholders as more valuable than darker blacks and that mulatto women were especially valued. This status carried over into freedom and seems to have remained strong as long as slavery provided a point of reference.[37]

Stanley Elkins pointed out almost a generation ago that planters often thought of their slaves as "Sambo," that docile and intensely loyal character. Apparently they were less likely to consider lighter-skinned slaves in these terms. Newspaper advertisements seeking the recovery of fugitive slaves were more likely to describe darker runaways as gentle and, ironically, as loyal. Mulattoes, on the other hand, were often described as rebellious and intelligent. The mulatto characteristics were generally attributed to the infusion of "white blood." This was seen as a dangerous combination that might explode in violence. Many whites would have agreed with one southern women's belief that in the mulatto "enough white blood [would] replace native humility and cowardice with Caucasian audacity."[38]

It is likely that such beliefs became, in part, self-fulfilling prophecies. Not all mulattoes were seen by whites as possessing these characteristics, but they were seen as different from darker blacks. If Winthrop Jordan is correct in his assertion that blackness itself, defined as the opposite of whiteness, carried negative connotations in a culture predisposed toward things white, it is surely understandable that mulattoes might have an advantage in dealing with white society.[39] These often conflicting images of mulattoes were of course most operative in those areas of large mulatto populations. Thus the mulatto populations in large Deep South cities seemed most affected. It is significant that port cities such as Charleston and New Orleans are so often used to illustrate color stratification in black society. These cities had large mulatto populations.[40]

Equally important, these southern port cities were greatly influenced by the more racially complex cultures that flourished in the West Indies. Williamson detailed the significant impact of Barbados patterns of race relations on South Carolina through the mid-nineteenth century. He examined the close connections, which began in the seventeenth century, between that British West Indian colony and South Carolina. Significant numbers of British settlers migrating from Barbados to Charleston brought with them racial views that distinguished mulattoes from darker blacks. These traditions help to explain why interracial marriage was never outlawed in South Carolina during the slavery era and why "the Palmetto state also refused to relegate free mulattoes to the status of blacks, slave or free." Apparently South Carolina whites agreed with a legislative commission appointed to investigate the Denmark Vesey slave conspiracy in Charleston that mulattoes were most likely to side with whites during times of racial upheaval. Light-skinned blacks were thus seen by many white South Carolinians as a protective buffer between the races and were treated with greater tolerance.[41]

Mulattoes in the French colonies of the Caribbean also formed a distinct and separate caste. Their's was a recognized, and often codified, social, economic, and political superiority to darker blacks in Latin and French culture. After the fall of Santo Domingo in the early nineteenth century, thousands of wealthy Haitian mulattoes who had remained loyal to France migrated to French New Orleans and to several other southern port cities in the United States. It was no accident that Charleston's exclusively mulatto Brown Fellowship Society was established by many of these mulattoes and was maintained throughout the antebellum period by their descendants.[42]

The French influence did not begin or end with the revolution in Santa Domingo. Social intercourse and trade between the United States and the Caribbean was maintained throughout the eighteenth and nineteenth centuries. Migrants from the West Indies, black or white, brought with them the tradition of a caste system favoring mulattoes. The constant sensitivity of the white populace in southern port cities to the presence of Haitian seamen is well known if not well analyzed. The favored position of mulattoes in the South was probably due to a combination of the color predilections of whites, mulatto family relationships with whites, and the influence of French and Latin traditions, which permeated the urban South.

These traditions were not as strong in northern cities where there were fewer African Americans and thus fewer mulattoes. The relative absence of paternalism of the type described for the plantation South by Eugene Genovese dictated less personal contact between free blacks and whites in the North. The capricious nature of southern society provided little if any protection for the safety or welfare of free blacks outside of the "good will" and patronage of a few "quality white folk." Thus in the South, for middle-class free blacks, often the most likely targets of racial hostility, a paternalistic relationship with an influential white was essential, and a light complexion might make it easier to acquire such protection. Being related to a wealthy white family would often ensure one's security. In this setting there was incentive for mulattoes to distance themselves from darker, poorer, and more vulnerable blacks.[43]

The absence of these traditions in Boston and Buffalo set them apart from Cincinnati. Not dependent on southern style paternalism, and with greater opportunity to protest racial injustice, northern mulattoes tended to be a more integral part of the black community. Residential patterns showed that Boston and Buffalo mulattoes were integrated into the black community. Such stratification as did exist tended to be along economic lines. Although mulattoes were generally more stable financially, it was this stability, rather than their color, that was the crucial variable. In Cincinnati there was a greater tendency for mulattoes to reside in areas of heavy mulatto concentration, economic stability being a less important factor.

Of the cities studied, Cincinnati was the most southernlike in terms of restrictions upon and hostility toward free blacks. The Black Laws of Ohio operated much like the black codes in southern cities, restricting the rights of all free blacks. Yet a strict interpretation of these codes would have allowed mulattoes the franchise while withholding it from darker African Americans. Here again enforcement in southern Ohio was often more harsh than in the northern regions of the state. Like the southern black codes, Ohio's Black Laws were enforced erratically, but darker blacks were more likely to be restricted in Cincinnati than, for example, in Cleveland, a city in northern Ohio with distinctly northern characteristics where African Americans generally received greater social and political tolerance.[44]

It is significant that 1829 and again in 1841 white mobs attacked Bucktown (in Cincinnati), driving blacks out of their homes—many out of the city and some out of the country. There were certainly advantages for mulattoes in not living in Bucktown. There were no comparable riots in Buffalo or Boston during that period. There was occasional violence directed at the black community in these cities, but it generally did not take the form of uncontrolled rioting.[45]

The color stratification among the African Americans in Boston and Buffalo was not as significant as that in Cincinnati. Conversely, such stratification in Cincinnati's black community was less rigid than that found in the port cities in the lower South. Compared to Boston and Buffalo, Cincinnati looked more southern. Compared to most southern cities, Cincinnati, with its sizable immigrant population and its commercial and industrial economic base, looked more northern. There is no doubt that a light complexion had real advantages in all these cities, but these advantages were less in northern-styled cities.

There was an additional complication of the status of mulattoes within the African American society, one which was a factor in all regions of the North. Some African Americans expressed feelings of hostility toward lighter members of the race. These feeling could arise as a reaction to real or imagined superior attitudes assumed by mulattos, jealousy of their more privileged position, or as displaced anger over white oppression. They could become strident during periods when, for reasons of politics or self-esteem, blacks felt the need to stress a pride in color. When in 1816 Daniel Coker of Baltimore was elected to the position of first bishop of the newly formed African Methodist Episcopal Church Conference, there was a storm of protest that eventually forced him to concede his position to rival Richard Allen. Allen, who was much darker than the nearly white Coker, was, many believed, a more suitable first leader of an African American national church association.[46]

Blackness might be accentuated whenever the race was attacked. Boston's David Walker, in his militant denunciation of theories of white supremacy expressed by Jefferson and others, argued that blackness was a human color that pleased both God and African Americans. It was wrong, he contended, to believe that "we are not as thankful to our God for having made us as it pleased himself as they [white people] are for having made them white."[47]

In the late 1840s and 1850s, black nationalism found favor among some African Americans who demanded greater respect for their blackness. Many went to considerable lengths to make clear their color pride. David Ruggles, New York abolitionist, wanted none to mistake his color. "I am a black man," he announced to any who doubted his racial loyalties.[48] Likewise, John S. Rock, Boston physician, attorney, and abolitionist, turned his attention to the issue of blackness in the late 1850s. Before a largely black crowd he delivered a "black is beautiful" speech in which he praised the rich color of his race and delighted his audience by arguing that mother nature had invested so much energy in the creation of black people that "when the white was created, nature was pretty well exhausted—but determined to keep up appearances, she pinched up his features and did the best she could under the circumstances."[49]

Politics were often at the heart of the mulatto issue for northern blacks. In the South racial mixture was understood to be almost exclusively the prerogative of wealthy and powerful white men, but in the North, where free black men were uncontrolled by the "civilizing" influence of slavery, the prospect of "race mixing" was more frightening. African Americans understood well the issue's explosive potential. Anti-abolitionist forces used it to discredit the antislavery movement among many in the North by claiming that miscegenation was the natural outcome of abolition. Many blacks reacted by arguing that there was little interest in their communities in marrying outside of the race. There was substantial ambivalence and little active black protest against anti-intermarriage laws in many northern states. Ruggles claimed that neither he nor "any colored man or women of [his] acquaintance" were interested in such an association with white people. Indeed, he expressed his personal opposition to miscegenation, assuming it to be the result of the rape of black women: "Nothing is more disgusting than to see my race bleached to a pallid and sickly hue by the lust of those cruel and fastidious white men."[50]

Under these conditions there was surely anxiety among many mulattoes about their place in black society. Some were ambivalent toward their own racial heritage, even in the face of their advantaged position within American and black society. Despite the public statements of some African American leaders, however, the demographic measures used in this study indicate that although there were regional differences, mulattoes had economic and social advantages. Further, marriage patterns suggested that mulatto men and financially and professionally successful darker men preferred mulatto women. As with most human beings, African Americans' private choices were sometimes at variance with their public pronouncements. The mulatto issue remained ambiguous and potentially divisive throughout the period.[51]

The mulatto advantage most evident in the South became less important among African Americans as they became a more northern people during the twentieth century. The Hershberg and Williams findings support this contention, and most scholars agree that the Great Migration, which brought millions of black southerners to the North, played a vital role in this change. The argument presented here helps explain the process. As more blacks became "northernized," as white paternalism became less important in the wake of rising black political power in the urban North, and as more blacks joined in interregional protest and demands for racial justice, the northern model, which played down the mulatto advantage, became dominant.

Yet even in the twentieth century we see the lasting effects of the French and Latin mulatto caste system. The vast majority of twentieth-century African American economic and political leaders—the "talented tenth," as W. E .B. Du Bois termed them—from Booker T. Washington to A. Phillip Randolph to Ralph Bunche, Adam Clayton Powell, Jr., and Du Bois himself, were mulattoes. The only notable exception was Marcus Garvey, a native of Jamaica, the black nationalist leader who in the 1920s rejected both integration and mulatto leadership. Even Malcolm X, Garvey's successor as the major black nationalist leader of this century, was a mulatto. Martin Luther King was the first truly national African American leader of dark skin in the twentieth century.[52]

By the late 1960s, when the black power movement reminded African Americans that light skin tone was a poor basis for social differentiation and that black could indeed be beautiful, such distinctions only marginally determined social status. Thereafter the color of black political and economic leadership changed, leaning toward a deeper shade of brown.[53]

There remains much to be understood about the role of mulattoes in black society, historically and currently. Until recently the volatility of this issue made it almost impossible to analyze dispassionately. Calls for black unity proclaimed a common experience and discouraged the analysis of historical conflict within the black community. Racism and the limitations it imposed has certainly marked the American experience of all black people. Yet that experience has varied significantly depending on time, place, and circumstance. As this study shows, it is important to see that although racial justice has been the chief concern of all blacks, local circumstances are of great significance. Mulattoes had different roles and statuses depending upon the demographics, economics, and the social traditions of the local and regional environment.

As a regional approach sheds light on the varied roles of color in black society, it also can help to reveal the variations of black community. As was true for the pattern of color stratification, the structure of black community life is complicated. It is counterproductive to see black society in simplistic terms, for, as with most significant structures, it is nuanced and incredibly complex—a matter not merely of black and white, but of many shades of color.

I Sell the Shadow to Support the Substance.

SOJOURNER TRUTH.

Sojourner Truth was one of the few black women who was able to blend her activism in the cause of women's rights with her vigorous support for racial equality. (Courtesy of The New-York Historical Society, New York City)

Chapter 7

Double Consciousness

African American Identity in the
Nineteenth Century

By the beginning of the nineteenth century, many African Americans could trace their American ancestry back more than a hundred years, yet they were not considered true Americans by European Americans, who were themselves relative newcomers to this land. Throughout the nation's first century, as more Europeans arrived to adopt an American identity, blacks remained non-Americans in the minds of most white people and in the policies of the government. By midcentury most whites no longer viewed blacks as African, but they still did not consider them permanent Americans. Before the Civil War, the Supreme Court in the case of Dred Scott decided that black people were not legally American citizens, a judgment African Americans roundly rejected. For them the question of identity was complicated but understood. Theirs was a "double consciousness," a "two-ness," as black scholar W. E. B. Du Bois saw it. At the turn of the twentieth century, he wrote, "One ever feels his two-ness,—an American, a Negro; two souls, two thoughts, two unreconciled strivings; two warring ideals in one dark body, whose dogged strength alone keeps it from being torn asunder."[1]

The American slave melting pot erased many of the national distinctions among blacks, so that Ashanti American and Ghanaian American, for example, became simply African American, but blacks were never simply American. Instead, they attempted to preserve both their racial heritage and their American heritage. As Du Bois continued, "The history of the American Negro is the history of . . . this longing to attain self-conscious manhood, to merge his double self into a better and truer self. In this merging he wishes neither of the old selves to be lost."[2] Although it was sometimes difficult to maintain ties to ancient traditions, slaves and free blacks passed their African heritage along through the generations.

By the nineteenth century, there was no thought of recreating old world Africa in America. Rather, those customs that worked best in the new setting were preserved and made a part of the new African American identity. The African American recognized practical advantages in retaining both aspects of his heritage. As Du Bois explained, "He would not Africanize America, for America has much to teach the world and Africa. He would not bleach his Negro soul in a flood of white Americanism, for he knows that Negro blood has a message for the world. He simply wishes to make it possible for a man to be both a Negro and an American, without . . . having the doors of opportunity closed in his face."[3]

This, then, was the invention of the African American, whose identity was shaped in part by the quest for American rights and privileges earned over centuries of unrelenting labor and patriotic service. This American identity blended with an African heritage that increasingly rested on a common racial identity and a collective struggle. Maintaining this complex identity in the face of hostile opposition required tenacity and encouraged a creativity partly derived from the marginality of black life.

The American Revolution profoundly affected the status and identity of African Americans. During the war tens of thousands of black slaves in the southern states fled the plantations for the safety of British lines. They were encouraged by British officials, among them Lord Dunmore, the colonial governor of Virginia, who issued the 1775 proclamation promising freedom for any slave who would bear arms for England against the colonial rebellion. Hundreds of black Americans fought with British regulars, but many more became independent guerrilla fighters, carrying out raids against southern plantations. In South Carolina these were the banditti, the interracial groups that had harassed planters and freed slaves since the 1750s. These free blacks, slaves, Indians, and poor whites were known to slaveholders as "notorious harbourers of runaway slaves." Blacks saw them as freedom fighters.[4]

Though troublesome before the war, attacks on southern plantations became even more intolerable and frightening when linked to the

British cause. In 1781 one white Virginian expressed the concern of his fellow slaveholders at the numbers of slaves who were running away and taking up arms against the supporters of slavery in that state: "We have had most alarming times this summer all along the shore, from a set of barges manned mostly by our own Negroes who have run off. . . . These fellows are really dangerous to an individual singled out for their vengeance whose Property lay exposed. They burnt several houses."[5]

Thousands of slaves who did not become combatants simply took the opportunity to escape slavery. In 1778 Thomas Jefferson estimated that thirty thousand were lost to Virginia plantations, South Carolina officials claimed a loss of twenty-five thousand, and Georgia lost ten thousand of its fifteen thousand slaves. At wars end, twenty thousand black loyalists withdrew from American ports with the British. Other former slaves sought refuge with the Seminoles of Florida or with Indian nations in areas west of the newly founded United States. Some continued the fight. Years after the Revolution was officially over, black troops calling themselves "King of England Soldiers" continued to harass planters in South Carolina and Georgia.[6]

The actions of black loyalists serving the king in the cause of freedom had an unmistakable impact on the general African American population. Black women in New York City were rumored to have named children in honor of Lord Dunmore, and in Philadelphia blacks were said to have been emboldened to a "display of disrespect" toward whites. One black fellow, accosted on the street by a group of whites, was reported to have threatened retribution when "lord Dunmore and his black regiment come."[7]

If some blacks seized the opportunity for freedom and to fight for liberty on the side of Great Britain, others joined the American cause for similar reasons. Although African Americans stood with the first minutemen at Lexington and Concord, and were part of the prerevolutionary uprisings, such as the Boston Massacre, General George Washington was reluctant to accept black troops into the Continental army. The necessities of war finally made a decision imperative. Despite southern opposition, after 1777 northern states and many of those in the upper South enlisted black soldiers and sailors. Slaves were promised freedom as a reward for service in freedom's cause. State authorities in Georgia and South Carolina did not follow suit, because the large number of slaves there rendered the prospect of arming blacks too frightening to contemplate. Still, five to eight thousand blacks from the North and upper South served the American cause, many receiving their freedom as a result.[8]

Blacks, whether they served with the American or the British forces, fought for the cause of their own freedom. Liberty held special meaning for a slave. If African Americans were committed to America, it was because they included themselves among the people who might benefit from the promised opportunity of this new nation. They saw in this daring experiment a possibility not merely for their freedom but also for their eventual acceptance as citizens, a rank earned through personal sacrifice. Decades after American independence was won, Philadelphia blacks reminded the U.S. Congress that blacks had "the highest claims to the privilege of citizenship, since the first blood shed upon the altar of American Republicanism, and consecrated its soul to liberty and independence, was that of Crispus Attucks, 'a colored man.'"[9]

Repeatedly, black children were told by their elders of the exploits of black revolutionary heroes. One child recalled listening to the stories told by black revolutionary veterans and becoming convinced that "I had more right than any white man in the town." It was this belief in the right of black people to enjoy the freedoms of the revolutionary ideal that brought one black editor, William J. Watkins, to ask white America, "Why should you be the chosen people more than me?" Blacks were convinced that they were entitled to full status as Americans.[10]

Revolutionary ideals also encouraged antislavery forces in the North and the upper South. African Americans drew allies in their fight for freedom from the ranks of Quakers, who had opposed slavery for a generation before the Revolution, and from more recent converts, who saw an inconsistency between emerging American principles and American slavery. Abigail Adams wrote to her husband John of her discomfort with African American bondage. "It has always seemed a most iniquitous scheme to me," she declared, "to fight ourselves for what we are daily robbing and plundering from those who have as good a right to freedom as we have." Abigail Adams did not stand alone in her opposition to slavery. In northern states, where there were relatively few blacks and slavery was less economically important than in the rich plantation areas of the South, the antislavery movement grew during the postrevolutionary period, attracting such notables as Benjamin Franklin of Pennsylvania, John Jay, Alexander Hamilton and Aaron

Burr of New York, and Moses Brown of Rhode Island. Slavery was a "national crime" declared Benjamin Rush of Pennsylvania.[11]

Even in the Chesapeake region, where the black population was large and slaveholding was profitable, many American patriots spoke of liberty as the natural right of human beings and of slavery as a blight on the new nation. Maryland attorney general Luther Martin called slavery "inconsistent with the genius of republicanism" and destructive to the principles of republican government. "It is contrary to the command of Christ to keep fellow creatures in bondage," proclaimed one Virginian. The abolition of slavery was favored by the likes of Gustavus Scott of Maryland, Patrick Henry, and George Mason and Thomas Jefferson of Virginia. When the question was called at the Confederation Congress in 1784, even a member of the delegation from North Carolina voted to outlaw slavery from the western territories, and most assumed the eventual demise of the institution throughout the nation. South Carolina and Georgia, the two hard-line states on the slavery issue, seemed out of step with a national swing toward one or another brand of emancipation.[12]

African Americans were encouraged by these expressions of antislavery sentiment. Most identified with the words and the spirit of the Declaration of Independence and the Revolution. They moved to secure as many of these rights as possible wherever they could. In New England slaves petitioned state governments for freedom in the name of human and natural rights. Often petitioners used the words of those who had only a few short years before accused England of violating American rights. Massachusetts blacks successfully pressed for the right to vote claiming "taxation without representation."[13]

There were significant victories. Decades of struggle by blacks and their white allies resulted in the abolition of slavery in the northern states, so that by the opening of the nineteenth century, human bondage had either disappeared or had been set on the road to extinction through programs of gradual emancipation. Although blacks had not generally secured the rights of citizenship, many had achieved release from bondage. By the 1820s slavery had been confined almost totally to the South.[14]

Northern blacks emerged from slavery into an uncertain freedom. Despite their significant presence in the American revolutionary forces, there were several early indications that the federal government did not consider them full citizens. The postwar national militia excluded blacks, and early laws limited naturalization to white aliens. In the first two decades of the nineteenth century, federal law forbade blacks to carry the federal mail or hold elective office in the District of Columbia.[15]

Nor did the Constitution protect free blacks from limitations imposed by the individual states. From 1820, when Maine joined the union, until after the Civil War, every new state denied the vote to free blacks, and many did not allow them to serve on juries or even to testify in court cases involving whites. The Constitution did not prevent states such as Ohio, Illinois, Indiana, and Oregon, or the territory of Michigan, from barring free blacks or from requiring substantial bonds as a prerequisite to their immigration. The Northwest Ordinance, adopted by Congress in 1787, forbade slavery in the north-central region, but it did not assure the civil rights of free blacks in the area. Even in states such as Massachusetts and Pennsylvania, which did not restrict black immigration, there was serious discussion of such action. Save for two votes in its constitutional convention of 1850, California would have barred blacks. By that time it was clear that across America whites did not consider black Americans citizens.[16]

The question of black citizenship was further complicated by the fact that although many states obviously precluded it, others did not. Before 1820 free black men in Massachusetts, New Jersey, Pennsylvania, New York, Maine, Vermont, Connecticut, Rhode Island, and New Hampshire voted on an equal basis with white men. Ironically they lost that right in New Jersey, Connecticut, and Pennsylvania before the Civil War. In New York, black voters were required to meet property ownership requirements that had been removed for whites during the democratic reforms of the Jacksonian era. Yet African American political participation in states where it was allowed lent additional legitimacy to the claim of citizenship for free blacks.[17]

Federal recognition of black rights was inconsistent. A few blacks received passports to travel abroad under the aegis of the United States in the 1840s and 1850s. In 1856 the State Department officially discouraged such action citing the 1821 opinion of Attorney General William Wirt that blacks were not citizens. The department was willing to issue certificates to blacks traveling abroad verifying that they were born in the United States, were free, and even acknowledging some governmental responsibility to provide assistance should they be mistreated by a foreign government, but this was not to imply citizenship.[18]

At times the federal government also moved to safeguard the

rights of free blacks at home. In response to the contentions of slave-holders that free blacks had a dangerous effect on slaves, in 1822 the South Carolina legislature passed the Colored Seamen's Act requiring the imprisonment of all free black seamen while their ships were in South Carolina ports. Moreover, ships' captains had to pay the cost of the seamen's imprisonment, an amount he often deducted from the sea-man's wages. If a captain refused, the seaman was sold into temporary slavery to compensate local authorities. Other southern states adopted similar laws. Because the sea offered a major source of employment for thousands of free blacks before the Civil War, this provision posed a sig-nificant threat to the free black community. In response to protests by free blacks and northern white reformers, a congressional committee in-vestigated these policies and determined that they violated the Constitu-tion. The committee did not express an opinion on the question of black citizenship, however. In 1823 the Supreme Court supported con-gressional judgment by declaring such laws unconstitutional, yet several southern jurisdictions continued the practice until the Civil War.

This open violation of the Supreme Court ruling by southern port cities was but another sign that constitutional guarantees did not pro-tect African Americans from discriminatory regulations. Blacks were well aware of their vulnerability. Standing before an Iowa religious con-vention in the 1850s, Sojourner Truth, women's rights advocate and an-tislavery speaker, delighted her audience with her analysis of the U.S. Constitution. With a dry wit that was her trademark on the abolitionist circuit, this former slave, the first black female antislavery speaker in the nation, compared the Constitution to the midwestern wheat that in the 1850s was suffering from the boll weevil blight. From a distance the countryside looked deceptively beautiful, but on a closer look one might see the ravishes of the blight.

The Constitution was much the same, she said. "I feel for my rights, but there ain't any there." As weevils besieged the wheat, preju-dice and bigotry threatened to undermine constitutional guarantees. As Truth saw it, American civil rights and liberties were endangered. The Constitution had "a little weevil in it." Most African Americans agreed. The Constitution did not generally protect their rights or secure for them a full partnership in the American venture. Clearly weevils abounded in the document and in the society at large.[19]

The first generation of free blacks in the northern states struggled to work out their identity in the context of this American malevolence.

They did so with the memory of an African culture kept alive by the last Africans among them. The decades of the 1750s and 1760s witnessed a rise in the importation of African slaves directly into the northern colonies. These Africans refreshed an Old World cultural awareness growing increasingly faint with each passing generation. At the end of the eighteenth century, as northern blacks established a community institutional life, the influence of this last African generation was clearly visible.

The churches and the fraternal and mutual-aid societies formed the core of black communities. These institutions served as the staging ground for reform and protest organizations and were the foundation of the social and economic structure of the society. They were central to an African American sense of identity. Because there were few opportunities for black people in the wider society, political, educational, and social ambitions found outlets in the institutions of the black community. Although some northern cities made provisions for the poor, most poor blacks looked to their own communities for aid. Sometimes this was accomplished through formal charities operated by the church, but often aid was provided informally by family and friends.

The names of early free black organizations and institutions left no doubt of the identity of their memberships. The Free African Society was organized in Philadelphia in May of 1787 to provide for the mutual aid of the city's "colored" population. In Boston a month later, the black masonic order was inaugurated as African Lodge No. 459.[20] That fall the African Free School was founded to educate New York City's black children, and before the turn of the century the African Church of St. Thomas and the Bethel African Methodist Episcopal Church had been organized in Philadelphia, and the African Society had been established by forty-four black Bostonians. Throughout the first generation of the nineteenth century, *African* remained the name of choice for most black groups. The Zion African Methodist Episcopal Church was founded in New York City in the fall of 1800, the African Meeting House was built in Boston to house the African Baptist Church and the African School in 1806, and the African Methodist Episcopal Church organized a national network of black churches in 1816. In 1827 the African Woolman Benevolent Society of Brooklyn, New York, undertook the construction of a black school, which, when completed, took the name African Public School No. 1. During this early period blacks clearly saw themselves as both Americans and transplanted Africans.

In the formation of their organizations, these African Americans also incorporated the structure of American institutions. Like most Americans, blacks patterned their community associations on the democratic model. Organizational principles and purposes were set forth in constitutions or similar documents in words reminiscent of the federal Constitution. Blacks identified themselves with Africa even while they used the language of their American heritage. "We, the African Members," began the Laws of the African Society founded in Boston in 1796. "We, the Subscribers . . . do form ourselves into an Association, for the benevolent purpose of raising funds . . . to aid and assist the widows and orphans of deceased members . . ." read the constitution of the New York African Clarkson Association in 1825. The opening of the constitution and bylaws of the Brotherly Union Society in Philadelphia in 1833 contained similar language. These documents were divided into articles and often prefaced by preambles. They provided for democratic functions, including the election of officers (presidents, vice-presidents, secretaries, and treasurers), and for policy decided by a majority vote of the membership.[21]

Thus African Americans were able to blend the two aspects of their heritage to their advantage. Even as their institutional names identified black Americans as an African people, they utilized many of the tools of American politics to organize themselves in their struggle for self-improvement and mutual support.

As the organization of community institutions was a symbol of a newfound freedom, so also was the adoption of new personal names. Blacks were eager to establish an identity different from that forced on them in bondage, as illustrated by their rush to change their names and those of their children from slave names to names of freedom. The classical slave names (Cato, Caesar, and Pompey) so fashionable among slaveholders were discarded by many African Americans as they became free. Biblical names, such as John, James, and Peter, not only signified Christian faith but also symbolized control over one's own identity.

African Americans selected last names that linked them to one another, to their friends and relatives, familiarly or geographically distant. Generally, a last name was taken from the father, if there was one, unless he had been unkind to the family or was in some way not a worthy person. The rejection of one's father's name became a strong symbolic gesture. Former slaves were often ambivalent about taking the name of a father who was white, especially if he had also been their master. As names were intimately linked with identity, one's connection with a white slaveholding father was a particularly difficult problem. Renaming was an attempt to break the bounds of a slave identity and, as one historian found for Philadelphia, the surnames of former masters were often avoided.[22]

First names were also important connectors, not only from father to son but also from mother to daughter and sometimes from grandparents to grandchildren. Among the slaves, names linked one generation to another, helping to define an identity based on a common heritage and experience. Some adopted the names of black heroes. In the directories of major nineteenth-century cities, the name Toussaint is likely to be found—chosen to honor Toussaint L'Ouverture, the black leader of the successful revolution against France that created the nation of Haiti. For a people limited in their ability to control important aspects of their own lives, this partial power over their identity was one affirmation of their humanity, individuality, and personal freedom. Significantly, many of these former slaves took the names of white American heroes. Washington was one of the favorite names selected, as were Jefferson and Monroe. Later Jackson was almost as popular. Blacks drew sharp distinctions between these heroes' public commitment to freedom and their personal commitment to slavery. This contradiction heightened black ambivalence toward their American identity.

Name changing linked both the American and the African identities of black people. Although many blacks adopted European names, the act of changing one's name in response to a change in life circumstance was rooted in West African tradition. Whereas a West African's "real name" might be kept secret to protect its bearer from the evil magic of an enemy, an assumed name might change several times. A change in name generally marked some rite of passage, some new stage of life, or some unforseen occurrence.[23]

During slavery it was not unusual for slaves to have one name known to their masters and another known only to fellow slaves. This was one way of retaining control over the core of one's identity. The coming of freedom was such a monumental event that for African people nothing was more natural than an accompanying name change, whether the new name identified the group as African or the individual more personally. Freedman, Freeman, or Newman were personal names that often marked the transition from slavery.[24]

Some blacks changed their names several times. Benjamin

Summons, who served in a Connecticut regiment during the Revolution, originally enlisted as Benjamin Black but soon changed his surname to Summons. When he left service, he adopted the name Benjamin Roberts, supposedly because that had been his father's name. By the end of his life he had taken the name Benjamin Freedman, presumably in honor of his status as a free person of color. Yet he still occasionally signed his mark "alias Benjamin Black."[25]

The use of *African* in the names adopted for black organizations and European first names embraced by black individuals serve to suggest the black double consciousness in the early nineteenth century. Blacks sought the rights of American citizenship even as they accepted an African heritage as a part of their identity. Yet the essential aspect of African American identity, more important than either an American birthplace or an African heritage, was a dark skin. Blacks knew well that their skin color was used by whites to justify slavery and the deprivation of their civil rights. They understood that in the eyes of most Americans a dark skin was the brand of natural, irreversible inferiority in all things necessary to civilized society. They knew white America to be terribly wrong in this belief, but they differed on how to correct that misconception. Most blacks hoped that the educational, political, and economic uplift of the race would expose the folly of racial prejudice. Yet these goals were difficult to achieve in the face of severe prejudice that greater opportunities might well have challenged.[26] Public identification with Africa took on a new significance among blacks as the last of the Africans died out and a new American organization gained attention with a program that threatened the American part of their dual identity. Assertions of African American citizenship faced a severe challenge from the activities of the American Colonization Society. Founded in 1816, this group sought to encourage the colonization in western Africa of free blacks and slaves subsequently freed. Some colonizationists hoped that if they could assure southern masters that free blacks would be settled outside the country, more would consent to manumit their slaves. Others saw the plan as an opportunity to rid the nation of troublesome free blacks. Thomas Jefferson was among those who saw African colonization as the only practical solution to the nation's "race problem." Although colonization never attracted wide support among free blacks, some expressed a willingness to emigrate to Africa. Early in the nineteenth century, Paul Cuffe, son of an African slave and an American Indian women, advocated African emigration and even transported a group of thirty-eight blacks to the British West African colony of Sierra Leone in 1815. One of the earliest Pan-Africanists, he hoped to stimulate African American business and trade between Africa and the United States. Cuffe's efforts encouraged white colonizationists such as Henry Clay, Daniel Webster, Supreme Court justice Bushrod Washington, Francis Scott Key, and others to establish the American Colonization Society a year later.[27]

By 1822 the society had purchased about one thousand square miles of land on the West African coast with the financial assistance of the federal government. There they established the colony of Liberia. In the next few years a small but enthusiastic settlement was established, drawing blacks from Maryland, Virginia, and several parts of the North, including Providence, Boston, and Philadelphia. Those who went saw their actions as a part of a grand effort to provide a circumstance in which blacks would be able to determine their own identity and secure greater future opportunity. A few emigrated as a result of their identification with "Mother Africa." For most, their motivation was not unlike that of the Europeans bound for the New World. These black immigrants sought a new and better life for themselves, for their children, and for their race. As one elderly traveler explained, "I go to set an example to the youth of my race. I go to encourage the young. They can never be elevated here. I have tried it for sixty years—it is in vain. Could I by my example lead them to set sail, and I die the next day, I should be satisfied."[28]

Despite the interest of many, most free blacks disapproved of colonization. In several mass meetings before 1820, Philadelphia blacks took the lead in protesting the plans of the new society. The colonizationist's acquisition of territory in West Africa heightened the interests of many southern free blacks, but nearly all northern blacks remained opposed. So strong was the opposition among northern blacks that when John Russwurm, cofounder of *Freedom's Journal,* the nation's first black newspaper (New York City, 1827), became a supporter of colonization, the resultant hostility forced him to leave the paper.[29]

There were several reasons for black opposition to the American Colonization Society. Most found the society's motives suspect, because several of the country's most prominent slaveholders were members. Free blacks feared an unstated agenda, their removal from the nation, thereby silencing the most vocal opponents of slavery and making slave holding more secure. Blacks also resented the notion, implicit in the colonization program, that they had no right to American citizenship. Black Americans aggressively claimed their national rights on the basis of their personal contributions and sacrifices for the country. "Let no man of us budge one step, and let slave-holders come to beat us from our country," one Boston spokesmen admonished. "America is more our country, than it is the whites—we have enriched it with our blood and tears."[30]

The Colonization Society portrayed its aims as enlightened philanthropy that realistically addressed the nation's race problem. Supporters of colonization believed it impossible that white Americans would ever accept blacks as fellow citizens. Many saw African colonization as the only humane alternative. African Americans disagreed—"We must not leave this continent," one leader argued. "America is our destination and our home." Most free blacks refused to willingly relinquish rights for which they paid dearly in the Revolution and again in the War of 1812.[31]

The black anticolonizationist struggle was thus an assertion of black American identity. Beginning in the early 1830s, African Americans met in national conventions to discuss and organize a response to the colonizationists and the "Slave Power." On 20 September 1830, approximately thirty delegates representing five states met in Philadelphia's Bethel Church for five days to develop a collective strategy. In the first line of the convention proceedings, these delegates proclaimed a commitment to the spirit of the Declaration of Independence. The next year delegates resolved that the declaration and the preamble of the Constitution be read at the opening of each convention. They asserted that "truths contained in the former document are incontrovertible and . . . the latter guarantees in letter and spirit to every freeman born in this country all the rights and immunities of citizenship."[32]

At national black conventions held throughout the antebellum period, resolutions expressed black identity and commitment—both racial and American. Blacks were both African and American. They were, in fact, special Americans, dedicated to the spirit of American liberty as few others were. They were not alienated Americans, even though for them American society was alienating. They were not discouraged Americans, even though the racial restrictions were discouraging. They were committed Americans, determined to improve the country's treatment of its people. As one black Bostonian put it, "This being our country we have made up our minds to remain in it, and to try to make it worth living in."[33]

There was, however, a subtle alteration of black perceptions during the second third of the century. Increasingly blacks identified themselves as Americans of African heritage rather than as Africans in America, as they had done a generation before. This shift in identification is evident in the names selected for black organizations formed after 1825. They were less likely to include the word *African*. The first black newspaper published in New York City, which became a forum for African American national news, was called *Freedom's Journal*. The periodic national gatherings of blacks were termed *colored conventions,* and in the minutes of those conventions, blacks referred to themselves as "people of color." Significantly, the African Baptist Church of Boston, founded in 1806, changed its name to the First Independent Church of the People of Color in the 1830s "for the very good reason that the name African is ill applied to a church composed of American citizens."[34] Although such changes were not universal—the African Episcopal Methodist Church, for example, retains its title to this day—the tendency to drop *African* as descriptive of black groups is both striking and understandable.

By the 1830s few African Americans had experienced Africa first-hand or even through the stories of parents or grandparents. To most Africa must have seemed farther removed than it had for preceding generations. Africans of the late eighteenth century, and their children who influenced the free black experience of the first decades, were less influential by the thirties. The American Colonization Society and its program might have been seen more favorably by a community of African-born black Americans. Indeed many of the early black supporters of colonization were African born or, like Paul Cuffe, first-generation Americans. In the 1830s Africa remained the mother country to many blacks, but there had been a change. Blacks were more like to draw their unique identity from their color and from their common struggle against slavery and for equal rights as American citizens.[35]

Free blacks of this period also played down their African identity in response to the program of the American Colonization Society, which they perceived as a threat to their American heritage. In opposing colonization, blacks asserted themselves as American citizens—disadvantaged citizens to be sure—but citizens nonetheless. There was considerable debate and strong differences of opinion on what blacks should call themselves. At the 1835 convention of blacks, a resolution was unanimously adopted calling for the removal of "the title of African from [black] institutions, the marbles of churches, and etc." A strong American identity was urged. Some blacks even opposed the term *colored* unless it was used in conjunction with the word *American.* Accordingly, in 1837 the New York City black newspaper *Weekly Advocate* changed its name to *Colored American.* The editor explained the change by saying, "We are Americans—colored Americans."[36]

Some favored the term *oppressed Americans* as most descriptive of the status of African Americans. In the pages of black newspapers, the debate among blacks over their proper designation continued throughout the pre–Civil War era. In 1837 Samuel Cornish, editor of the *Colored American,* explained:

> Many would rob us of the endeared name, "Americans," a distinction more emphatically belonging to us than five-sixths of this nation, one that we will never yield. In complexion, in blood and nativity, we are decidedly more exclusively "American" than our white brethren; hence the propriety of the name of our people, Colored Americans, and of identifying the name with all our institutions, in spite of our enemies, who would rob us of our nationality and reproach us as exoticks.[37]

This statement was aimed at refuting the colonizationist plan and their charge that blacks were foreigners and "exoticks."

There was, therefore, wide agreement among African Americans that they must maintain their American nationality, and although they did downplay their African identity, they did not reject their racial heritage. The identification that free blacks felt with the plight of blacks in bondage was especially strong and publicly expressed among northern blacks whose environment was more tolerant of protest. Northern blacks who had already gained their freedom were the most active members of the Underground Railroad, which helped to bring slaves out of the South and assisted them with food, shelter, medical care, and legal as well as extralegal protection once they arrived in the North.

Black opposition to slavery was more than philosophical. In a nation where, by 1860, four million blacks were slaves and only a half million were free, it was likely that every free black person had a friend or family member in bondage. Slavery touched the lives of virtually all blacks, and a steady stream of communication flowed between the regions, carried by black sailors, boatmen, and other black travelers.[38]

In all regions of the country, blacks increasingly identified themselves as Americans. They particularly identified with the stated ideals of the nation's Declaration of Independence and with its constitutional expressions of concern for civil liberties and minority rights. In speeches, in print, from political platform and church pulpit, blacks reminded America of the vast gap between its ideals and its reality, attacking American hypocrisy, striking at the national conscience, and challenging the inconsistencies of American idealism. Free blacks vowed, in the words of a New York group writing in the mid-1830s, to "fill every continent and island with the story of the WRONGS done to our brethren, by Christian, church-going, psalm-singing, long prayer-making, lynching, tar and feathering, man-roasting, human-flesh-dealing America." Further they determined to "preach the DECLARATION OF IN-DEPENDENCE, till it begins to be put in PRACTICE."[39] Here African Americans carved out still another identification. They were voice of the true America, the keepers of the flame ignited by the words of the declaration and carried forth on the shoulders of revolutionary soldiers, black and white. This role became a traditional part of black identity and became even more important during the twentieth century.

Thus the point of identification for eighteenth-century blacks, their birthplace, either in Africa or in America, became more attached to color and struggle, freedom and slavery during the antebellum years. In both instances common concerns and familial connections helped to bridge these potential divisions among African Americans. The Civil War and emancipation greatly affected these points of identity. After 1865 all blacks were free, but it quickly became clear that freedom remained both precarious and ambiguous. Depending on region, wealth, and shade of skin color, freedom was more or less circumscribed. In the Deep South where the black population was largest, the civil rights and liberties of African Americans were severely limited by law and through violent enforcement of extralegal custom. One rule of thumb, generally but not universally true, was that blacks received greatest tolerance in areas where their numbers were small and where they posed no political, economic, or social threat to the white citizenry. Another traditional cushion against racial hostility and violence was protection given by influential whites. Wealth and light skin, indicating familial connections to the white world, were likely to ensure that advantage.[40]

Reconstruction saw the rise of black political influence in many southern states and the adoption of constitutional amendments guaranteeing civil rights to blacks. The Thirteenth Amendment made slavery unconstitutional, and the Fourteenth Amendment provided for black citizenship, reversing the Supreme Court's ruling in the Dred Scott case. The Fifteenth Amendment instituted universal manhood suffrage. Taken together, these amendments codified black identity and seemed to answer the question of black "two-ness." Finally, being black was not constitutionally incompatible with being American. In states with the largest black populations, South Carolina, Mississippi, and Louisiana, former slaves joined those who had been free before the war in writing new progressive state constitutions. These documents laid the groundwork for public schools, more equitable tax policies, improved funding of hospitals and other state-supported institutions, more just divorce laws, and greater guarantees of civil liberties for all citizens.[41]

The federal government appeared to sanction black political rights in the North and in all the states of the former Confederacy, where blacks voted in substantial numbers. Almost all blacks voted for the Republican party of Abraham Lincoln, the "Great Emancipator." Republican votes brought black and white progressive legislators into state, local, and federal offices. Blacks served as mayors in Natchez and other urban areas of the Deep South. They were elected state legislators, served as secretaries of state and as speakers of the house in South Carolina and elsewhere. Louisiana had a lieutenant governor and an acting governor who were black.[42]

On the national level, southern blacks were elected to both houses of the U.S. Congress. Through the efforts of black and white progressive legislators in Congress and at the state, county, and local levels, laws were passed that seemed to affirm the identity of African Americans as citizens of the United States entitled to all the rights and privileges of that status. Federal law supported state statutes that made racial segregation in public facilities and on public transportation illegal. Although most public schools in the South were segregated, and many remained so in the North, many black children in both regions attended integrated schools.

There were a few significant signs that some white Americans—southerners and northerners—were willing to accept the evolving post-Emancipation identity of black people. In the South, however, much confusion remained about the nature of race relations under this new freedom. Some whites tried to return blacks to a position of dependency, and others sought new methods of racial control and labor stabilization. Labor contracts, sharecropping, and tenant farming replaced the old system of slavery. Blacks reunited families, formalized and legalized their marriages (legal marriage had been impossible under slavery), and accommodated themselves to the new system of work relationships.

Fairly administered, these changes might well have led to the creation of a new African American identity and a fulfillment of the promise of the American experiment. But the rise of political terrorism carried out by the Ku Klux Klan and other groups, and the willingness of the federal government to bargain away the protection of southern blacks in return for economic and political stability in the South, ensured that the progress of the post–Civil War years was short lived. By the closing decades of the nineteenth century, with most black voters forcibly stripped of the franchise and most Republicans—black and white—driven from office in the South, it was clear that the pattern of race relations in America would be one based on white supremacy. Although blacks continued their traditional struggle for an American identity and the rights inherent in that status, the obstacles were great indeed. In the 1890s a few blacks elected to leave the country for the sanctuary of Africa, but as in times past, their numbers were tiny.

At the end of the nineteenth century, most of the factors, except for slavery, that had limited black opportunity in America remained important complicators of black identity. A further complexity was the fact that black Americans increasingly identified with regions of the American nation. These regional identifications had always existed, but with slavery ended they were brought into sharp relief. No less than white Americans, blacks considered themselves New Englanders, northerners, westerners, and—most important—southerners. A southern identity was most complex for an African American. Southern civilization was rooted first in slavery and later in the policies of legalized racial segregation. It was almost impossible to be a true southerner without supporting, or at least accepting, both systems. Most blacks did neither. Yet black people, especially during the nineteenth century, were so obviously tied to the culture of the South, and the South was so obviously influenced by African and African American culture, that it was impossible not to identify the vast majority of blacks as southern people. This was but another complication in the complex pattern of African American identity.

The nineteenth century was a confusing and multifaceted period for American black people. During the first part of the century, the vast majority of African Americans were enslaved in a region and in a country most called home. They were enslaved by a people most ambivalently called countrymen. There was a love of country and a hatred of the evil practiced within that country. For free blacks who found it possible to protest that evil, the protest itself became a vital part of identity. Black citizenship became defined in part by the role of African Americans as national conscience, which would not allow America to sleep soundly as long as human bondage and injustice remained the bases upon which American opportunity rested. Sometimes it was necessary for blacks to emphasize their American rights and roots over their African heritage, but that heritage was never abandoned. Instead, the individual African heritages were merged into the African American racial identity, creating one of the truest melting pots this nation has ever witnessed.

3

Race and Ethnicity

The nineteenth-century city was a far more integrated place than its counterpart of the twentieth century. Residents lived within walking distance of their work, making distinctions between residential area and business districts less significant than they are in today's city. There was also less residential separation along lines of race and ethnicity. African Americans, American-born whites, and immigrants shared neighborhoods, and, although there was some residential clustering, the solid urban racial or ethnic ghetto of the twentieth century had not yet developed. These nineteenth-century urban living patterns ensured that daily contacts between blacks and whites were more common than in the modern city, but the nature of this contact varied with economic and political conditions. This section explores the relationships between blacks and whites in two very different mid-nineteenth century cities in two different ways.

Chapter 8, "Blacks and Germans in Mid-nineteenth Century Buffalo," examines relations between these two groups and compares them to the relations between blacks and the Irish. It finds associations between African Americans and Germans to have been relatively harmonious, particularly in contrast to the violence and acrimony that marked contact between blacks and Irish immigrants. Traditional notions of black-immigrant relations in the nineteenth century have focused on black-Irish conflict. In cities such as Boston, New York, Cincinnati, and

Philadelphia, hostility between these groups sometimes erupted into open and bloody violence. Few studies have contrasted these relations with those that blacks were able to establish with other immigrant groups. The information provided in Chapter 8 serves to reveal both a more nuanced picture of black-immigrant relations and much about the economics of prejudice and racism.

If African Americans and Irish immigrants often competed for scarce resources, they did so with a similar American dream of success. There are two tenets of that dream that seem so obvious to many privileged Americans that most take them for granted. One is that hard work is rewarded with economic success, and the other is that education clears a path to advancement. Chapter 9 examines the impact of literacy on black economic advancement in the years after the Civil War. "Race, Occupation, and Literacy in Reconstruction Washington, D.C." concludes that education was not enough to lift the thousands of poor blacks who flooded the federal city during the 1860s and 1870s from the lowest rungs of the occupational ladder. Although it proved a path toward the American dream for many immigrants, education did not benefit African Americans to the same extent. Blacks, no matter how educationally advantaged, were often passed over in the labor market for those whose privileged skin color overshadowed their foreignness in the eyes of would-be employers.

Further, this chapter illustrates the evolutionary roots of the liberal policy assumptions that became the foundation of the social welfare state of the twentieth century. The social program designed by post–Civil War liberal Republican reformers for the benefit of the newly free people of color triumphed in its attempt to bring literacy. Yet as social reformers endorsed a gradualist approach to betterment focusing largely on education, political forces were depriving blacks of the franchise, thus denying them the power that might have made their educational accomplishments economically meaningful. Education was then acceptable to both liberal reformers and political moderates, partly because the removal of the potential of black political power guaranteed that its acquisition would not appreciably alter the economic relationships or threaten the security of social authority in Reconstruction Washington. Some sought the gradual evolution of racial uplift through individual improvement; others understood the importance of controlling the routes to economic and political power.

The complexities of the interaction between blacks and immigrants are as integral to the development of issues of class and race in the twentieth century as they are to the development of protest strategies and political alliances within black society and between blacks and whites.

Engraved by J.C Buttre

William Wells Brown, escaped slave and Underground Railroad worker, was almost as widely known an abolitionist as Frederick Douglass. He combined his antislavery work with a writing career. His *Clotel* was the first novel published by an African American. He also wrote three major volumes on black history. (Courtesy of The New-York Historical Society, New York City)

Chapter 8

African Americans and Germans in Mid-nineteenth Century Buffalo

JAMES OLIVER HORTON AND HARTMUT KEIL

In the last few years there have been several good historical studies of blacks and of immigrants in the decades before the American Civil War. Few, however, have focused on the relationships between blacks and immigrants during this era. Antagonism between these groups is generally assumed, and the abundant evidence of hostility is often cited to illustrate the widespread social disorder of this period. Mob violence in 1829 drove hundreds of African Americans from Cincinnati. Similar incidents in Philadelphia, New York City, Pittsburgh, Washington, D.C., and other cities during the 1830s and 1840s show hostility turned violent, largely targeting black workers, who many immigrants saw as economic competitors. Recent studies of racial violence in New York City confirm the disproportional participation of immigrants in assaults on black communities during the 1820s and 1830s.[1]

Irish immigrants shared with these blacks a position at the economic bottom of American society, and they were blacks' most notorious adversaries. In the three decades before the Civil War, more than 1.8 million Irish people came to America. Most arrived during the decade of the fifties, escaping the effects of the potato blight that began in Ireland during the mid-forties. They came from the Irish countryside, bringing few skills fit for their new urban homes. In cities such as Boston, Philadelphia, and New York, most lived in poverty and faced discrimination from native-born whites. The addendum No Irish Need Apply often appeared in the want ads of the major newspapers of these port cities, signaling the restrictions on secure employment open to Irish immigrants. The work that was available to many of them was generally low paying and less desirable. Free blacks, also the victims of job discrimination, were their strong employment competitors. This economic rivalry frequently spawned violence, which continued sporadically throughout the nineteenth century.[2]

Historians generally accept economic competition as the root of the hostility between blacks and Irish immigrants. But what of those immigrants not in economic competition with black labor? Was there racial/ethnic hostility between blacks and other groups of immigrants? And was it as strong or as violent? In an attempt to address these questions, consider the other major immigrant group of the antebellum period—the Germans. Much of what is considered black-immigrant relations is in reality black-Irish relations. Less is known about contacts between blacks and Germans. Like the Irish, many German immigrants came to America to escape economic hardship. Almost 1.5 million Germans arrived during the antebellum decades, but unlike the Irish, most did not arrive destitute. Often they could afford to take up farms in the open land of the Midwest. Even so, tens of thousands of Germans remained in the cities of the East. Some were unskilled workers, but many quickly gained work as skilled craftsmen and business owners.[3]

This chapter will investigate the economic structures of the German and African American communities in Buffalo in the mid-nineteenth century. It will seek to shed light on the relationships between these groups as compared to relations between blacks and Irish immigrants. Evidence suggests that black relations with Germans, although not always friendly, were far less hostile than those with the Irish. A comparison of the relations between these groups will aid in understanding the importance of economic issues in the formation of racial attitudes. Further, it will suggest a more complex relationship between blacks and non-native whites than that which fails to differentiate between immigrant groups.

Buffalo, perched on the shores of Lake Erie, a major commercial transit point connecting western New York state to New York City, is the site of this study. Demographically it is well suited to this kind of comparison, because it had a substantial immigrant population. By the mid-nineteenth century almost half of the city's seventy-two thousand people were foreign born.[4] Germans were the single largest immigrant group of the period, about 39 percent of the city's population. The Irish constituted the second largest immigrant group, but their proportion of Buffalonians was less than half the Germans'. Buffalo also had a small but highly visible African American population. Buffalo's black society was composed of slightly more than seven hundred people by the mid-nineteenth century, about 1 percent of the city's household heads. By 1860 Buffalo's black population had increased to more than eight hundred but was never so large as to be threatening to those who were uncomfortable with an African American presence in the city.[5]

The lives of all Buffalo's people, immigrant and native born, black and white, were tied to the local economy and influenced by local social and political conditions. The Queen City was a regionally dominant commercial city, hub of the Great Lakes trade system linking the hinterland areas of the eastern Midwest with western New York State and the East. It took its economic and cultural bearings from the East Coast. As the western terminus of the Erie Canal, it was part of the commercial sphere of New York City and thereby connected to the economies of Europe. After the economic boom ushered in by the completion of the canal in 1825, Buffalo's economic fortunes rose and fell with the fluctuations of the eastern economy and the weather, always unpredictable and potentially disruptive. By the 1840s growing competition from the railroad was making a revolutionary impact on the region's transportation and general economic system, and by the mid-1850s it threatened the canal's preeminence.

Buffalo grew rapidly from twenty-five hundred residents at the time the canal was completed to just under nine thousand by 1830. During the next fifteen years the population leaped to seventy thousand and to more than eighty thousand by the time of the Civil War. Many laborers, drawn by the building of the canal, stayed to take advantage of the commercial expansion it brought. By midcentury there was employment for unskilled and semiskilled workers at the city's ten major grain elevators. By 1855 ironworking and manufacturing provided at least two thousand jobs. The docks and construction work also provided significant employment for the city's manual laborers.[6]

These were important occupations for Buffalo's blacks, the vast majority of whom (67 percent of those reporting employment) held the lowest-paying and least-stable jobs in the city. African American men were overrepresented among dock laborers and at least seven times as likely to serve on the lake, river, and canal boats as their proportion of the general population would indicate. Black women were disproportionately domestic servants. Significantly, many blacks, men and women (30 percent), reported no occupation at all. Indeed, an overwhelming three-quarters of the black work force reported either no job or an unskilled job.[7]

A significant minority of African Americans held more reliable employment. Almost one-third were professionals or skilled workers. These included four ministers, two teachers, several seamstresses and dressmakers, and a few skilled workers in the construction trades. There was also a small group of entrepreneurs. As in other northern cities of the period, the largest group of black businesses were run by barbers, many of whom owned their own shops. Some of these barbers served a white clientele, but many also had black customers, and often their shops served as important community gathering places. The occupational structure of the Buffalo black community was, then, one of a largely unskilled or lower-skilled majority with a small, but important and influential, middling minority.

There was little employment competition between Buffalo's African Americans and Germans. Germans were employed in different and substantially better occupations. Almost two of every five German workers (37 percent) held more stable skilled jobs. They represented a majority of the city's skilled construction workers, 70 to 80 percent of the masons, more than 60 percent of the cabinetmakers and ironworkers, and more than half of the carpenters. Of all German men in Buffalo in the mid-1850s only 42 percent, or about half the rate for black workers, reported either no occupation or an unskilled occupation. The situation was even better for younger German workers, many of whom found apprenticeship positions under the supervision of their skilled countrymen. The proportion of German household heads under the age of thirty holding a skilled job in the mid-1850s was 44 percent.[8]

In the black community there was no special advantage for younger workers. There were few black craftsmen to train them, and few white craftsmen would take on a black apprentice. Thus their occupational levels remained no better than that of other black workers. Of the thirty-nine younger (under thirty years of age) black household heads in Buffalo in 1855, only nine (23 percent) held a job at the skilled or professional level. Almost as many (eight) reported no job. Others were unskilled or semiskilled workers; the largest group, ten or 26 percent of all younger black household heads, worked as cooks.[9]

The economic distance between African Americans and Germans

is more striking when persistence rates are considered. Among Germans residing in Buffalo for more than fourteen years, the proportion of un- skilled workers dropped to 13 percent. By contrast, 77 percent of black workers who had lived fourteen years or longer in the city still reported either no job or a job at the unskilled level. Whereas German workers seemed to have improved their occupational position as they lived longer in the city, the occupational position for black longtime residents grew worse.[10]

The difference in occupations between Germans and blacks was reflected in property-holding statistics. Substantial numbers of Germans were property holders (40 percent in 1855), and their number increased with advancing age. About one-quarter of German household heads in their twenties owned property. That proportion almost doubled by mid- dle age and continued to rise, so that by the time German heads of household reached old age (sixty years or older) the proportion of prop- erty owners among them was at its greatest (47 percent).[11]

Property ownership among blacks was a different story. By 1855 only one-quarter of all black household heads held property. Among younger household heads, property holders were a mere 5 percent, and although property holding was more widespread by the time these blacks reached middle age, peaking during their fifties (at 35 percent), it dropped again after age sixty (to 20 percent). This pattern was unusual. For American-born whites, as for Germans, old age was the time of greatest property holding.

There were, then, important economic differences that defined the social distance between Buffalo's blacks and Germans. Spatially, howev- er, the distance between these two groups was not as great. Almost three-quarters of African Americans lived in the adjacent Fourth, Fifth, and Sixth wards in the eastern quadrant of the city. These wards were also home to more than half of the city's German-born population. Blacks could hardly have escaped the ever-present Teutonic social and cultural stamp imposed on these neighborhoods. They could count on from 55 to 90 percent of their neighbors being Germans.

Although there was some clustering of black households in these wards, blacks and Germans often lived side by side, sharing exterior and sometimes interior space. Forty percent of black families lived un- der the same roof with white families, and three-quarters of these whites (fifty-eight of seventy-six) were Germans. The vast majority of these living arrangements (92 percent) were in the heavily German Sixth

Ward. Here a black cook's family from Washington, D.C., shared a house with a family of seven from Württemberg. Nearby lived a black waiter and his family of four in the same building as two German families headed by a grocer and a tailor and the family of an Alsatian blacksmith.[12]

Sometimes special circumstances, suggesting complex social interaction, brought Germans and African Americans together, as when two German widows, each with young children, shared a house with a black widow and her children. There were a few blacks who boarded with German families. One Prussian couple took fourteen black men into their boardinghouse. Recent arrivals, widowers, the elderly, and laborers contributed disproportionately to these racially mixed living arrangements.

Less important numerically, but of great symbolic significance, were the marriages between African Americans and Germans. In 1855 there were forty-eight interracial couples in Buffalo. Half of the white partners in these unions were foreign born and almost half of these foreign-born partners were Germans. There were few German-born spouses, only twelve, but it is significant that Germans were four times as likely to marry blacks than were Irish immigrants, a rate twice that expected, given their proportion of Buffalo's population. Most of the spouses were women, but three German men took black wives. The contact represented by these marriages was greater than simply that between two partners, because in several cases these couples lived in extended-family households. In Buffalo's Fourth Ward, for example, a twenty-seven-year-old Bavarian watchmaker was married to a young black women. The couple lived with the woman's parents in a house shared with three other German and Alsatian households.

These marriages were particularly significant considering German reluctance to marry outside their ethnic, religious, or even their regional group. The vast majority of Germans took spouses from their own province within Germany. As one historian suggested, "Marriage between Bavarians and Prussians would be unusual . . ." Thus for a German to choose an African American mate, even though often of the same religious faith, was noteworthy.[13]

The fact that they lived in the same neighborhoods did not necessarily make blacks and Germans competitors for the same housing. Blacks lived in homes valued at an average of eleven hundred dollars. These were mainly buildings of wood and planking. Only 12 percent of blacks lived in more substantial brick or stone homes.[14] Germans could afford slightly better housing, with an average value of almost thirteen hundred dollars. Fourteen percent of their homes were built of brick or stone. Both Germans and blacks lived far below the level of housing enjoyed by native-born white Americans, whose homes, one-third of which were brick or stone, were valued at an average of thirty-eight hundred dollars. German housing was, however, somewhat better than African American housing.

When ownership rates are taken into consideration, the situation becomes even clearer. Germans owned many more of the homes in which they lived and were less likely to compete with blacks for rentals. This is significant, because in cities where blacks and Irish lived in the same neighborhoods—Boston, for example—their similar economic levels forced them to compete for the same poor quality rental property. In Buffalo, as might be expected, blacks and Irish immigrants occupied housing of similar quality. The average Irish family lived in a house of wood and planking (only 10 percent constructed of brick or stone) valued at about one thousand dollars. They ordinarily did not compete for housing with blacks in Buffalo, however, because they lived in different parts of the city.[15]

Germans and African Americans, then, did not generally come together as competitors on the job or in the housing market, but they did live as neighbors and often established social relationships. Occasionally they associated as employees and employers. Domestic servants were considered a necessity in nineteenth-century middle-class homes, and a few blacks filled this role within German households. Several African American domestic workers commuted to work, making their proximity to the German community convenient and practical. Although a review of the New York state census of 1855 suggests that most of these workers were young black men, because women's occupations were less likely to be listed in that year, there is surely an undercount of black women among these domestics. Most of these black servants lived in the homes of native-born whites, but about one-third lived in German households.[16]

An analysis of the 1860 U.S. census provides further evidence of the undercount. There is an unlikely rise in the employment rate of black female workers from 1 percent in 1850 (about 7 percent in the 1855 New York state census) to a more substantial and a more believable 30 percent in the 1860 census. An examination of the 1860 census also changes the picture of live-in domestic service for black women. Whereas earlier censuses indicated insignificant numbers of black women living in white households, the 1860 census reported this proportion to be more than 43 percent, most in the homes of native-born white Buffalonians. Although a few blacks were live-in domestics in German homes, most Germans were not wealthy enough to afford that luxury.[17] Interestingly, there were also a few German servants living and working in black households. These were all women and all in their twenties except for one ten-year-old girl. When nonrelated blacks and Germans lived in the same family setting, they were more likely to board with one another than to be live-in servants.

The relationship that existed between blacks and Irish in the city was quite different. They were far more likely to share the same work space as competitors. Like blacks, Irish workers were most likely to hold jobs in the lowest-paying, least-secure, and most-unskilled sector of the city's economy. Almost 70 percent of Irish workers labored on the docks, did domestic work, or were low-skilled transportation workers. Like blacks, they were not likely to be property holders. Only about 23 percent of Irish households held property, actually three percentage points less than black Buffalonians. Also like blacks, they experienced a decline of property holding in old age. The proportion of Irish property holders surpassed that of blacks for those in their twenties but fell behind for those greater than thirty years of age.[18]

There were similarities between the Irish and blacks in household and family structure. Two-parent households predominated in both groups. The census reported that 80 percent of black and Irish households had two parents, but this was below the rate for both native-born white Americans (85 percent) and Germans (90 percent). The poverty of both Irish and black Buffalonians explains in part the somewhat lower rate of two-parent households. There were, however, interesting differences in the marriage patterns of Irish and black men that were also involved. Black men remained single longer than Irish men. Half of all Irish adult males were married by age twenty-five. Black men started to marry in their early twenties, but the rise in the proportion of black married men progressed more slowly, so that even by age thirty only half were married. This slow rate of marriage continued. By their mid-thirties about two-thirds of black men were married, rising to more than 70 percent by age forty. By contrast almost 70 percent of the other American-born men in the city were married before thirty years of age.[19]

Many of these single black men worked at menial jobs and, without a family to support, perhaps they were willing to work for lower wages than those demanded by their economic competitors. A local newspaper explained one outbreak of racial violence as resulting from the willingness of Buffalo's blacks to "labor and receive a fair compensation therefore."[20] The Irish, also unskilled but more likely to be head of a family, saw black workers as a direct threat to their families. These competing groups, living at a distance from one another, were likely to come into contact mainly at the workplace, the site of their most direct antagonism. It is not difficult to understand the potential for violence in that contact.

This racial hostility was intimately tied to politics. Early on the Democratic party recognized and encouraged racial antipathy among immigrants and used it to their political advantage against the Whigs in the 1840s and against the Republicans a decade later. During the struggle for black voting rights in New York state in the 1840s, for example, Democrats called Whigs anti-Catholic, anti-immigrant "fanatics" who would put up "truckling, ignorant and subservient Negro[es]" to diminish the power of immigrant voters. The city's German press echoed this charge. Early in the decade, the Buffalo *Der Weltbürger,* the city's first German-language newspaper (begun in 1837), spoke out against the Whig party, which it believed was more likely to stand for black enfranchisement than for immigrant rights. This conservative journal praised the Democrats as the "progressing element" likely to stand for the rights of all while disparaging Whigs as those who "reject all progress . . . [for the] benefit of the few and [to] the cost of the many . . ."[21]

Buffalo's immigrants were likely to back these sentiments with their votes. When the state referendum on black enfranchisement was posed in 1846, it was soundly defeated throughout the city. Voters in the immigrant wards were especially opposed to this measure. Eighty-seven percent of those in the heavily Irish First Ward voted against black enfranchisement. Significantly, the measure was defeated in the predominantly German Fourth Ward by the same margin.[22]

Using this racial appeal, Democrats played on the immigrant defensiveness induced by the rising tide of nativism during the pre–Civil War decades. By the mid-1850s most immigrants were Democrats, opposing the conscience Whig and Republican programs which they equated with radical abolitionism and anti-immigrant zeal. Their anger, generated by discrimination that limited immigrant political, economic, and social opportunity, was often directed at the black community. In this context Democratic racial tactics were especially meaningful. But not all immigrants exhibited hostile racial attitudes to the same degree.

Although most Germans were Democrats in the 1840s and early 1850s, and many no doubt accepted the party line on race, there was a strong intellectual tradition that ran counter to such arguments. During the late 1840s, a small but influential group of German intellectuals arrived in the United States seeking escape from the consequences of the unsuccessful revolution in their homeland. These were political radicals, socialists with a strong commitment to individual rights and freedoms. Like earlier German liberal thinkers who had questioned America's continued sanctioning of slavery, these German radicals challenged the blatant racism of the Democratic party. It would be an overstatement to portray these intellectuals as racial egalitarians, but many of them opposed slavery as a violation of humanitarian principles. These forty-eighters, as they were called, were important in the shift of German political support away from the Democrats and toward the Republican party during the middle and late 1850s.[23]

The Irish also had a strong traditional commitment to freedom. Having suffered centuries of British oppression, there was a sensitivity and a social radicalism among them that in some ways paralleled that of the German intellectuals. The Fenian revolutionaries in Ireland and the Sinn Fein movement, which established a headquarters in New York City before the Civil War, dedicated themselves to the liberation of Ireland and espoused a general commitment to human rights. However, for Irish Americans this did not translate into even the tentative liberalism on questions of human freedom observed among the Germans.[24] Irishmen were never attracted in significant numbers to antislavery or the Republican party of the 1850s. Generally their intolerance of class privilege did not extend to a condemnation of the southern slaveholding aristocracy. Few sympathized with the plight of free blacks or slaves. When Charles Lenox Remond, a black abolitionist from Boston, returned from Europe with an antislavery petition bearing the signatures of sixty thousand citizens of Ireland, Irish Americans refused to endorse it. Clearly Irish Americans perceived their loyalties and the plight of black Americans differently than did those on the Emerald Isle.[25]

During the early 1850s, the rise of the nativist Know-Nothings encouraged political conservatism and a swing toward the Democrats among all of Buffalo's immigrants. But the nativist appeal declined after the defeat of Buffalo's own Millard Fillmore in his bid for the presidency in 1856. In the late 1850s, many Germans were moving cautiously toward the Republicans and a more liberal political stance on slavery. The Irish, however, stood fast on the bedrock of political conservatism, and racial hostility. The appeal of Republicanism from the standpoint of the Germans was more economic than humanitarian. They were drawn by the Republican Free-Soil platform and its pledge to maintain the western territories for free labor. Even the conservative *Der Weltbürger,* claimed that the German newspapers in America opposed the abandonment of the Missouri Compromise, which restricted the spread of slavery into the northern areas of the western territories.[26]

German support for the Republican party or for antislavery did not signal a general affinity toward African Americans. Buffalo's Germans were more inclined to denounce slavery, often in strong language, than to accept free blacks as equals. Despite the fact that there were many examples of the integration of blacks into German neighborhoods, Germans often spoke in the racially charged language of the time. In the pages of *Der Weltbürger* blacks were referred to as "monsters" and "animals." The report of a rape of a German woman by a "mulatto" who "executed the act of disgrace" to satisfy his "bestial lust" was typical of the newspaper's use of racially inflammatory rhetoric. Despite the realities of Buffalo's residential patterns, most of the city's Germans wanted to keep the number of blacks small in the city and in the North generally. Most agreed that "we don't want Negroes in the northern states because we don't expect anything good from the mixture of the black and white races."[27]

Yet despite these illustrations of racial intolerance, by the late 1850s German racial attitudes were changing, at least on the question of black suffrage. By 1860 several local German politicians endorsed equal voting rights for New York blacks. Most did so on the grounds of bringing uniformity to state voting regulations. Some German organizations, however, supported the measure on egalitarian grounds. In the largest German ward in the city, voters gave Lincoln 57 percent in his 1860 presidential victory. Although the enfranchisement measure failed once again in Buffalo, German wards voted 42 percent in favor, the highest percentage in any wards in the city. Irish voters remained anti-Republican and continued their strong opposition to black voting.

The distinction between German and Irish racial attitudes was most obvious during the anti-black violence that erupted in many northern cities in the early 1860s. Racial violence had occurred periodically in Buffalo in the 1850s as black and immigrant workers, mostly Irish, clashed on the docks and in the city's shipyards. One historian reported that such conflict "frequently pitted the Irish in fierce battles with blacks, who at times attempted to work as sailors and longshoremen and were brought into competition with Irish men."[28]

These confrontations were relatively limited compared to the full-scale riot in the early 1860s, which erupted when black workers were used as strikebreakers. Three blacks were killed and twelve severely injured in this conflict. Several black families had to be evacuated from their homes by police. Even under police protection, blacks were surrounded by crowds of whites and beaten. "This we fear is but the beginning of the end," concluded one contemporary observer. Yet this Buffalo violence was just one of many race riots during the Civil War years, riots resulting from job competition and the impact of the military draft. Irish immigrants figured most prominently in these confrontations.[29]

Buffalo's Germans were not as visible in these riots. Their absence is noteworthy and due in part to the relatively noncompetitive nature of black-German relationships in the city. As Germans were not as likely as the Irish to see blacks as immediate threats to their community, their reaction to African Americans was less extreme. Germans were hardly committed to notions of racial equality, but neither were they likely to attack blacks. Crime records for antebellum Buffalo suggest that Germans were not likely to be involved in violent crimes. There were few instances of Germans jailed for such crimes. Further, during the antebellum years the only recorded incidence of German collective violence was in 1842 when a group of twenty German men stoned a brothel.[30]

During the racial violence of the 1860s, Germans even attempted to control the Irish rioters. A recent study of the New York draft riots of 1863 shows that Germans took part in the early stages of the riot when it was largely directed against the draft law. They dropped out, however, when it turned violent and directed its venom toward the city's blacks, killing and mutilating more than one hundred. Before the riot was over, one newspaper reported that "the Germans organiz[ed] their forces and . . . enrolled about three hundred men who will be sworn in to act as special police." The efforts of these men saved the lives of many black New Yorkers.[31]

Historians have argued effectively that "mob action" is more than a random outburst of irrational emotion. It is often the violent expression of deeply felt political and social beliefs. An analysis of mob composition and the object of its attack can explain much about the group dynamics and the ethnocultural politics of the period. The Irish saw themselves as victims, defending what little they had against black competitors. Germans, higher on the economic scale and less competitive with black workers, were less likely to see African Americans as economically threatening. German and Irish actions carried their own rationality.[32]

Thus the relations between blacks and immigrants were more complex than is often recognized. They depended in large part on local social, political, and, perhaps most important, economic conditions. Strong occupational competition could combine with other local factors to turn antagonism to violence. It was also likely that a specific social atmosphere and perhaps a degree of social integration might act to mute the most violent manifestations of intergroup antipathy.

Sociological and anthropological work in the area of human conflict suggests that group violence may be lessened between those linked by a variety of social contacts. Sociologist Donald Black uses the term *relational distance* to describe "the scope, frequency, and length of interaction between people, the age of their relationship, and the nature and number of links between them in a social network." He argues that groups with decreased relational distance were less prone to riot or mob violence against one another. Black drew support for his theory from the anthropological work of Max Gluckman and Elizabeth Colson, who used the term *cross-cutting ties* to suggest the links that bind groups together lessening the likelihood of intergroup violence.[33]

Historians have used these theories to provide a context for understanding racial violence in America. Neighbors may clash over personal issues, but recent studies suggest that widespread, large-group violence is less likely to occur between those engaged in regular, positive social interaction. In her study of the Springfield, Illinois, race riot of 1908, Roberta Senechal found that those who took part in that riot were working-class whites experiencing "status insecurity," feeling directly threatened, economically and socially, by a growing African American presence in that city. She argued that those who lived in or near black neighborhoods were least likely to take part in the anti-black violence. "If you plot rioters' residence on a map, you find that the further away you get from black residences, the more rioters you find." She found that 70 percent of the rioters lived in "all-white streets and all-white blocks." Allen D. Grimshaw, studying urban violence nationally, came to similar conclusions.[34]

In light of this argument, the residential configuration in mid-nineteenth century Buffalo takes on additional importance. It may be directly connected to and a partial explanation of the behavior of Germans toward blacks in that city. The absence of strong economic tension and the presence of spacial and social links may be important elements underlying the nature of German-black relations. If this is so, it may have crucial implications for understanding the impact of racial integration on group interaction today. There is obviously much more to learn about the history of ethnic and racial relations. It is hoped that this study will contribute to that effort.

The black church was the sanctuary in which people of color found relief from the pressures of the outside world and were able to come to grips with the secular and spiritual complexity of their identity. (Library of Congress)

Chapter 9

Race, Occupation, and Literacy in Reconstruction Washington, D.C.

JAMES OLIVER HORTON AND LOIS E. HORTON

Education and economic mobility are inextricably bound in American ideology. Education is believed to be an important road to occupational success for all Americans. During Reconstruction, education for black Americans became a major element of federal policy.

The focus of this chapter is on the development of Reconstruction federal policy for blacks—a policy that placed greater and greater reliance on education. It relates events in Washington, D.C., where the federal government had the greatest power and impact on local affairs. Primarily using records of the Bureau of Refugees, Freedmen and Abandoned Lands (Freedmen's Bureau) and federal census data, it will attempt to examine the extent to which reformers' faith in education for blacks was well founded.

The Civil War years and the following decades brought dramatic changes to the nation's capital. The conduct of the war concentrated greater power in the federal government, expanding the federal payroll, attracting legions of government contractors, and transforming the southern village into a cosmopolitan town. The population of Washington, D.C., grew from slightly more than 60,000 in 1860 to more than 100,000 ten years later. The striking increase in the black population during those years, rising from almost 11,000 to more than 35,000, was particularly distressing to many Washingtonians. As war disrupted the institution of slavery in the Maryland and Virginia countryside and as slavery was abolished in the District of Columbia in 1862, thousands of blacks poured into the city for the shelter of federal protection.

Mainly former slaves, these blacks brought the problems of their poverty to the already overburdened city, overwhelming the resources of the local government and private agencies. As in other areas of the South, the federal government assumed responsibility for the amelioration of the war-related problems of Reconstruction. The urban character of Washington presented unique problems for federal programs, but federal involvement in the city also presented unique opportunities for experimentation and the formulation of social policy. Destitute blacks were in need of relief, housing, health care, employment, and education, and the Freedmen's Bureau instituted in 1865, undertook programs in all of these areas.

Supplementing private efforts, the bureau employed visiting agents who distributed food, clothing, and fuel to more than two thousand people in Washington from 1866 to 1868. Subsidized housing was located in the city's outskirts; dispensaries and hospitals were operated by the bureau. Bureau employment agents found employment for thousands of workers, and the bureau provided about half of the support for Washington's expanding educational system.

The political and philosophical realities of the era demanded that any assistance provided to the former slave be temporary. Slavery had engendered dependency, most believed, and an important task was to promote self-reliance. "These refugees, as readily spoiled as children, should not be treated with weak and injurious indulgence," warned the Freedmen's Inquiry Commission. "Even-handed justice, not special favor, is what they need." Any social program should emphasize "mild firmness" to encourage "self-support."[1]

Emancipation had created the possibility for black independence. Radical Republicans and black leaders argued that enfranchisement of the freedmen was necessary to safeguard freedom, promote self-respect, and encourage independence. In late 1865 Senator Benjamin Wade introduced a measure to provide blacks in Washington with the right to vote. In the House, radicals such as George Julian, representative from Indiana, supported black voting in the District as a part of a broad vision of justice for both blacks and women. Others saw black enfranchisement as retribution for southern disloyalty. Locally, those who viewed voting as the blacks' right included the postmaster of Washington, Sayles J. Bowen, and the city's blacks. Led by George T. Downing, a longtime black abolitionist; Lewis H. Douglass, the son of Frederick

Douglass; and John F. Cook, a black teacher, twenty-five hundred black Washingtonians petitioned Congress in support of the Wade bill.[2]

White Washingtonians generally opposed the measure. Many argued that America was the white man's country and voting was white man's business. Blacks, they said, were not capable of responsible citizenship. Besides, many argued, enfranchisement would only aggravate the racial antagonism already excited by rapid black population growth. A straw vote taken among whites in the district in December 1865 confirmed the overwhelming white opposition to black enfranchisement. The city council rejected a moderate declaration, explaining that the opposition to blacks voting was based on the inability of most blacks to read or write, and the council passed a more blatantly racist explanation, saying that only those who possess "mental and moral qualifications acceptable to an enlightened public" ought to be allowed to vote. Local whites, led by Mayor Richard Wallach and prominent members of the board of aldermen, were not moderate on the question of black enfranchisement in the district.[3]

Luckily for blacks, the decision on suffrage was not made at the local level. Through the early months of 1866 debate raged in the House and the Senate. Conservatives dismissed black suffrage in the district as a folly that might set a dangerous precedent for the rest of the nation. Moderates also opposed black suffrage in the district, but their argument was more subtle. Francis Thomas, representative from Maryland, pointed to the hypocrisy of northern representatives who supported black suffrage in Washington but did not support it in their home states. Other moderate Republicans, Carl Schurz, Sen. William Pitt Fessenden of Maine, and Sen. John Sherman of Ohio, believed blacks must be educated before they were allowed to vote.

The campaign for the black vote was spearheaded by radical Republicans. Leadership in the House included Julian and Thaddeus Stevens; in the Senate, Wade was joined by Charles Sumner, Benjamin F. Butler, and Jacob Howard. Despite local and congressional opposition and a presidential veto, the bill granting black suffrage in the District of Columbia became law in 1867.

By the time of the 1867 district elections, black and white Republicans had organized for the exercise of political power. Although blacks were only about one-third of the population, they constituted nearly half of the registered voters.[4] On election day they came early and stood in long lines at the polls to cast this historic vote. In a perverse protest, many whites boycotted the election, ensuring an impressive Republican victory. By the election of 1869, the power of the black Republican vote was apparent, as only three Democrats served on the fourteen-member board of aldermen and none remained on the common council. Indeed, in 1869 nine blacks were elected to public office. Under the threat of growing black political power and with the promise of federal backing for expanding public works, powerful business interests joined with concerned white Washingtonians to exchange home rule for territorial government in 1871. The process of the disfranchisement of all Washingtonians was completed by 1874, when a commission form of government was instituted. With the loss of the vote, an important radical program for promoting black self-reliance failed in the District of Columbia. Black political power in the district was greatly diminished. What seemed to remain, then, was to pursue those policies that would promote black independence without severely disrupting the existing social and political structure.

As early as 1868, most of the Freedmen's Bureau's relief and civil rights functions had waned or disappeared. Only its educational program remained. Education was the cornerstone of moderate Republican postwar reform and of Freedmen's Bureau activities. By the late 1860s, most moderate reformers still agreed with an earlier statement issued by the Federal Educational Commission that "the instruction most needed by the blacks . . . [was] that which should lead them to appreciate the advantages of civilized life . . . and to learn the duties and responsibilities of free men."[5] In 1865 a special committee of the common council of Washington declared that illiteracy was a major impediment to black advancement.

Blacks themselves had long viewed education as an important means of advancement. "If we ever expect to see the influence of prejudice decreased and ourselves respected," an early national black conference declared, "it must be by the blessing of an enlightened education."[6] Washington's first black school was established in 1807 by the free black community. It experienced constant financial difficulties and was forced to close in 1822. The next year another black school was established in the city by a former slave, enrolling as many as one hundred students.[7] By 1862 there were six private schools for black primary education in the district. In that year a bill was introduced in the Senate that called for the establishment of public support of black education through the diversion of 10 percent of the taxes paid by Washington's black community. The first black public school was actually opened in March 1864, in the black Ebenezer Methodist Church.[8]

Schools proliferated in Washington during and after the war, so that in 1866 there were forty-five day schools, fifteen night schools, and twenty Sabbath schools serving the black population and supported by a combination of public aid, private benevolent-society funds, and the free blacks themselves.[9] By 1867 the school system had achieved some success in accommodating the city's children, with about one-third of the black children and more than half of the white children between the ages of six and seventeen attending school. Many black adults were also being educated—so many, in fact, that the percentages of the total black and white populations under instruction were virtually the same.[10]

By 1870 Washington public schools educated both black and white children in a well-rounded curriculum that included English grammar, spelling, arithmetic, penmanship, geography, and history. Standardized written and oral examinations were conducted regularly for all children. Before a child completed the ninth grade in 1871, for example, he or she was required to spell and understand a long list of words from "abridgment" to "zoophyte." Other tasks included naming "four memorable events in Jefferson's first term."[11] There was also training in manual trades and domestic arts. Black children between the age of six and seventeen attended public school in greater proportions than white children of the same age throughout the 1870s. The percentage of black children in this age group actually enrolled in public school, always above 50 percent during this decade, rose to more than 70 percent by the 1878–79 school year.[12] The curriculum for adults was often less elaborate than that for the children. It generally concentrated on reading, writing, spelling, and arithmetic.

Although the education of Washington's blacks faced some local opposition, it received support from high levels of the federal government. In addition to the passage of legislation by Congress, President Grant expressed great interest in black schools. He favored the establishment of a federal bureau of education in 1867 in order to assure federal involvement in the free slaves' education.[13]

By the mid-1870s the educational programs of moderate reformers eclipsed radical reform. The radical Republicans of the mid-1860s had advocated the redistribution of Confederate lands to freedmen, the enforcement of civil rights legislation, and the protection of black suffrage as a means of repaying blacks for their servitude and bringing them to full citizenship. The passage of the Fourteenth and Fifteenth amendments was a part of their program to assure black rights. Within a decade in the District of Columbia and in many parts of the South, radical programs had been successfully circumvented.[14] Political feasibility then rested with moderate reform.

The philosophy of social Darwinism espoused by the moderates served to justify their position and to explain the "failure" of the radicals. The radical philosophy was grounded in transcendentalism, with its belief in the perfectibility and equality of the brotherhood of men and the possibility of immediate social change. The application of Charles Darwin's theory of evolution to human society and American race relations gained prominence throughout the postwar period. Writers as diverse as Josiah C. Nott, Thomas Huxley, and Herbert Spencer agreed that only through centuries of evolutionary progress could blacks approach "the highest places in the hierarchy of civilization."[15]

In the field of social welfare, proponents of social Darwinism influenced by the extreme laissez-faire aspects of this philosophy argued that government activity in the welfare sphere was wasteful and inefficient. Moreover, it afforded the inferior members of the race artificial protection from the laws of nature, which promoted "the survival of the fittest." One reformer went so far as to suggest that "the killing off of one-third of the black population of the South would probably prove a benefit to civilization. It would work like the thinning out of a forest jungle, leaving room for the sun and air to reach the survivors; but the law has not yet authorized this process of scientific weeding out of the unfittest."[16]

Moderate Republicans argued that the radical goals had been unrealistic, failing to recognize the necessity for the evolutionary development of the black race. In 1865 the Washington City Council asked rhetorically, "If it took the ancient Briton a thousand years to emerge from his only half-civilized condition . . . to reach the point to qualify him for the exercise of this right [the vote], how long would it reasonably take the black man, who but about two hundred years ago was brought from Africa . . ."[17] To extend the vote to ignorant and easily manipulated blacks, they believed, invited political corruption by unscrupulous municipal party bosses. The mayoral election of Sayles J. Bowen in 1868 was cited as an example in Washington of the corrupt machine politics that plagued New York and other major cites. Black votes had ensured Bowen's election. Charges of dishonesty helped ensure his defeat in 1870.[18]

Moderates believed that government policy must be carefully designed. It should not provide assistance that might engender dependency, nor should it endanger democracy by forcing the rights of citizenship on those not ready for its responsibilities. Policy must be compatible with the laws of nature, encouraging the gradual, evolutionary growth of the former slaves. Black progress would only be assured when the freed men and women overcame the "slave habits" that were the "inheritance of generations."[19] Education was the key that would open the door to economic and political progress. The radicals had promoted black education as a part of a program that attacked the problems of newly freed slaves on many fronts. For the moderates, however, education alone was sufficient to guarantee eventual black uplift.

In order to test the validity of this moderate assumption, it is necessary to examine the status of blacks in both educational and economic pursuits. It can be estimated that the rate of black illiteracy stood at about 80 percent in Washington, D.C., at the close of the Civil War. (This assumes a 95 percent illiteracy rate for the thirty thousand freed men and women who entered the city during and immediately after the war, a 95 percent rate for slaves freed in Washington by compensated emancipation, and a 30 percent rate for free blacks recorded in the district prior to emancipation.) As a result of educational programs, illiteracy among the district's blacks was drastically reduced in the postwar period. By 1870 it was about 70 percent, and by 1880 it was about 50 percent.[20] This compares with 27.6 percent for Washington's total adult population in 1870 and 20.1 percent in 1880. Thus even in 1880, black illiteracy was still nearly two and a half times higher than that of the total Washington population.

The question of whether this educational progress was reflected in economic progress is of crucial importance. Because the population of the District of Columbia changed so drastically during the Civil War,[21] it is extremely difficult to make comparisons between 1860 and 1870. It can be estimated, however, that of the blacks residing in Washington, D.C., in 1870, about 10 percent had been skilled workers and about 89 percent had been semiskilled or unskilled workers in 1860.[22]

All data that follow on occupation and literacy in 1870 and 1880 were compiled from the manuscript federal census of those years.

Table 6
Black Occupational Levels and Illiteracy Rates in Washington, D.C., 1870 and
1880 (in percentages)

	1870 (N=408)	1880 (N=411)
Occupational level		
High white collar	0.2	0.5
Low white collar	3.2	3.4
Skilled	12.7	14.1
Semiskilled and unskilled	83.8	82.0
Illiteracy rate	68.6	51.1

Note: The table includes both those listed as black and those listed as mulatto. Due to rounding, occupational level totals may not be 100 percent.

Table 7
White Occupational Levels and Illiteracy Rates in Washington, D.C., 1870 and
1880 (in percentages)

	1870 (N=610)	1880 (N=615)
Occupational level		
High white collar	5.2	9.3
Low white collar	36.6	40.7
Skilled	30.3	29.8
Semiskilled and unskilled	27.9	20.3
Illiteracy rate	5.6	5.4

Note: Statistically significant at the .0175 level. Due to rounding, occupational level totals may not be 100 percent.

Systematic random samples were taken from each ward in each census, with a sampling fraction of $\frac{1}{50}$ for 1870 and $\frac{1}{70}$ for 1880. From a total population of 131,700 in 1870, a sample of 2,623 was taken; and from a total population of 177,624 in 1880, a sample of 2,533 was taken.

The sample of the black population in 1870 shows little economic progress measured in terms of occupation (see Table 6). By 1880 there was still little progress. If the highest occupational category, in which only a few blacks were employed, is eliminated for statistical computations, there was no difference between black occupational status in 1870 and 1880. Whites, on the other hand, show a significant upward mobility during this period (see Table 7).

Table 8
Occupational Levels and Illiteracy Rates among Mulattoes in Washington, D.C., 1870 and 1880 (in percentages)

	1870 (N=63)	1880 (N=98)
Occupational level		
High white collar	1.6	0.0
Low white collar	6.3	3.1
Skilled	23.8	16.3
Semiskilled and unskilled	68.3	80.6
Illiteracy rate	52.3	33.9

Source: Federal manuscript census returns for 1870 and 1880.
Note: Due to rounding, occupational level totals may not be 100 percent.

Table 9
Occupational Levels and Illiteracy Rates among Irish-born Whites in Washington, D.C., 1870 and 1880 (in percentages)

	1870 (N=104)	1880 (N=67)
Occupational level		
High white collar	3.8	13.4
Low white collar	20.2	23.9
Skilled	13.5	23.9
Semiskilled and unskilled	62.5	38.8
Illiteracy rate	(N=157)	(N=103)
	21.7	19.4

Source: Federal manuscript census returns for 1870 and 1880.
Note: Significant at .0074. Due to rounding, occupational level totals may not be 100 percent.

For mulattoes the situation appears especially confusing. Mulattoes had a higher rate of literacy than other blacks in both 1870 and 1880. They also showed slightly greater progress in education than other blacks during this decade. Yet their economic position actually deteriorated in these years (see Table 8). Conversely, one group of whites, those born in Ireland, showed little change in literacy but remarkable economic gains (see Table 9).

The lack of information on various levels of education makes it impossible to assess their importance for occupational mobility. It seems

Table 10
Pearson's Correlation Coefficient between Literacy and Occupational Status in
Washington, D.C., 1870–1880

Blacks	.1369
Mulattoes	.2408
Whites (total)	.2774
Irish-born whites	.3526

Source: Federal manuscript census returns for 1870 and 1880.
Note: Significant at .01 level.

unreasonable to assume, however, that a high level of education would have been necessary or sufficient to move from semiskilled and un-skilled work to skilled work.

The fact that blacks had made virtually no economic progress does not necessarily warrant the assumption that reformers' faith that education would eventually bring about progress was misplaced. They acknowledged that progress would be slow. A better test of the link be-tween education and economic advancement can be made by assessing the relationship between literacy and occupational status in 1870 and 1880. If education was the key to economic progress, literate individu-als should have had a higher occupational standing than illiterate indi-viduals.

Assuming that in the nineteenth century even a low level of educa-tional accomplishment might provide occupational mobility, the follow-ing analyses are based on the census reporting of the ability to read only. Only a few more people were able to read than could both read and write.[23] A strong positive relationship did exist in 1870 and 1880 between literacy and occupational status. For the total population, liter-acy did tend to mean a higher occupational standing. At first glance this supports the reformers' belief that improved educational achievement would mean improved economic status for blacks. The data is more troublesome, however, when the factor of race is taken into account.

A clue explaining the perception that education improved eco-nomic positions can be found in the experience of Irish-born workers. The occupational gains of the Irish did not appear to depend on gains in literacy, yet literacy was important to the status of the Irish worker. The correlation between literacy and occupational status was stronger for the Irish-born than for any other workers. If the same factors had been

Table 11
Pearson's Correlation Coefficients among Race, Literacy, and Occupational
Status in Washington, D.C., 1870 and 1880

	1870	1880
Race and literacy	.6575	.5779
Literacy and occupational status	.4925	.4304
Race and occupational status	.5313	.5796

Source: Federal manuscript census returns for 1870 and 1880.
Note: Significant at .01 level.

as important for blacks as they were for other essentially lower-class
workers, then education would indeed have held promise (see Table 10).
However, education was not equally important as a factor in economic
mobility for all groups of blacks and whites. Whereas about 12 percent
of the variation in occupational status for the Irish-born can be accounted for by variations in literacy and about 8 percent of the variation can be accounted for by variations in literacy for all whites, only 6
percent for mulattoes and 2 percent for other blacks can be accounted
for in this way. Clearly education promised much more economic
mobility for lower-class whites than it did for lower-class blacks.

If there was a strong relationship between literacy and occupational status for some, how can blacks' lack of economic progress be explained in the light of their greatly increasing literacy? Simply by the
fact that although literacy was a factor in determining economic status,
race was an even stronger factor. Much of the relationship between literacy and economic status is attributable to the fact that both literacy
and economic status were correlated with color (see Table 11). Reformers rightly identified illiteracy as a particular problem for blacks, but
they failed to see that race was an even greater handicap to black economic mobility. As black literacy increased, race became more important, and literacy less important, in determining occupational status.

Despite the fact that education was not providing greater economic mobility for most blacks, many Republicans continually touted education as the means to black achievement. Although many Democrats
agreed with James Brooks, representative from New York, that blacks
were incapable of benefiting from any but the most basic forms of training, others, such as South Carolina planter and politician Wade Hamp-
ton and writer Joel Chandler Harris, expressed conviction that former

slaves were making impressive educational and economic progress.[24] These moderate Democrats and Republicans refused to recognize, publicly at least, that schooling was not ensuring racial progress. They were, of course, not racial egalitarians, and most never believed that blacks could achieve the level of white "excellence."

It was the philosophy of moderate reformers, rooted in social Darwinism, that enabled them to continue their effort in education. In addition to pointing to exceptional black achievers and to asserting "realistic" occupational goals for blacks, moderates, such as Oliver O. Howard and John Eaton of the Freedmen's Bureau, were convinced that progress eventually would be made. They were, in fact, willing to wait a very long time for evidence of success. "There is, perhaps, no better parallel for the education of a race than the education of a child," it was said, "only for every five years we must take five hundred. Men *fall* into vice, but they *climb* into virtue."[25]

Secure in their faith and sincere in their work, moderates toiled diligently to improve educational opportunity for blacks. Under the Public School Law of 1862, the importance of black education in the District of Columbia had been recognized by Congress. In 1864 Congress directed proportional funding for white and black schools. The Washington city government, however, provided only a few hundred dollars for black education and almost $25,000 for white schools. It took federal pressure and additional legislation by Congress to increase the black share of the city's total educational budget to slightly more than 20 percent by 1869. By that year more than $250,000 had been allocated for all the district schools, with black schools receiving slightly more than $50,000. Even this much higher amount was $25,000 less than they should have received according to the 1867 Commissioner of Education's Report.[26]

The fight to improve funding equity in black education in the district was an example of the extent to which reformers took seriously the importance of schooling as a means for black improvement. It was also a sign of their determination to see their program realistically implemented. It was the limited expectations of the moderate reformers, rather than a lack of sincerity, that prevented them from seeing the flaws in their program. These reformers were committed to black progress, but they could not accept the radical vision of rapid achievement. Charles Sumner had stressed the need for blacks to protect themselves through political power as a means of securing the advantage that education made possible. "The ballot is a schoolmaster," he said. "Reading and writing are of inestimable value, but the ballot teaches what these cannot teach. It teaches manhood."[27] Moderate reformers saw this as radical folly—as moving too far, too fast.

Blacks only a few years out of slavery, the moderates argued, were not ready for full equality with whites. Any attempt to force artificial equality would be disastrous for both races. In this the moderate view was compatible with the majority view in Washington. The program of providing for separate education for blacks was far more acceptable to white Washingtonians than the radical vision of black political power. Whites in the city were willing to go to great lengths to blunt such power, even if it meant placing Washington under the colonial control of the federal government.

Moderates offered something for each side of the question. To the radicals and blacks, they offered the traditional route to mobility in American society—education. To the more conservative, they offered a restoration of white control of the district, unhampered by black political influence and promising nondisruptive social reform. Given the strong tradition of compromise in American politics, the radical program for Reconstruction in the district had only a dim chance of success. Instead, the radicals served the important function of defining the left. Blacks and radical white Republicans, although not always in agreement, illustrated the possibility of black political power. As white fears flared, the moderate program for evolutionary change through black segregated education seemed reasonable.

Thus the greatest achievement of federal Reconstruction policy in the District of Columbia, education of the newly freed blacks, was the most acceptable reform. It would not create dependency, moderates argued; at the same time it would prepare former slaves for freedom. Yet as a few radicals realized, and as the data clearly demonstrate, education alone could do little to promote black economic mobility as long as they were deprived of the tools of citizenship and race remained the chief deterrent to progress.

Afterword

By the end of the antebellum years, free people of color in the urban North had established well-defined communities providing formal and informal supports and services not generally available elsewhere to African Americans. The institution of slavery was a focal point among a diverse black people, even for those who had not personally experienced its horrors. Its presence profoundly shaped the relationships, activities, and ideas of the free black society.

The Civil War ended slavery, but the political and economic failures of the postwar period foreclosed the possibility for true freedom and brought a new structure of racial control. For free northern blacks, the end of slavery meant fewer restrictions for southern relatives and friends, although they were not totally freed from the inhumane consequences of the South's peculiar institution. Many former slaves exercised their new mobility and migrated from the South to the cities of the North and the Midwest. Their numbers did not approach those of the World War I Great Migration, but they did significantly increase the urban black population in the North. Detroit's black population increased by two-thirds during the 1860s, with more than two-thirds of its migrants coming from the South. There were similar population explosions in Cleveland, Boston, New York, and Philadelphia.

The presence of slavery complicated the lives of free blacks before the Civil War; emancipation made its own demands. Urban black communities strained to cope with the needs of the incoming southern rural migrants. Northern white workers, uncomfortable with the growing urban black population and always sensitive to any increased occupational competition, resisted black employment in any except unskilled jobs. Northern society at first resisted the participation of blacks in the emerging factory economy, then limited the protections afforded them by organized labor unions.

Thus economic and social pressures from outside, complicated by racial prejudice, continued to constrict opportunities and exacerbate differences within the African American community. Many issues that delineated internal differences before the Civil War persisted into the twentieth century. Gender roles, the contradictions between racial and national identity, and the need for continuing protest and political action remained. Charity work and educational reform among the freed slaves replaced the unifying activities of antislavery work and the Underground Railroad. African Americans remained united in their commitment to racial progress, but their differences over means and even short-term ends became more visible. The fierce struggles between the forces of protest and those of accommodation, symbolized by the Booker T. Washington and W. E. B. Du Bois debates in the early twentieth century, moved from the interior of black society to a more public stage. Without the undeniable evil of slavery, common ground was more elusive. Mutual support activities remained important throughout the twentieth century, and there continued to be many instances of concerted effort and cooperation among those in the diverse African American community. Yet modern industrial forces restructured social and economic relationships in black America, magnifying the existing diversity. In the preceding pages I have tried to illustrate both the diversity and the commonality in mid-nineteenth century free black society. The mutual support, if not constant agreement, among African Americans of that era is highly visible and easily described. It is more difficult to explore divisions dispassionately, for they often carry meaning beyond their academic interest. Yet understanding the history of black people in America in all of its subtlety demands a straightforward acknowledgment of interior conflict as well as traditional strengths.

Once several years ago, after having given a lecture at North Carolina State University on the subject of gender conflict among African Americans in the antebellum North, I was confronted by a young black man who questioned whether such a sensitive subject was a fit topic for public airing in an interracial forum. "Aren't such issues better left private?" he asked. I had considered that question before and did again later as I revised the lecture to write the chapter that appears here as "Freedom's Yoke." Over and over again as I wrote on equally delicate subjects, I debated this issue with colleagues and friends. The question is not unique to African American history. Is it proper for a southerner to deal frankly and forthrightly with slavery, segregation, racial violence, and other unflattering episodes of southern history? How should a scholar of upper-class background treat historical abuses of power by the political and economic elites? Should one seek to recount the entire truth about American foreign policy even when such truth indicts one's country before the world?

These questions are, of course, rhetorical. A scholar must reject a selective historical presentation in favor of one more broadly instructive, even if personally discomforting. Because black suffering has often been attributed to the internal disorganization and divisiveness of black society, the weight of scholarly responsibility falls heavily on the African American historian. It is tempting to minimize internal conflict among black people in favor of emphasizing legitimate traditional strengths. Yet to do so is to fall short, to miss the opportunity to discover a fully usable past. Obviously the traditions of cooperation and self-help are not to be ignored, but they take on additional meaning when set against the diversity and differences of those who disagree even as they work together for progressive ends. Contemporary black society remains divided on many of the significant issues presented here, and successful action to address conflict requires historical context and understanding. African American folk wisdom concerning questions of unity and diversity generally consists of two opposing myths. One holds that black people did not cooperate with one another but were torn by petty jealousies. The other contends that external pressure forged an unswerving racial unity. Both of these notions are misleadingly absolute and historically incorrect. Yet there is also some truth in each. Unity was the major theme of the black community studies of the 1970s, a positive response balancing the 1960s scholarship, which focused on black divisiveness. But old arguments and sensitivities should not continue to define historical inquiry. Historical tensions and divisions must be explored, even if they embarrass, or incite, or resurrect conflict. To do less is to ignore the rich complexity of black life—to reveal a disrespect for African American history and the resiliency of those who struggled to cope with and survive it.

Notes

NORTHERN FREE BLACKS

1. Revolutionary War Pension Records (London Hazard), Records of the Continental and Confederation Congress, Record Group 360, National Archives (hereafter cited as Revolutionary War Pension Records [with name of applicant]).

2. Gary B. Nash and Jean R. Soderlund, *Freedom by Degrees: Emancipation in Pennsylvania and Its Aftermath* (New York: Oxford University Press, 1991).

3. For a discussion of the social policy debates of the 1960s and 1970s on the question of black family and community, see Michael B. Katz, *The Undeserving Poor* (New York: Pantheon Books, 1989); William Julius Wilson, *The Truly Disadvantaged: The Inner City, The Underclass, and Public Policy* (Chicago: University of Chicago Press, 1987).

4. Kenneth Stampp, *The Peculiar Institution: Slavery in the Antebellum South* (New York: Knopf, 1956). The first full-length scholarly study of slavery was Ulrich B. Phillips, *American Negro Slavery* (New York: D. Appleton & Co., 1918). In this and his later *Life and Labor in the Old South* (Boston: Little, Brown & Co., 1929), Phillips pictured slavery as a benign institution, sympathized with the planter South, and displayed a belief in black inferiority. For an excellent discussion of the historiography of slavery, see Peter Parish, *Slavery: History and Historians* (New York: Harper & Row, 1989).

5. Lee Rainwater and William L. Yancey, *The Moynihan Report and the Politics of Controversy* (Cambridge: Harvard University Press, 1967), 76. See also Kenneth Clark, *Dark Ghetto: Dilemmas of Social Power* (New York: Harper & Row, 1965) and E. Franklin Frazier, *Negro Family in the United States* (New York: Citadel Press, 1948).

6. Nathan Glazer and Daniel Patrick Moynihan, *Beyond the Melting Pot: The Negroes, Puerto Ricans, Jews, Italians and Irish of New York City* (Cambridge: MIT Press, 1963), 53. For an important study of these issues and their impact on historians of the mid- to late twentieth century, see Peter Novick, *That Noble Dream: The "Objectivity Question and the American Historical Profession"* (New York: Cambridge University Press, 1988). Although I generally agree with Novick's analysis, I think that he underestimates the extent to which the harsh and superior tone of Moynihan and Glazer offended

blacks and many whites in the 1960s. Almost as much as the message their condescension fueled the fire of reaction. Moynihan and Glazer ignored the work of anthropologist Melville J. Herskovits, who a generation before had provided a great deal of evidence that black Americans retained much of African heritage and cultural style. See Herskovits, *The Myth of the Negro Past* (1941; reprint, Boston: Beacon Press, 1958).

7. William Ryan, *Blaming the Victim* (New York: Vintage Books, 1976).

8. John W. Blassingame, *The Slave Community* (New York: Oxford University Press, 1972); Eugene D. Genovese, *Roll Jordan Roll* (New York: Pantheon Books, 1974); Herbert Gutman, *The Black Family in Slavery and Freedom, 1750–1925* (New York: Pantheon Books, 1976); Leslie Howard Owens, *This Species of Property* (New York: Oxford University Press, 1976). For a complete review of slavery historiography, see Parish, *Slavery: History and Historians*.

9. For an imaginative and innovative look at black American culture, see Lawrence W. Levine, *Black Culture and Black Consciousness: Afro-American Folk Thought from Slavery to Freedom* (New York: Oxford University Press, 1977). One of the most important and controversial quantitative studies of slavery is Robert W. Fogel and Stanley L. Engerman's two-volume work, *Time On the Cross* (Boston: Little, Brown, 1974).

10. Leon F. Litwack, *North of Slavery: The Negro in the Free States, 1790–1860* (Chicago: University of Chicago Press, 1961), vii; Howard Zinn, *The Southern Mystique* (New York: Simon & Schuster, 1964).

11. Benjamin Quarles, *Black Abolitionists* (New York: Oxford University Press, 1969). See also Carleton Mabee, *Black Freedom: The Nonviolent Abolitionists from 1830 through the Civil War* (New York: Macmillan, 1971).

12. For a complete description of the Philadelphia Social History Project, see "A Special Issue: The Philadelphia Social History Project," *Historical Methods News Letter* 9 (March–June 1976).

13. Theodore Hershberg, "Free Blacks in Antebellum Philadelphia: A Study of Ex-Slaves, Freeborn, and Socioeconomic Decline," *Journal of Social History* 5 (December 1971): 183–209.

14. See Theodore Hershberg and Henry Williams, "Mulattoes and Blacks: Intra-Group Color Differences and Social Stratification in Nineteenth-Century Philadelphia," 392–435 and Frank Furstenberg, Jr., Theodore Hershberg, and John Modell, "The Origins of the Female-Headed Black Family: The Impact of the Urban Environment," 435–55, both in Theodore Hershberg, ed., *Philadelphia: Work, Space, Family and Group Experience in the 19th Century* (New York: Oxford University Press, 1981). The Furstenberg, Hershberg, and Modell article was originally published in *Journal of Interdisciplinary History* 6 (September 1975): 211–33.

15. Also see Robert C. Dick, *Black Protest: Issues and Tactics* (Westport, Conn.: Greenwood Press, 1974).

16. Jane Pease and William Pease, *They Who Would be Free* (New York: Atheneum, 1974), 297; see also their *Black Utopia: Negro Communal Experiments in America* (Madison, Wis.: State Historical Society of Wisconsin, 1963).

17. Frederick Cooper, "Elevating the Race: The Social Thought of Black Leaders, 1827–50," *American Quarterly* 24 (December 1972): 604–25.

18. See, for example, Jane Pease and William Pease, "Black Power—The Debate in 1840," *Phylon* 39 (Spring 1968): 19–26. E. Franklin Frazier condemned what he saw as the pretentiousness of the black middle class in his *Black Bourgeoisie* (Glencoe, Ill.: Free Press, 1957).

19. Hershberg, "Free Blacks in Antebellum Philadelphia."

20. Ibid., 283.

21. Victor Ulman, *Martin R. Delany: The Beginnings of Black Nationalism* (Boston: Beacon Press, 1971); Earl Ofari, *"Let Your Motto Be Resistance": The Life and Thought of Henry Highland Garnet* (Boston: Beacon Press, 1971); Joel Schor, *Henry Highland Garnet: A Voice of Black Nationalism in the Nineteenth Century* (Westport, Conn.: Greenwood Press, 1977).

22. Floyd J. Miller, *The Search for a Black Nationality: Black Emigration and Colonization, 1787–1863* (Urbana: University of Illinois Press, 1975).

23. Also see Leonard I. Sweet, *Black Images of America, 1784–1870* (New York: W. W. Norton, 1976). Several pioneering studies, generations ahead of their time, offered useful information on free blacks in the antebellum South. James M. Wright, *The Free Negro in Maryland, 1634–1860* (New York: Columbia University Press, 1921); John Russell, *The Free Negro in Virginia, 1619–1865* (1913; reprint, New York: Negro Universities Press, 1979); Luther P. Jackson, *Free Negro Labor and Property Holding in Virginia, 1830–1860* (1942; reprint, New York: Russell & Russell, 1971); John Hope Franklin, *The Free Negro in North Carolina, 1790–1860* (1943; reprint, New York: Russell & Russell, 1969).

24. Ira Berlin, *Slaves Without Masters: The Free Negro in the Antebellum South* (New York: Pantheon Books, 1974); the opening chapter of David Katzman, *Before the Ghetto: Black Detroit in the Nineteenth Century* (Urbana: University of Illinois Press, 1973); and Kenneth L. Kusmer, *A Ghetto Takes Shape: Black Cleveland, 1870–1930* (Urbana: University of Illinois Press, 1976) also provided a valuable framework for later antebellum black community studies.

25. Ira Berlin, "Time, Space and the Evolution of Afro-American Society," *American Historical Review* 85 (February 1980): 44–78; Berlin, "The Structure of the Free Negro Caste in the Antebellum United States," *Journal of Social History* 9 (Spring 1976): 297–318.

26. James Oliver Horton and Lois E. Horton, *Black Bostonians: Family Life and Community Struggle in the Antebellum North* (New York: Holmes & Meier, 1979). Important information on this topic is also provided in Donald M. Jacobs, "David Walker: Boston Race Leader, 1825–1830," *Essex Institute Historical Collections* 107 (January 1971): 94–107; and also in his "William Lloyd Garrison's Liberator and Boston's Blacks, 1830–1865," *New England Quarterly* 44 (June 1971): 259–77.

27. Leonard P. Curry, *The Free Black in Urban America, 1800–1850: The Shadow of the Dream* (Chicago: University of Chicago Press, 1981).

28. Robert Cottrol, *The Afro-Yankees: Providence's Black Community in the Antebellum Era* (Westport, Conn.: Greenwood Press, 1982). Cottrol also suggested social and economic class as a significant point of diversity within Providence's black community that deserved further study.

29. Joseph Reidy, " 'Negro Election Day' and Black Community Life in New England, 1750–1860," *Marxist Perspective* 1 (1978): 102–17; Levine, *Black Culture and Black Consciousness;* see also Dena J. Epstein, *Sinful Tunes and Spirituals: Black Music to the Civil War* (Urbana: University of Illinois Press, 1977). For the innovative use of folklore in the study of slave community, see Charles Joyner, *Down By the Riverside: A South Carolina Slave Community* (Urbana: University of Illinois Press, 1984). For an example of the recent use of folklore to study northern free blacks and slaves, see William D. Pierson, *Black Yankees: The Development of an Afro-American Subculture in Eighteenth-Century New England* (Amherst, Mass.: New England University Press, 1988). John Michael Vlach has contributed significantly to the expanding use of black folklore. See his *By The Work of Their Hands: Studies in Afro-American Folklife* (Ann Arbor, Mich.: UMI Research Press, 1991).

30. Emma Jones Lapsansky, "Friends, Wives, and Strivings: Networks and Community Values Among Nineteenth-Century Afro-American Elites," *Pennsylvania Magazine of History and Biography* 108 (1984): 3–24; R. J. M. Blackett, *Building an Antislavery Wall: Black Americans in the Atlantic Abolitionist Movement, 1830–1860* (Baton Rouge: Louisiana State University Press, 1983). Several other studies should be cited as among the most important of the period: Emma Jones Lapsansky, "Since They Got Those Separate Churches: Afro-Americans and Racism in Jacksonian Philadelphia," *American Quarterly* 32 (Spring 1980): 54–78 and "South Street, Philadelphia, 1762–1854: 'A Haven for Those Low in the World'" (Ph.D. diss., University of Pennsylvania, 1975); Carleton Mabee, *Black Education in New York State* (Syracuse: Syracuse University Press, 1979); Hershberg, *Philadelphia*; Phyllis F. Field, *The Politics of Race in New York: The Struggle for Black Suffrage in the Civil War Era* (Ithaca, N.Y.: Cornell University Press, 1982); Juliet E. K. Walker, *Free Frank: A Black Pioneer on the Antebellum Frontier* (Lexington: University Press of Kentucky, 1983); V. P. Franklin, *Black Self-Determination* (Westport Conn.: Lawrence Hill & Co., 1984); Richard Blackett, *Beating Against the Barriers: Biographical Essays in Nineteenth-Century Afro-American History* (Baton Rouge: Louisiana State University Press, 1986); Julie Winch, *Philadelphia's Black Elite: Activism, Accommodation, and the Struggle for Autonomy, 1787–1848* (Philadelphia: Temple University Press, 1988); and David E. Swift, *Black Prophets of Justice: Activist Clergy Before the Civil War* (Baton Rouge: Louisiana State University Press, 1989).

31. Gary B. Nash, *Forging Freedom: The Formation of Philadelphia's Black Community, 1720–1840* (Cambridge: Harvard University Press, 1988). For more specialized studies on this subject by Nash, see his "Slaves and Slaveowners in Colonial Philadelphia," *William and Mary Quarterly* 30 (April 1973): 223–56 and "To Arise Out of the Dust: Absolom Jones and the African Church of Philadelphia, 1785–95," in Nash, *Race, Class, and Politics: Essays on American Colonial and Revolutionary Society* (Urbana: University of Illinois Press, 1986). Nash's latest contribution, *Race and Revolution* (Madison, Wis.: Madison House Publishers, 1990) expands still further the debt owed him by our profession.

32. Shane White, *Somewhat More Independent: The End of Slavery in New York City, 1770–1810* (Athens: University of Georgia Press, 1991); W. Jeffrey Bolster, "To Feel Like a Man: Black Seamen in the Northern States, 1800–1860," *Journal of American History* 76 (March 1990): 1173–99. See also W. Jeffrey Bolster, "African American Sailors: Race, Seafaring Work and Atlantic Maritime Culture, 1750–1860" (Ph.D. diss., Johns Hopkins University, 1991). Lonnie Bunch, *Black Angelenos: The African American in Los Angeles* (Sacramento: State of California, 1988).

33. Dorothy B. Porter, ed., *Early Negro Writing, 1760–1837* (Boston: Beacon Press, 1971); Bert James Loewenberg and Ruth Bogin, eds., *Black Women in Nineteenth-Century American Life* (University Park: Pennsylvania State University Press, 1976); John Blassingame, ed., *Slave Testimony* (Baton Rouge: Louisiana State University Press, 1977); Charles Blockson, ed., *The Underground Railroad* (New York: Prentice-Hall, 1987); Ann Allen Shockley, ed., *Afro-American Women Writers, 1746–1933* (New York: New American Library, 1989). Earlier collections of primary documents that are invaluable for free black studies include Carter G. Woodson, ed., *Negro Orators and Their Orations* (1925; reprint, New York: Russell & Russell, 1969); Carter G. Woodson, ed., *The Mind of the Negro as Reflected in Letters Written During the Crisis, 1800–1860* (Washington, D.C.: Associated Publishers, 1926); Dorothy B. Porter, ed., "Early Manuscript Letters Written by Negroes," *Journal of Negro History* 24 (April 1939): 199–210; Philip Foner, ed., *The Life and Writings of Frederick Douglass*, 5 vols. (New York: International Publishers, 1950–75).

34. Dorothy Sterling, *Speak Out in Thunder Tones* (Garden City, N.Y.: Doubleday, 1973); Philip S. Foner and George E. Walker, eds., *Proceedings of the Black State Conventions, 1840–1865*, 2 vols. (Philadelphia: Temple University Press, 1979–80); Howard H. Bell, ed., *Minutes of the Proceedings of the National Negro Conventions, 1830–1864* (New York: Arno Press, 1969). Donald Jacobs has provided a valuable index to major black antebellum newspapers with his *Antebellum Black Newspapers* (Westport, Conn.: Greenwood Press, 1976).

35. C. Peter Ripley et al., eds., *The Black Abolitionist Papers* (New York: Microfilm Corp. of America, 1981–83). Some of these documents are being published in book form; see Peter Ripley et al., eds., *The Black Abolitionist Papers*, 5 vols. projected (Chapel Hill: University of North Carolina Press, 1988–). See also Paul Finkelman, ed. *Free Blacks, Slaves and Slaveowners in Civil and Criminal Courts*, 2 vols. (New York: Garland Publishing, 1988).

36. Kenneth L. Kusmer, "The Black Urban Experience in American History," in Darlene Clark Hine, ed., *The State of Afro-American History: Past, Present, and Future* (Baton Rouge: Louisiana State University Press, 1986), 91–122. For a broad range of discussions on this topic, see also Kenneth L. Kusmer, ed., *Black Communities and Urban Development in America, 1720–1990*, 10 vols. (Hamden, Conn.: Garland Publishing, 1991).

37. Clarence E. Walker, *Deromanticizing Black History: Critical Essays and Reappraisals* (Knoxville: University of Tennessee Press, 1991), xvi.

38. See Berlin, "Evolution of Afro-American Society."

CHAPTER 1: BLACKS IN ANTEBELLUM BOSTON

1. For the purpose of this study, a *migrant* is defined as anyone not born in Massachusetts. Many of those born in Massachusetts were not born in Boston and might also qualify as migrants to Boston. The antebellum U.S. census, from which much of this chapter's data are taken, did not provide information on city of birth. It is thus impossible to determine which of the Massachusetts-born blacks were born in Boston. It is significant, though, that Boston had the state's largest and most concentrated black community between 1800 and 1860.

Wherever possible census data have been combined with data gathered from city directories and tax records. Much of the anecdotal data was gathered from the Records of the Veterans Administration for Civil War. Of particular interest here was information gathered from individual pension records. By using these varied data sources in combination with more traditional manuscript and newspaper data, I have sought to overcome many of the difficulties inherent in each individual source.

For the general problem of census underenumeration, see John B. Sharpless and Ray M. Shortridge, "Biased Underenumeration in Census Manuscripts: Methodological Implications," *Journal of Urban History* 1 (1975): 409–39. For problems with city directory data, see Peter Knights, "City Directories as Aids to Antebellum Urban Studies: A Research Note," *Historical Methods Newsletter* 4 (1969): 1–10, and Curry, *The Free Black*.

2. There are several important recent studies. See Kusmer, *A Ghetto Takes Shape*; Katzman, *Before the Ghetto*; Elizabeth H. Pleck, *Black Migration and Poverty, Boston 1865–1900* (New York: Academic Press, 1979). Pleck finds far greater fragmentation in post–Civil War Boston than I do in antebellum Boston. This may be explained, in part, by the fact that slavery, the most important issue for blacks and one that obscured most divisions, was no longer an issue after the war. More recently James Borchert, *Alley Life in*

Washington (Urbana: University of Illinois Press, 1980) explains the formal and informal adjustment process for recent migrants to the nation's capital. Borchert's migrant alley communities tend to be isolated from the more established black community, but the adjustment process is quite similar to that of antebellum Boston.

3. Lorenzo J. Greene, *The Negro in Colonial New England* (Port Washington, N.Y.: Kennikat Press, 1942).

4. For a detailed look at Boston's black community before the Civil War, see Horton and Horton, *Black Bostonians.*

5. Ibid.

6. Ibid. The proportion of black migrants was comparably high for New Bedford, the second largest concentration of African Americans in the state, just under 58 percent.

7. See chapter 3, "Generations of Protest," in this volume.

8. The black population of Boston as recorded in the U.S. censuses of 1850 and 1860 has been subjected to computer analysis. All quantitative data that appear in this chapter for those years are from that analysis unless otherwise noted.

9. Carter G. Woodson, *The Mind of the Negro as Reflected in Letters Written During the Crisis* (Washington, D.C.: Association for the Study of Negro Life and History, 1926), 624.

10. Wilbur H. Siebert, *The Underground Railroad from Slavery to Freedom* (New York: Russell & Russell, 1898), 246.

11. Quarles, *Black Abolitionists,* 200.

12. See Pleck, *Black Migration and Poverty.*

13. Peter Randolph, *From Slave Cabin to Pulpit* (Boston: J. H. Earle, 1893), 103, 109.

14. Preliminary findings of the Afro-American Communities Project (a research project that compares various northern antebellum cities on the question of racial tolerance and opportunity) indicate that Boston was indeed one of the most racially tolerant cities in the North. It may not, however, have offered the greatest economic opportunity for blacks.

15. There was significant tension between the Irish immigrants and the blacks of Boston during this period. Although basically economic in nature, it often was manifested in terms of race. See Horton and Horton, *Black Bostonians* for a fuller treatment of this subject.

16. Charlotte L. Forten, *The Journal of Charlotte L. Forten: A Free Negro in the Slave Era* (New York: Collier Books, 1961).

17. For the story of John S. Rock, see chapter 3, "Generations of Protest."

18. Civil War Pension Records (Washington Perkins) Records of the Veterans Administration, Record Group 15, National Archives (hereafter cited as Civil War Pension Records [with name of applicant]).

19. *Boston Evening Transcript,* 29, 30, 31 May 1854.

20. Laurence A. Glasco, "The Life Cycles and Household Structure of American Ethnic Groups: Irish, Germans and Native-Born Whites in Buffalo, New York, 1855," in *Family and Kin in Urban Communities, 1700–1930,* ed. Tamara K. Hareven (New York: New Viewpoints, 1977), 122–43.

21. Stuart A. Blumin, "Rip Van Winkle's Grandchildren: Family and Household in the Hudson Valley, 1800–1860," in Hareven, *Family and Kin,* 100–102.

22. John Modell and Tamara K. Hareven, "Urbanization and the Malleable Household: An Examination of Boarding and Lodging in American Families," in Hareven, *Family and Kin,* 164–87.

23. For a discussion of the African augmented family, see Melville J. Herskovits, *The Myth of the Negro Past* (Boston: Beacon Press, 1941). For a description of the aug-

mented black family in slavery, see Gutman, *Black Family in Slavery and Freedom*. In her book *All Our Kin* (New York: Harper & Row, 1974), Carol B. Stack shows how the black family is extended in contemporary America. See also Elizabeth R. Bethel, *Promiseland* (Philadelphia: Temple University Press, 1981); Elmer P. Martin and Joanne Mitchell Martin, *The Black Extended Family* (Chicago: University of Chicago Press, 1978); Theodore Kennedy, *You Gotta Deal With It* (New York: Oxford University Press, 1980).

24. Civil War Pension Records (Arthur B. Lee).

25. Civil War Pension Records (Joseph Henry Green).

26. John Tidd to Arthur Jones, 6 April 1834, William L. Garrison Papers, Boston Public Library.

27. Civil War Pension Records (Elias Hall).

28. Ibid.

29. A few historians have argued that the black church was a conservative force, largely detached from community political action. See, for example, George A Levesque, "Inherent Reformers—Inherent Orthodoxy: Black Baptists in Boston, 1800–1873," *Journal of Negro History* 4 (1975): 491–525. I am not persuaded by this argument. The church provided a strong moral voice, much of the leadership, and was often the gathering and organizing place for protest action. This was as true for the mid-nineteenth century as it was for the mid-twentieth century. For the story of the importance of the African Baptist Church as a center for community activism, see Horton and Horton, *Black Bostonians*.

30. Civil War Pension Records (James McCloud).

31. Ibid.

32. John Daniels, *In Freedom's Birthplace* (1914; reprint, New York: Johnson Reprint Corp., 1968).

33. Civil War Pension Records (William H. Lee).

34. Ibid.

35. "Commonwealth v. John Robinson and Sophia Robinson," in *Judicial Cases Concerning American Slavery*, ed. Helen Tunnicliff Catterall (Washington, D.C.: Carnegie Institution of Washington, 1926–37), 501.

36. Austin G. Elbridge, *Statement of the Facts Connected with the Arrest and Emancipation of George Latimer* (Boston, 1842); Original Papers of Chapter 69 of the Personal Liberty Act and Petition, 24 March 1843, Massachusetts State Archives.

37. Boston Committee of Vigilance account book, Massachusetts Historical Society, Boston.

38. Horton and Horton, *Black Bostonians*.

39. Ibid.

40. Several recent studies of the Great Migration are available. See James R. Grossman, *Land of Hope* (Chicago: University of Chicago Press, 1989) and Nicholas Lemann, *The Promised Land* (New York: Vintage Books, 1991).

CHAPTER 2: GENERATIONS OF PROTEST

1. There is some disagreement about Prince Hall's exact date of birth; Donn A. Cass, *Negro Freemasonry and Segregation* (Chicago: E. A. Cook, 1957).

2. Cass, *Negro Freemasonry*.

3. They had tried but failed to obtain a charter from the American Masonic Order and became the first American lodge chartered directly from the English Order; William C. Nell, *The Colored Patriots of the American Revolution* (1835; reprint, New York: Arno Press, 1968); Cass, *Negro Freemasonry*, 26.

4. Cass, *Negro Freemasonry;* Nell, *Colored Patriots,* 61–64.

5. Nell, *Colored Patriots.*

6. *Baptist Magazine* 16 (1831); Unidentified newspaper clipping, Boston, 1905, as reprinted in Charles L. Coleman, "A History of the Negro Baptists in Boston" (Master's thesis, Andover Newton Theological School, 1956).

7. *Baptist Magazine* 16 (1831); First Baptist Church of Boston Records, 25 July 1805; Second Baptist Church of Boston Records, 26 July 1805; Minutes of the Boston Baptist Association, 1849, 26; *Liberator,* 19 November 1858.

8. There is some question about the identity of the Nathaniel Paul who preached in the African Baptist Church when Thomas Paul was away. One source, Minutes of the Boston Baptist Association, 1812–1867, cited in Coleman, "History of the Negro Baptists," identifies him as Thomas's son. J. Marcus Mitchell, "The Paul Family," *Old Time New England* (January–March 1973): 73–77, lists a Nathaniel among Thomas's six brothers. Swift, *Black Prophets of Justice,* 5, lists a Nathaniel as Thomas's younger brother. Still another source, Henry J. Young, *Major Black Religious Leaders* (Nashville, Tenn.: Abingdon Press, 1977), identifies Nathaniel Paul as having been born in 1755, eighteen years before Thomas was born. There may have been three Nathaniels: one, Thomas's father or uncle; a second, Thomas's son; and a third, Thomas's younger brother. This would make sense on a number of levels. First, names were often repeated in the Paul family from one generation to the next. Also, the Nathaniel who was born in 1755 would have been in his eighties when he was traveling in England as an antislavery speaker and when he married a young English woman. Although both these things are possible, they appear unlikely. Probably the Nathaniel who lectured in England in the 1830s and who married the English woman was Thomas's younger brother.

9. Wendell Phillips Garrison and Francis Jackson Garrison, eds., *William Lloyd Garrison* (New York, 1885), 1:222; *Liberator,* 7 September 1831; Swift, *Black Prophets of Justice;* Mitchell, "The Paul Family."

10. *Liberator,* 13 April 1833; Membership list, Boston Female Anti-Slavery Society; "Liberator Extra," 1840, Boston Female Anti-Slavery Society; Annual Report of the Boston Female Anti-Slavery Society, 1836; Proceedings of the Anti-Slavery Convention of American Women, 1838, Philadelphia; *Liberator,* 26 December 1835, 17 May, 15 February 1834.

11. Susan Paul to William Lloyd Garrison, 1 April 1834, William Lloyd Garrison Papers, Boston Public Library.

12. *Baptist Magazine* 16 (1831); First Baptist Church of Boston Records, 25 July 1805; *Liberator,* 19 November 1858; Nell, *Colored Patriots.*

13. *Freedom's Journal,* 19 December 1828; Nell, *Colored Patriots,* 343–46; Cass, *Negro Freemasonry,* 27; William Wells Brown, *The Rising Sun; or the Advancement of the Colored Race* (1874; reprint, New York: Negro Universities Press, 1970).

14. *First Annual Report of the Board of Managers of the New England Anti-Slavery Society* (Boston, 1833), 7–8; *First Annual Report of the American Anti-Slavery Society* (New York, 1834), 35.

15. George W. Forbes, in his "typescript Biographical Sketch of William Cooper Nell" (date unknown), says William G. Nell was never captured but that the *General Gadsden* was chased into Boston harbor by a British ship; Nell, *Colored Patriots;* Robert P. Smith, "William Cooper Nell: Crusading Black Abolitionist," *Journal of Negro History* (July 1970): 182–99.

16. Smith, "William Cooper Nell."

17. Nell, *Colored Patriots;* Boston Negro Proceedings (1855), original records.

18. Forbes, "Sketch of William Cooper Nell."

19. Nell, *Colored Patriots;* Boston Negro Proceedings.
20. Nell, *Colored Patriots;* Boston Negro Proceedings.
21. Martin R. Delany, *The Condition, Elevation, Emigration, and Destiny of the Colored People of the United States* (1852; reprint, New York: Arno Press, 1968), 123.
22. *Liberator,* 12 December 1845.
23. Boston Negro Proceedings; List of members, *Laws of the African Society* (1796); *Boston City Directory* (various copies, 1830 to 1860).
24. Boston Negro Proceedings; List of members, *Laws of the African Society.*
25. First Baptist Church of Boston Records, 1805; Nell, *Colored Patriots; Boston City Directory.*
26. Bureau of the Census, *U.S. Census,* 1840, 1850; Boston Committee of Vigilance account book; "List of Qualified Voters in the City of Boston" (1838, 1839, 1844, 1845), Massachusetts Historical Society, Boston.
27. *First Annual Report . . . New England Anti-Slavery Society,* 7–8; *First Annual Report of the American Anti-Slavery Society,* 35; Howard H. Bell, *A Survey of the Negro Convention Movement 1830–1861* (New York: Arno Press, 1969).
28. Boston Committee of Vigilance account book.
29. *Liberator,* 11 April 1851.

CHAPTER 3: LINKS TO BONDAGE

1. See Siebert, *Underground Railroad;* William A. Breyfogle, *Make Free: The Story of the Underground Railroad* (Philadelphia: Lippincott, 1958).
2. Quarles, *Black Abolitionists.*
3. Carter G. Woodson, *The Education of the Negro Prior to 1861* (1919; reprint, New York: Arno Press, 1968); Charles Wesley, "The Negroes of New York in the Emancipation Movement," *Journal of Negro History* (1939): 62–81. Herbert Aptheker, *The Negro in the Abolitionist Movement* (New York: International Publishers, 1941); Litwack, *North of Slavery.*
4. Larry Gara, *Liberty Line: The Legend of the Underground Railroad* (Lexington: University of Kentucky Press, 1967).
5. Ibid.
6. Cooper, "Elevating the Race." For an insightful critique of Cooper's thesis, see Peter P. Hinks " 'We Must and Shall Be Free': David Walker, Evangelicalism, and Antebellum Black Resistance" (Ph.D. diss., Yale University, forthcoming).
7. *Frederick Douglass' Paper,* 13 April 1855.
8. Carol V. R. George, "Widening the Circle: The Black Church and the Abolitionist Crusade, 1830–1860," in Lewis Perry and Michael Fellman, eds., *Antislavery Reconsidered* (Baton Rouge: Louisiana State University Press, 1979), 88.
9. Revolutionary War Pension Records (James W. Watson).
10. Historian Lawrence Friedman described their dedication as "the most intense moral expression of a larger evangelical missionary subculture . . ." Lawrence J. Friedman, *Gregarious Saints: Self and Community in American Abolitionism, 1830–1870* (New York: Cambridge University Press, 1982), 21.
11. Quarles, *Black Abolitionists,* viii.
12. For a description of the abolition of slavery in the North, see Arthur Zilversmit, *The First Emancipation: The Abolition of Slavery in the North* (Chicago: University of Chicago Press, 1967).
13. Revolutionary War Pension Records (Richard Cozzens).

14. These figures were taken from the computerized files of the Afro-American Communities Project, National Museum of American History, Smithsonian Institution, Washington, D.C., compiled from the Bureau of the Census, *U.S. Census, 1850*.

15. Levi Coffin, *Reminiscences of Levi Coffin* (1899; reprint, New York: Arno Press, 1968).

16. Stanley W. Campbell, *The Slave Catchers: Enforcement of the Fugitive Slave Law, 1850–1860* (Chapel Hill: University of North Carolina Press, 1970); Schor, *Henry Highland Garnet*.

17. Allan Nevins, *The Emergence of Lincoln: Prologue to Civil War, 1850–1861* (New York: Scribner, 1950), 2:31; Campbell, *Slave Catchers*, 137; Peter Hinks, "Frequently Plunged into Slavery: Free Blacks and Kidnapping in Antebellum Boston" (Unpublished paper, 1991); Carol Wilson, "Living in the Shadow of Slavery: Black Response to Kidnapping in the Mid-Atlantic Region" (Unpublished paper, 1991).

18. Horton and Horton, *Black Bostonians*, 103.

19. "The Sons of Africans: An Essay on Freedom" (Boston, 1808) reprinted in Porter, *Early Negro Writing*, 25.

20. Horton and Horton, *Black Bostonians*, 32.

21. *Liberator*, 19 April 1834; Alexander Crummell, *The Eulogy of Henry Highland Garnet, D.D. Presbyterian Minister, etc.* (Washington, D.C., 1882), 25–26.

22. Charles C. Andrews, *The History of the New York African Free Schools* (New York: Negro Universities Press, 1969).

23. "Report of the Condition of the People of Color in the State of Ohio" (April 1835), reprinted in Herbert Aptheker, ed., *A Documentary History of the Negro People in the United States* (New York: Citadel Press, 1965), 157–58.

24. Ibid.

25. Horton and Horton, *Black Bostonians*, 123, 90.

26. Howard H. Bell, *A Survey of the Negro Convention Movement, 1830–1861* (New York: Arno Press, 1969).

27. Foner and Walker, *Proceedings* 1:188.

28. Ibid., 223. See also William Cheek and Aimee Lee Cheek, *John Mercer Langston and the Fight for Black Freedom, 1829–65* (Urbana: University of Illinois Press, 1989).

29. Ibid., 225.

30. See, for example, *Colored American*, 20 November 1841.

31. Blassingame, *Slave Testimony*, 143.

32. Pauli Murray, *Proud Shoes: The Story of an American Family* (1956; reprint, New York: Harper & Row, 1978), 99.

33. Ibid.

34. George, "Widening the Circle," 90; "Frederick Douglass at Home," *Weekly Anglo-African*, 16 June 1860.

35. Horton and Horton, *Black Bostonians*, 108.

36. James McCune Smith, "Sketch of the Life and Labors of Henry Highland Garnet," in Henry Highland Garnet, *A Memorial Discourse by Rev. Henry Highland Garnet . . . February 12, 1865* (Philadelphia: J. M. Wilson, 1865); Crummell, *Eulogy of Henry Highland Garnet*; Schor, *Henry Highland Garnet*.

37. Roi Ottley and William J. Weatherby, eds., *The Negro in New York: An Informal Social History, 1626–1940* (New York: New York Public Library, 1967), 80; Union Baptist Church records, 1837, Union Baptist Church, Cincinnati.

38. Elizabeth Buffum Chace, "My Anti-slavery Reminiscences," in her *Two Quaker Sisters* (New York: Liveright Publishing, 1937), 159–60, 110–83.

39. John F. Watson, *Annals of Philadelphia and Pennsylvania, in the Olden Times,* vol. 2 (Philadelphia: Whiting & Thomas, 1856–1857).

40. *St. Louis Daily Union,* 7 September 1846; *Louisville Daily Courier,* 21 January 1859.

41. For the story of the train ticket swindle, see Horton and Horton, *Black Bostonians.*

42. Daniel Drayton, *Personal Memoir of Daniel Drayton for Four Years and Four Months a Prisoner in Washington Jail. Including a Narrative of the Voyage and Capture of the Schooner Pearl* (Boston: Bela Marsh, 1854); John H. Paynter, *Fugitives of the Pearl* (Washington, D.C.: Associated Publishers, 1930).

43. *Liberator,* 24 September 1841.

44. Blassingame, *Slave Testimony,* 143–44.

45. Catherine Dupre Lumpkin, "The General Plan was Freedom: A Negro Secret Order on the Underground Railroad," *Phylon* (Spring 1967): 70.

46. William Still, *Underground Railroad Records* (Philadelphia: Porter & Coates, 1872).

47. Wendell P. Dabney, *Cincinnati's Colored Citizens: Historical, Sociological and Biographical* (1926; reprint, New York: Negro Universities Press, 1970).

48. Union Baptist Church records, 1837, Union Baptist Church, Cincinnati.

49. "Manuscript Records of Allen Temple, Cincinnati, Ohio, 1824"; George, "Widening the Circle," 91.

50. Randolph, *From Slave Cabin to Pulpit,* 103, 109.

51. For an excellent account of the role of religion and the church in the slave South, see Albert J. Raboteau, *Slave Religion: The Invisible Institution* (New York: Oxford University Press, 1978); James Oliver Horton and Lois E. Horton, "Black Theology and Historical Necessity," in *Transforming Faith: The Sacred and Secular in Modern America,* ed. Miles L. Bradbury and James B. Gilbert (Westport, Conn.: Greenwood Press, 1989).

52. John O'Brien, "From Bondage to Citizenship: The Richmond Black Community, 1865–67" (Ph.D. diss., University of Rochester, 1975), 69. I thank Marie Tyler-McGraw, of the Valentine Museum, Richmond, Virginia, for bringing this dissertation to my attention. For more information about the First African Baptist Church of Richmond see Marie Tyler-McGraw and Gregg D. Kimball, *In Bondage and Freedom: Antebellum Black Life in Richmond, Virginia* (Richmond: Valentine Museum; Chapel Hill: University of North Carolina Press, 1988).

53. Martha S. Putney, *Black Sailors: Afro-American Merchant Seamen and Whalemen Prior to the Civil War* (Westport, Conn.: Greenwood Press, 1987); W. Jeffrey Bolster is doing a comprehensive study of black seamen during the nineteenth century. His forthcoming study on the subject will greatly expand our knowledge of the importance of the sea to black occupational structure and the importance of seamen to the economic and political life of the black community. See Bolster's "To Feel Like a Man," 4, and "African American Sailors."

54. Douglas Henry Daniels, *Pioneer Urbanites: A Social and Cultural History of Black San Francisco* (Philadelphia: Temple University Press, 1980); *Daily Evening Gazette* (St. Louis), 18 August 1841.

55. Union Baptist Church records, 1834, Union Baptist Church, Cincinnati.

56. Records of the Treasurer's Office, 1843, Oberlin College Archives.

57. *Richmond Enquirer,* 15 November 1850.

58. Horton and Horton, *Black Bostonians,* 97; Alan Frank January, "The First Nullification: The Negro Seamen Acts Controversy in South Carolina, 1822–60" (Ph.D. diss., University of Iowa, 1976).

59. Clement Eaton, "A Dangerous Pamphlet in the Old South," *Journal of Southern History* 2 (August 1936), 326–29. I thank Peter Hinks for bringing this article to my attention. His work cited above will be a valuable addition to our knowledge of the impact of such radical literature on the relationships between blacks in the North and the South during the antebellum years. Hinks speculates that Cunningham was more involved in this matter than he admitted to local official.

60. Horton and Horton, *Black Bostonians,* 98.

61. William Wells Brown, *Narrative of William W. Brown, A Fugitive Slave, Written by Himself* (Boston: Anti-Slavery Office, 1848), 107–8.

62. Frederick Douglass, *The Life and Times of Frederick Douglass* (New York: Collier Books, 1962). This story is yet another example of what Larry Gara argued in 1967, that is, that the Underground Railroad was more likely to be an informal, loosely connected group of people often working independently providing aid to fugitives on a personal, noninstitutional basis.

63. Jennifer Williams, "The Civil Rights Struggle in Antebellum San Francisco: One Aspect of Black Politics," working paper series, The Afro-American Communities Project, Smithsonian Institution (unpublished, 1982).

64. Foner and Walker, *Proceedings* 2:126.

65. Ibid., 149, 142.

66. Rudolph M. Lapp, *Blacks in Gold Rush California* (New Haven: Yale University Press, 1977), 266.

67. Philip Foner, *History of Black Americans* (Westport, Conn.: Greenwood Press, 1983), 3:91–97.

68. Seamen represented one-fifth of the employed black male population of Boston in 1860 and almost 35 percent of that in Cincinnati in the same year. In San Francisco the largest proportion of black male workers were employed in restaurants and boardinghouses as waiters and cooks. Although many of these may have been seamen employed temporarily in port, I have been able to identify only 123 black men of the city's 732 black male work force as definitely being seamen in 1860. Most of the others were indirectly linked to the sea through the sailors they served. Figures compiled from the *U.S. Census, 1860.*

CHAPTER 4: VIOLENCE, PROTEST, AND IDENTITY

1. Frederick Douglass, *The Life and Times of Frederick Douglass* (London: Collier-MacMillan, 1962), 143. Also see David W. Blight, *Frederick Douglass' Civil War* (Baton Rouge: Louisiana State University Press, 1989). Ronald T. Takaki makes the argument that because of Douglass's experience of cruelty at the hands of southern white men and relatively gentle treatment by white women he came to associate the brutality of slavery with white men of the South. It was this belief, Takaki argued, that lead him later in life to suggest that perhaps violence alone would make white southern men understand that slavery must be ended. This is a suggestive and interesting thesis with which Blight disagrees and about which there is some question. See Ronald Takaki, *Violence in the Black Imagination: Essays and Documents* (New York: Putnam, 1972).

2. Charles Rosenberg, "Sexuality, Class and Role in Nineteenth Century America," in Elizabeth Pleck and Joseph E. Pleck, eds., *The American Man* (Englewood Cliffs, N.J.: Prentice-Hall, 1980), 219–57.

3. E. Anthony Rotundo, "Learning About Manhood: Gender Ideals and the Mid-

dle Class Family in Nineteenth-Century America" (Paper delivered at Smith-Smithsonian Conference on the Conventions of Gender, Smith College, South Hadley, Massachusetts, 16–17 February 1984).

4. Grady McWhiney, *Cracker Culture: Celtic Ways in the Old South* (University: University of Alabama Press, 1988); Bertram Wyatt-Brown, *Southern Honor: Ethics and Behavior in the Old South* (New York: Oxford University Press, 1982); Elizabeth Fox-Genovese, "Cavaliers and True Ladies, Bucks and Mammies: Gender Conventions in the Antebellum South" (Paper delivered at Smith-Smithsonian Conference on Conventions of Gender, Smith College, South Hadley, Massachusetts, 16–17 February 1984).

5. Thomas Dew, *Review of the Debate of the Virginia Legislature of 1831 and 1832* (1832; reprint, Westport, Conn.: Negro Universities Press, 1970); William Drayton, *The South Vindicated From the Treason and Fanaticism of the Northern Abolitionists* (New York: Negro Universities Press, 1836), 246; Thomas R. R. Cobb, *An Inquiry into the Law of Negro Slavery in the United States of America* (1858; reprint, New York: Negro Universities Press, 1968), quoted in George M. Fredrickson, *The Black Image in the White Mind* (New York: Harper & Row, 1971), 54.

6. William Craft, *Running a Thousand Miles for Freedom: Or The Escape of William and Ellen Craft From Slavery* (London: William Tweedle, 1860), 14–15.

7. Published in two parts in the *National Anti-Slavery Standard*, 20, 27 October 1842, reprinted in Blassingame, *Slave Testimony*, 152.

8. *New York Times*, 14 January 1862, reprinted in Blassingame, *Slave Testimony*, 170.

9. William Still, *The Underground Railroad* (1872; reprint, New York: Arno Press, 1968); Benjamin Drew, *A North-Side of Slavery* (Boston: J. P. Jewett, 1856); Blassingame, *Slave Testimony*, 157.

10. For an analysis and discussion of this antislavery emblem, see Jean Fagan Yellin, *Women and Sisters* (New Haven: Yale University Press, 1989).

11. David Walker, *Walker's Appeal,* edited with an Introduction by Charles M. Wiltse, 3d ed. (New York: Hill & Wang, 1965), 16, 12.

12. Ibid., 21, 62.

13. Merton L. Dillon, *Slavery Attacked* (Baton Rouge: Louisiana State University Press, 1990), 146–47.

14. Walker had lived in Charleston, South Carolina, about the time that Denmark Vesey's slave rebellion plot was revealed. Historian Peter Hinks speculates that Walker was influenced by the arguments and general sentiment that gave rise to Vesey's actions. See Hinks, " 'We Must and Shall Be Free.' "

Others also understood the link between the spirit of freedom overseas and the slaves' desire for liberty in America. In Baltimore white children anxious to aid Greek children turned their attention to the plight of slaves upon learning that the Greeks no longer needed their help; Dillon, *Slavery Attacked*.

15. Benjamin Quarles, *Black Mosaic* (Amherst: University of Massachusetts Press, 1988).

16. Ibid., 165, 162.

17. Peter Brock, *Radical Pacifists in Antebellum America* (Princeton: Princeton University Press, 1968); *Liberator,* 8 January, 3 September 1831.

18. Henry J. Cadbury, "Negro Membership in the Society of Friends," *Journal of Negro History* 21–22 (April 1936): 151–213. There was considerable controversy among the Friends over the admission of blacks to the Society. Often African Americans were rejected on account of color, even though they were considered models of Quaker virtue.

The implication is that those blacks who applied for membership were likely to be at least as acceptable on grounds of principle, including that of pacifism, as whites who did so. Many blacks were accepted into the Society.

19. Marilyn Richardson, ed., *Maria Stewart, America's First Black Woman Political Writer* (Bloomington: Indiana University Press, 1987), 57.

20. Rotundo, "Learning About Manhood," 6.

21. *Liberator,* 1 January 1831; William Lloyd Garrison to the Reverend Samuel J. May, 14 February 1831, in Donald M. Jacobs, "William Lloyd Garrison's *Liberator* and Boston's Blacks, 1830–1865," *New England Quarterly* (June 1971), 260.

22. Wesley, "The Negroes of New York," 96.

23. Dillon, *Slavery Attacked,* 205–6. Hammond also wrote a fictionalized autobiographical account of the life of Julius Melbourne in which black troops are recruited and funded by abolitionists for an attack on southern slavery. See Jabez Delano Hammond, *Life and Opinions of Julius Melbourne* (Syracuse, N.Y.: Hall & Dickson, 1847).

24. Peter Paul Simons, "Speech Delivered before the African Clarkson Association," New York, 23 April 1839, reprinted in Ripley et al., *The Black Abolitionist Papers* 3:288–93.

25. *Liberator,* 6 August 1836.

26. Ibid., 13 August 1841.

27. "Speech by Henry Highland Garnet delivered before the National Convention of Colored Citizens, Buffalo, New York, 16 August, 1843," reprinted in Ripley et al., *The Black Abolitionist Papers* 3:403–412, quotes 408–10.

28. Ibid., 407, 410.

29. David Blight argued that Douglass was committed to nonviolence as a tactic rather than a moral position. In this way he was never a nonresistant in the Garrisonian sense of that term. See Blight, *Frederick Douglass' Civil War.*

30. *North Star,* 12 May 1848.

31. Foner, *History of Black Americans,* vol. 2.

32. For an excellent discussion of Garrison and his relationship with antebellum blacks in Boston, see Jacobs, "William Lloyd Garrison's *Liberator*" and Horton and Horton, *Black Bostonians.*

33. Horton and Horton, *Black Bostonians;* Smith, "William Cooper Nell," 182–99.

34. Horton and Horton, *Black Bostonians.*

35. William S. McFeely, *Frederick Douglass* (New York: W. W. Norton, 1991); *Frederick Douglass' Paper,* 2 June 1854.

36. Dillon, *Slavery Attacked.*

37. Jayme A. Sokolow, "The Jerry McHenry Rescue and the Growth of Northern Antislavery Sentiment During the 1850s," *Journal of American Studies* 16, no. 3 (December 1982): 427–45, 431.

38. *Liberator,* 7 July 1854.

39. Drew, *A North-Side of Slavery,* 248–51.

40. William Whipper to Gerrit Smith, Esq., Columbus, Pennsylvania, 22 April 1856, in Benjamin Quarles, ed., "Letters from Negro Leaders to Gerrit Smith," ed., Benjamin Quarles, *Journal of Negro History* 27, no. 4 (October 1942): 432–53, 450–51. Smith had issued his criticism in a speech entitled "Right of Suffrage" printed in *Frederick Douglass' Paper.* In his text he had used the term *black men* to refer to the objects of his remarks. Whipper obviously took offense at the use of the all inclusive term and in his answer he placed the words in quotation marks each time he used them. Whipper's reaction, perhaps overreaction, indicated his extreme sensitivity on the issue of black manhood.

41. Horton and Horton, *Black Bostonians;* Benjamin Quarles, *Allies For Freedom: Blacks and John Brown* (New York: Oxford University Press, 1974), 69.

42. *Weekly Anglo-African,* 31 January 1863; Douglass, *The Life and Time,* 338.

43. See Deborah Gray White, *Ar'n't I a Woman?* (New York: W. W. Norton, 1985). White argues that female slaves were more likely to feign illness to escape work than were men. Because childbearing was a primary expectation for slave women, this was a practical and effective tactic.

44. Silvia Dubois, "Silvia Dubois," in *Black Women in Nineteenth-Century American Life,* ed., Bert James Loewenberg and Ruth Bogin (University Park: Pennsylvania State University Press, 1976), 39–47. Many other examples might be cited. See Blassingame, *Slave Testimony;* Blockson, *The Underground Railroad;* Still, *The Underground Railroad;* Norrece T. Jones, Jr., *Born a Child of Freedom, Yet a Slave* (Hanover, N.H.: University Press of New England, 1990).

45. Jacqueline Bernard, *Journey Toward Freedom* (New York: The Feminist Press at The City University of New York, 1990); Douglass, *The Life and Time,* 142.

46. Bonnie Kettel, "The Commoditization of Women in Tugen (Kenya) Social Organization," in *Women and Class In Africa,* ed. C. Robertson and I. Berger (New York: Holmes & Meier, 1986), 50–51.

47. Barbara Welter's delineation of the "cult of true womanhood" identified a middle-class ideal that stressed piety, purity, and domesticity as the most natural and desirable nineteenth-century female characteristics. Ronald W. Hogeland expanded this view, calling the "true woman" *Romanticized Womanhood* and adding three additional ideals: The *Ornamental Woman,* typified by the ideal of genteel white womanhood in the Old South, was characterized by delicacy and decorum. *Evangelical Womanhood* was a practical response to the frontier, allowing women a more active role while engaged in social reform. And *Radical Womanhood,* an ideal that emerged before the Civil War, accepted the innate characteristics of true womanhood but encouraged the active assertion of feminine virtues in the public arena. Barbara Welter, "The Cult of True Womanhood, 1820–1860," *American Quarterly* 18 (Summer 1966): 151–74; Ronald W. Hogeland, "'The Female Appendage:' Feminine Life-Styles in America, 1820–1860," *Civil War History* 17, no. 2 (June 1971): 101–14.

48. Daniel R. Payne, *History of the African Methodist Episcopal Church* (Nashville: Publishing House of the AME Sunday School Union, 1891), 301.

49. Charles B. Ray, "Female Education," *Colored American,* 18 March 1837, Black Abolitionist Papers Microfilm, Reel 1, Frame 1008. For further discussion on this point and an analysis of black newspapers' contributions to gender education, see chapter 5, "Freedom's Yoke: Gender Conventions among Free Blacks."

50. *North Star,* 17 March 1848.

51. Hogeland, "'The Female Appendage,'" 113.

52. Truth quoted in Elizabeth Cady Stanton et al., *History of Woman Suffrage* (Rochester, N.Y.: Susan B. Anthony; Charles Mann, 1881–1922), 2, 152.

CHAPTER 5: GENDER CONVENTIONS AMONG FREE BLACKS

1. Zora Neale Hurston, *Their Eyes Were Watching God* (Urbana: University of Illinois Press, 1978), 29. Among several good studies of black women are Sharon Harley and Rosalyn Terborg-Penn, eds., *The Afro-American Woman: Struggles and Images* (New York: Kennikat Press, 1978); Gloria T. Hull, Patricia Bell Scott, and Barbara Smith, eds., *All the Women Are White, All the Blacks Are Men, But Some of Us Are Brave: Black*

Women's Studies (Old Westbury, N.Y.: Feminist Press, 1982); and Dorothy Sterling, ed., *We are Your Sisters: Black Women in the Nineteenth Century* (New York: W. W. Norton, 1984).

2. Literacy rates among northern blacks depending on location. Boston blacks were very literate, equaling Virginia whites of the period. Blacks in Cincinnati were less so. These newspapers were available to the illiterates of the community because they were often read aloud by those who could read. "Readers" drew special status from their ability. For details on the urbanization of free blacks, see Berlin, *Slaves Without Masters;* Curry, *The Free Black;* and Horton and Horton, *Black Bostonians.*

3. For a detailed description of emancipation in the postrevolutionary North, see Arthur Zilversmit, *The First Emancipation: The Abolition of Slavery in the North* (Chicago: University of Chicago Press, 1967).

4. Berlin, "Time, Space, and the Evolution."

5. Jacqueline Jones, "My Mother Was Much Of A Woman: Black Women, Work, and the Family under Slavery," *Feminist Studies* 8 (Summer 1982): 235–69. Also see Jacqueline Jones, *Labor of Love, Labor of Sorrow: Black Women, Work, and the Family from Slavery to the Present* (New York: Basic Books, 1985); and Gerda Lerner, ed., *Black Women in White America: A Documentary History* (New York: Vintage Book, 1973), esp. pt. 3.

6. Joseph P. Reidy, "Negro Election Day," 102–17.

7. A. Leon Higginbotham, Jr., *In the Matter of Color: The Colonial Period* (New York: Oxford University Press, 1978), 84.

8. Benjamin Quarles, *The Negro in the American Revolution* (New York: W. W. Norton, 1961), 44.

9. Cited in Sidney Kaplan, *The Black Presence in the Era of the American Revolution, 1770–1800* (Washington, D.C.: Education Department, National Portrait Gallery, 1973), 11.

10. Horton and Horton, *Black Bostonians,* 40–41.

11. Peter N. Stearns, *Be A Man! Males in Modern Society* (New York: Holmes & Meier, 1979), 45.

12. *Colored American,* 14 September 1839.

13. *Freedom's Journal,* 11 May, 15 June 1827.

14. *Aliened American,* 9 April 1853; *Colored American,* 17 August 1839.

15. *North Star,* 29 September 1849. Even in slavery a skill passed from parent to child was an important inheritance.

16. *Colored American,* 17 June 1837.

17. Ibid., 23 November 1839.

18. Ibid., 18 April 1840.

19. Ibid., 24 June 1837.

20. For the connections between class and sexuality, see Carroll Smith-Rosenberg, "Beauty, the Beast, and the Militant Woman: A Case Study in Sex Roles and Social Stress in Jacksonian America," *American Quarterly* 23 (October 1971): 562–84; for the connection between race and sexuality, see Winthrop Jordan, *White over Black: American Attitudes towards the Negro, 1550–1812* (Chapel Hill: University of North Carolina Press, 1968).

21. *Colored American,* 18 March 1837.

22. Genovese, *Roll, Jordan, Roll,* 482.

23. Gutman, *The Black Family.*

24. Frederick Douglass, "My Escape to Freedom," *Century Magazine* 23 (November 1881): 125–31, cited in *The Black Worker: A Documentary History from Colonial*

Times to the Present, ed. Philip S. Foner and Ronald L. Lewis (Philadelphia: Temple University Press, 1978), 1:135–37.

25. *Colored American,* 16 September 1837.

26. Ibid., 18 March 1837; 8 September, 3 November 1838.

27. Revolutionary War Pension Records (Thomas Watson). Bell Hooks explains that slave men "regarded tasks like cooking, sewing, nursing, and even minor farm labor as women's work." See Bell Hooks, *Ain't I A Woman: Black Women and Feminism* (Boston: South End Press, 1981), 44. Also see Ann Firor Scott, *The Southern Lady: From Pedestal to Politics, 1830–1930* (Chicago: University of Chicago Press, 1970).

28. Sterling, *We Are Your Sisters,* 92.

29. Ibid., 93.

30. Horton and Horton, *Black Bostonians,* 20–21.

31. *Weekly Advocate,* 4 January 1837.

32. *Colored American,* 23 March 1839.

33. Lerone Bennett, Jr., *Pioneers in Protest* (Baltimore: Pelican, 1969), 123–24.

34. Sterling, *We Are Your Sisters,* 156–57.

35. Quarles, *Black Abolitionists,* 179.

36. Sterling, *We Are Your Sisters,* 176–77.

37. Foner and Walker, *Proceedings* 1: 153–54.

38. Revolutionary War Pension Records (Titus Kent).

39. *Colored American,* 17 August 1839; for a contemporary analysis of black men and their emotional relationships with black women, see Ronald L. Braithwaite, "Interpersonal Relations between Black Males and Black Females," in *Black Men,* ed. Lawrence E. Gary (Beverly Hills: Sage, 1981), 87–88.

40. Horton and Horton, *Black Bostonians,* 24.

41. Ibid., 19–20.

42. Blacks were generally more likely than whites of similar economic level to board. In Boston in 1850 and 1860, between 32 and 36 percent of adults were boarders. In Cincinnati during the same period, the rate was 36 and 38 percent; 75 to 80 percent of all adult black migrants boarded and most of those who boarded in the homes of black families were young women. Male boarders were more likely to board in boarding houses.

43. Rosetta Douglass Sprague, "My Mother As I Recall Her," *Journal of Negro History* 8 (January 1923): 98.

44. Sterling, *We Are Your Sisters,* 143–47.

45. Bert James Lowenberg and Ruth Bogin, eds., *Black Women in Nineteenth-Century American Life: Their Words, Their Thoughts, Their Feelings* (University Park: Pennsylvania State University Press, 1976), 78–88.

46. Sterling, *We Are Your Sisters,* 100–101.

47. Jim Bearden and Linda Jean Butler, *Shadd: The Life and Times of Mary Shadd Cary* (Toronto: NC Press, 1977). I thank Carla Peterson for providing me with information on Mary Shadd Cary from her forthcoming study.

48. Sterling, *We Are Your Sisters,* 132.

49. For the story of William and Ellen Craft, see Horton and Horton, *Black Bostonians,* 103–4; for the Purvis family, see Janice Sumler-Lewis, "The Forten-Purvis Women of Philadelphia and the American Anti-Slavery Crusade," *Journal of Negro History* 66, no. 4 (1981–82): 281–88.

50. Foner and Walker, *Proceedings,* 99.

51. *British Banner,* 20 November 1855.

52. Foner and Walker, *Proceedings,* 227–28, 43.

53. *Colored American,* 8 September 1838.

54. Ibid., 23 November 1839. See also Rosalyn Terborg-Penn, "Black Male Perspectives on the Nineteenth-Century Woman," in Harley and Terborg-Penn, *The Afro-American Woman,* 28–35.

55. *Cleveland Morning Leader,* 25 August 1854; *Daily Cleveland Herald,* 25, 26 August 1854.

56. Sharon Harley, "Northern Black Female Workers: Jacksonian Era," in Harley and Terborg-Penn, *The Afro-American Woman,* 12. Also see William Wells Brown, *Clotel; or, The President's Daughter* (London: Partridge & Oakey, 1853) for a traditional view of black women and the special sufferings they experienced in slavery because of their helplessness.

57. Sumler-Lewis, "The Forten-Purvis Women," 285.

58. Black Abolitionist Papers Microfilm, Reel 2, Manuscript Division, Library of Congress, Washington, D.C.

59. Bearden and Butler, *Shadd,* 45, 201, 188.

60. Hooks, *Ain't I a Woman,* 195.

CHAPTER 6: THE MULATTO IN THREE ANTEBELLUM NORTHERN COMMUNITIES

1. Sterling Brown, "Negro Character as Seen by White Authors," *Journal of Negro Education* 2 (1933): 180–201. Lawrence Glasco provides a valuable analysis of twentieth-century literature on mulattoes in black society in "The Mulatto: A Neglected Dimension of Afro-American Social Structure" (Unpublished paper, 1974).

2. Joel Williamson, *New People* (New York: Free Press, 1980).

3. Edward Byron Reuter, *The Mulatto in the United States: Including a Study of the Role of Mixed-Blood Races Throughout the World* (Boston: Richard G. Badger, 1918); E. Franklin Frazier, *The Negro in the United States* (Chicago: University of Chicago Press, 1966). For a discussion of racist thought in the early twentieth century that includes information on white attitudes toward mulattoes, see I. A. Newby *Jim Crow's Defense: Anti-Negro Thought in America, 1900–1930* (Baton Rouge: Louisiana State University Press, 1965).

4. Carl N. Degler, *Neither Black Nor White* (New York: Macmillan, 1971), 102.

5. Robert Brent Toplin, "Between Black and White," *Journal of Southern History* 45 (1979): 185–200, quote 188; Leonard R. Lempel, "The Mulatto in United States Race Relations: Changing Status and Attitudes" (Ph.D. diss., Syracuse University, 1979). Lempel's is a creative study of the status of mulattoes in the slaveholding South and an important addition to the field.

6. Williamson, *New People.*

7. Data for this study was taken from the Afro-American Communities Project data file of the Bureau of the Census, *U.S. Census,* 1850 and 1860.

8. In addition to studies of slave community already noted, see Berlin, *Slaves Without Masters.*

9. Bureau of the Census, *Negro Population of the United States, 1790–1915,* 221. See also Berlin, *Slaves Without Masters,* 178 for figures.

10. Ibid.

11. Ibid.

12. Berlin, *Slaves Without Masters,* 275–78.

13. This chapter is based on data being analyzed for a much broader study of antebellum northern black communities. The conclusions presented here should be considered

tentative. They are an early attempt to explain differences that seem to be emerging from the first stages of analysis.

14. Most scholars agree that the term *mulatto* as it appeared in the census was most accurately a designation of skin tone rather than of heritage, although, of course, it may have been both. For a discussion of this question, see Hershberg and Williams, "Mulattoes and Blacks," 392–431.

15. These persistence rates are much lower than I expected and lower that I am aware any historian has found for a comparable size population. Although time does not permit it for this study, I plan to recheck the linkages used here. It is partly because of the low rates of persistence that hamper any use of the linkage test that I have turned to the second record linkage test. I regard this second test as more reliable. The Regimental Description books for the Fifty-fourth and Fifty-fifth Massachusetts regiments and the Fifth United States Colored Troop located in the Department of War Records collection at the National Archives in Washington, D.C., were used in this test. The skin color possibilities were black, very dark, dark, copper, and brown, all of which I judged might logically be seen by the census taker as "black" to mulatto, yellow, light, very light, and white, which I judged to be seen as "mulatto" by any reasonable measure.

16. Richard C. Wade, *The Urban Frontier: Pioneer Life in Early Pittsburgh, Cincinnati, Lexington, Louisville, and St. Louis* (New York: Negro Universities Press, 1959), 53–59.

17. Almost 60 percent of Cincinnati's officially recorded black population was southern born. If a correction is made to include only adults, thus excluding the large number of children born in Ohio, the proportion rises to more than 70 percent born in the South. Because these figures do not include the hundreds of fugitive slaves in the city, they are sure to underestimate the true proportion of southern-born blacks. See Carter G. Woodson, "The Negro of Cincinnati Prior to the Civil War," *Journal of Negro History* 1 (January 1916); Richard C. Wade, "The Negro in Cincinnati, 1800–1830," *Journal of Negro History* 39 (January 1954); David A. Gerber, *Black Ohio and the Color Line, 1860–1915* (Urbana: University of Illinois Press, 1976).

18. Unless otherwise noted, all population figures presented in this paper were taken from the U.S. Census for the appropriate year. Cincinnati's percentage of mulattoes in its free black population was higher than that of the Midwest, including Ohio, Indiana, Illinois, Michigan, and Wisconsin. See Williamson, *New People*, 58.

19. Gilbert C. Fite and Jim E. Reese, *An Economic History of the United States* (Boston: Houghton Mifflin, 1959), 235.

20. Oscar Handlin, *Boston Immigrants* (Cambridge: Belknap Press of Harvard University Press, 1959).

21. Horton and Horton, *Black Bostonians*.

22. David L. Calkins, "Before the Ghetto: Black Residence and the Walking City, 1819–1959" (Unpublished paper, n.d.). Calkins and Henry Taylor have done the best research on nineteenth-century black Cincinnati. See Henry Taylor, "The Use of Maps in the Study of the Black Ghetto-Formation Process: Cincinnati, 1802–1910," *Historical Methods* 17 (1984). The index was computed from the U.S. Census for Boston and Cincinnati for 1860. For further information on the index and for the index as computed for other cities, see Berlin, *Slaves Without Masters*, 257–58. The index of dissimilarity, an indicator of residential separation measured at the ward level, was 34.8 when computed for darker blacks' and mulattoes' residence in Cincinnati for 1860. It shows that there was as much residential separation between darker blacks and mulattoes in the "Queen City" at the ward level as there was between blacks and whites in Brooklyn (35.5) or San Francisco (34.6). Taylor is rightly critical of the index of dissimilarity for exaggerating the degree of

racial segregation of nineteenth-century cities. It is used here not as a measure of segregation within a city but only as a striking point of comparison between ward-level residential separation of the races in San Francisco and Brooklyn and that of mulattoes and blacks in Cincinnati.

23. Horton and Horton, *Black Bostonians*.

24. Mulattoes, 37 percent of Boston's blacks by 1860, were very slightly underrepresented in the Sixth Ward (35 percent). They were overrepresented in the Fifth Ward (72 percent), but this figure is misleading because there were only 275 African Americans in that ward, whereas there were more than 1,430 in the Sixth Ward.

25. Boston was one of the most residentially segregated cities in the North. Its index of dissimilarity for 1860 was 20.3, substantially less than that for Cincinnati (47.9). Again, this index most be regarded with care. It is used here only as a comparative indicator.

26. An index of dissimilarity was computed for Buffalo for 1850 and 1860 in an effort to gain a greater understanding of the changing residential patterns of the city. I am currently attempting to overcome the problem of ward-level data by computing residential patterns using the near-neighborhood concept, which divides wards into small groupings of six houses. Perhaps this smaller grouping of homes will clarify the residential pattern in antebellum Buffalo.

27. Horton and Horton, *Black Bostonians*, 8–10.

28. Curry, *The Free Black*.

29. Robert C. Reinders, "The Free Negro in the New Orleans Economy," *Louisiana History* 6 (1965): 274–75.

30. Horton and Horton, *Black Bostonians*; quote taken from Carlton Mabee, *Black Education in New York State: From Colonial to Modern Times* (Syracuse: Syracuse University Press, 1979), 76; Philip Foner, *Essays in Afro-American History* (Philadelphia: Temple University Press, 1978).

31. For a discussion of black education during the period, see Curry, *The Free Black*, 147–71.

32. Joana C. Colcord, comp., *Roll and Go: Songs of American Sailormen* (Indianapolis: Bobbs-Merrill, 1924), 17.

33. This phenomenon has been noted by many sociologists studying the twentieth century, but it has never before been statistically documented for antebellum northern cities. For a detailed look at marriage patterns in Boston, see Horton and Horton, *Black Bostonians*, 21–23. For a fuller discussion of the link between light skin and desirability of African American women, see chapter 5, "Freedom's Yoke: Gender Conventions among Free Blacks," in this volume.

34. Hershberg and Williams, "Mulattoes and Blacks."

35. Ibid.

36. Marcus Cunliffe, "North and South, East and West: The Polarizing of American Values" (Unpublished paper, 1983).

37. Lempel, "Mulatto in United States Race Relations."

38. Stanley Elkins, *Slavery: A Problem in American Institutional and Intellectual Life* (Chicago: University of Chicago Press, 1959). For an analysis of ads for fugitive slaves, see Lempel, "Mulatto in United States Race Relations"; quoted from Mrs. L. H. Harris, "A Southern Woman's View," *Independent*, 18 May 1899, p. 1354–55.

39. Jordan, *White Over Black*.

40. For a discussion of stereotyping, see John G. Mencke, *Mulattoes and Race Mixture: American Attitudes and Image 1865–1918* (Ann Arbor: University of Michigan Research Press, 1976).

41. Williamson, *New People*, 16–18. See also Rachel N. Klein, *Unification of a Slave State: The Rise of the Planter Class in the South Carolina Backcountry, 1760–1808* (Chapel Hill: University of North Carolina Press, 1990).

42. C. L. R. James, *The Black Jacobins* (New York: Vintage Books, 1963); E. Horace Fitchett, "The Traditions of the Free Negro in Charleston, South Carolina," *Journal of Negro History* 25 (1940): 139–51.

43. See Genovese, *Roll Jordan Roll.*

44. For information on the racial climate in mid-nineteenth century Cleveland, see Kenneth L. Kusmer, *A Ghetto Takes Shape: Black Cleveland, 1870–1930* (Urbana: University of Illinois Press, 1976).

45. Dabney, *Cincinnati's Colored Citizens.*

46. Daniel Alexander Payne, *Recollections of Seventy Year* (reprinted New York, 1968).

47. David Walker, *Walker's Appeal in Four Articles* (Boston, 1830; reprint, New York, 1969), 19.

48. David Ruggles, *The "Extinguisher" Extinguished! or David M. Reese M.D. "Used UP" Together with Some Remarks Upon a Late Production entitled 'An Address on Slavery and Against Immediate Emancipation with a Plan of their Being Gradually Emancipated and Colonized in Thirty-Two Years. By Herman Howlett'* (New York, 1834), 7.

49. *Liberator,* 12 March 1858.

50. Ruggles, *"Extinguisher" Extinguished,* 12–17. For a discussion of the crusade against anti-intermarriage laws in Massachusetts, see Louis Ruchames, "Race, Marriage and Abolition in Massachusetts," *Journal of Negro History* 40 (1955): 250–73.

51. One might well imagine the ambivalent feelings of those who were the children of slaveholders toward their fathers who were also their masters. James Mercer Langston, the mulatto son of a Virginia planter, was apparently able to accept his father and their father-son relationship better than most. See Cheek and Cheek, *John Mercer Langston.*

52. For a discussion of mulatto leadership in the black community, see F. James Davis, *Who Is Black: One Nation's Definition* (University Park: Pennsylvania State University Press, 1991). Although Martin Luther King was darker than most black leaders before him, apparently he too was of mixed ancestry, with an Irish grandmother on his father's side of the family.

53. It is significant that politically conservative Supreme Court justice Clarence Thomas, selected and supported largely by conservative white politicians for the position, is much darker than former Justice Thurgood Marshall, whom he replaced. The typical nineteenth-century model would have had a mulatto as the most likely collaborator with powerful whites. This nineteenth-century pattern is discussed by Thomas Holt as it appeared in Reconstruction South Carolina when mulattoes tended to be more politically conservative than darker blacks. See Thomas Holt, *Black Over White: Negro Political Leadership in South Carolina during Reconstruction* (Urbana: University of Illinois Press, 1977).

CHAPTER 7: AFRICAN AMERICAN IDENTITY IN THE NINETEENTH CENTURY

1. W. E. B. Du Bois, *The Souls of Black Folk* (Chicago: A. C. McClurg, 1903), 17. Dred Scott was a slave who sued for in freedom on the grounds that he had lived for an extended period in a free territory. In 1857 the Court denied his claim and went on to declare that black people had never been and could never be citizens of the United States.

See Don Fehrenbacher, *The Dred Scott Case: Its Significance in American Law and Politics* (New York: Oxford University Press, 1978).

2. Ibid.

3. Ibid.

4. Klein, *Unification of a Slave State*.

5. Quarles, *The Negro in the American Revolution*, 153.

6. *Pennsylvania Gazette*, 12 June 1780.

7. Quoted in Quarles, *The Negro in the American Revolution*, 31.

8. Ellen Gibson Wilson, *The Loyal Blacks* (New York: Putnam, 1976), 21; John Hope Franklin, *From Slavery to Freedom* (New York: Alfred A. Knopf, 1974), 92.

9. *Memorial of Thirty Thousand Disfranchised Citizens of Philadelphia, to the Honorable Senate and House of Representatives* (Philadelphia, 1855), 13. For an account of Crispus Attucks's role in the Boston Massacre, see Quarles, *The Negro in the American Revolution*.

10. Sweet, *Black Images of America*, 45.

11. Abigail Adams to John Adams, 22 September 1774, Lyman H. Butterfield et al., ed., *Adams Family Correspondence* (Cambridge: Belknap Press, Harvard University, 1963), 1:162.

12. Quoted in Nash, *Race and Revolution*, 11, 19, and 18.

13. "Petition of Paul Cuffe and Other Blacks, February 10, 1780," in *Am I Not a Man and a Brother*, ed. Roger Bruns (New York: Chelsea House Publishers, 1977), 454–56.

14. Zilversmit, *The First Emancipation*. States in the upper South, such as Virginia and Maryland, had not only slaves but also sizable and highly visible free black communities. Further south and west in the region, however, free blacks were rare. As the new cotton-growing states of the Deep South—Alabama, Mississippi, and Louisiana—joined the Union during the first quarter of the century, they became the area of greatest slave concentration. Almost all the blacks in the lower South were slaves. Only a few large cities, such as New Orleans and Charleston, had significant numbers of free African Americans. For a complete picture of free blacks in the South, see Berlin, *Slaves Without Masters*.

15. Leon Litwack, "The Federal Government and the Free Negro, 1790–1860," *The Journal of Negro History* 43, no. 4 (October 1958): 261–78.

16. Paul Finkleman, "Prelude to the Fourteenth Amendment: Black Legal Rights in the Antebellum North," *Rutgers Law Journal* 17, nos. 3 and 4 (Spring and Summer 1986): 415–82.

17. Ibid; Litwack, *North of Slavery*.

18. Litwack, *North of Slavery*.

19. Quoted in Lerone Bennett, Jr., *Before the Mayflower: A History of Black America* (New York: Penguin Press, 1984), 182.

20. This lodge had originally been established in Boston in July 1776 as African Lodge No. 1. The white Masons of Boston refused to grant the proper charter to the black group. They were also refused by Massachusetts masonry. Finally Prince Hall, the group's leader, applied for and was granted a charter from the British order in 1787. The official group was renamed the African Lodge No. 459.

21. *Laws of the Sons of the African Society, Instituted at Boston, Anno Domini, 1798* (Boston, 1802).

22. Nash, *Forging Freedom*.

23. Herskovits, *Myth of the Negro Past*.

24. Gutman, *The Black Family*.

25. Revolutionary War Pension Records (Benjamin Summons).

26. Jordan, *White Over Black;* Fredrickson, *The Black Image.*

27. Lamont D. Thomas, *Rise To Be A People: A Biography of Paul Cuffe* (Urbana: University of Illinois Press, 1986).

28. Sweet, *Black Images of America,* 32.

29. Woodson, *The Mind of the Negro,* 160–65.

30. Walker, *David Walker's Appeal,* 76.

31. Delany, *Colored People of the United States,* 79.

32. Bell, *Minutes of the Proceedings,* 4–5.

33. Horton and Horton, *Black Bostonians,* 123.

34. Ibid., 91. For estimates of percentages of African-born and American-born blacks during the eighteenth and nineteenth centuries, see Fogel and Engerman, *Time On the Cross.*

35. *Liberator,* 14 August 1840. For an excellent analysis of this change, see William Gravely, "The Dialectic of Double-Consciousness in Black American Freedom Celebrations, 1808–1863," *Journal of Negro History* 67, no. 4 (Winter 1982–83): 302–17.

36. *Minutes of the Fifth Annual Convention for the Improvement of the Free People of Color . . . 1835* (Philadelphia, 1835), 15; *Weekly Advocate,* 25 February 1837.

37. *Colored American,* 4 March 1837.

38. See chapter 2 of this volume.

39. *Colored American,* 22 August 1840, quoted in Gravely, "Dialectic," 311–12.

40. Joel Williamson, *The Crucible of Race: Black-White Relations in the American South Since Emancipation* (New York: Oxford University Press, 1984).

41. There are several excellent accounts of African American social history during Reconstruction. See Leon F. Litwack, *Been in the Storm So Long: The Aftermath of Slavery* (New York: Knopf, 1979); Holt, *Black Over White;* W. E. B. Du Bois, *Black Reconstruction: an essay toward a history of the part which black folk played in the attempt to reconstruct democracy in America* (New York: Russell & Russell, 1935).

42. For a recent description and analysis of the Reconstruction period, see Eric Foner, *Reconstruction: America's Unfinished Revolution, 1863–1877* (New York: Harper & Row, 1988).

CHAPTER 8: AFRICAN AMERICANS AND GERMANS IN MID-NINETEENTH CENTURY BUFFALO

1. Paul A. Gilje, *The Road to Mobocracy: Popular Disorder in New York City, 1763–1834* (Chapel Hill: University of North Carolina Press, 1987); Edward Raymond Turner, *The Negro in Pennsylvania* (Washington, D.C.: American Historical Association, 1911).

2. Dennis Ryan, *Beyond the Ballot Box: A Social History of the Boston Irish, 1845–1917* (Amherst: University of Massachusetts Press, 1989). For a study that traces these issues and the resulting violence into the twentieth century, see William M. Tuttle, Jr., *Race Riot: Chicago in the Red Summer of 1919* (New York: Atheneum, 1970).

3. Randell Miller, ed., *States of Progress: Germans and Blacks in America Over 300 Years* (Philadelphia: German Society of Pennsylvania, 1989), is one of the few studies on this subject.

4. Laurence A. Glasco rightly suggested that a more meaningful figure, removing children from the count, revealed that three-quarters of Buffalo's heads of households were immigrants. See Laurence A. Glasco, *Ethnicity and Social Structure* (New York: Arno Press, 1980).

5. For a history of blacks in mid-nineteenth century Buffalo see Monroe Fordham, "A Profile of the Colored Population of Buffalo, N.Y., in 1850" (Unpublished essay, 1974). The earliest study of black family structure in Buffalo is Herbert G. Gutman and Laurence A. Glasco, "The Buffalo, New York, Negro, 1855–1875: A Study of the Family Structure of Free Negroes and Some of its Implications" (Unpublished essay, 1966). A recent and very useful study of black Buffalonians is T. J. Davis, "A Historic Overview of Black Buffalo: Work, Community, and Protest" (Unpublished essay, 1989).

6. Glasco, *Ethnicity and Social Structure*; Davis A. Gerber, *The Making of an American Pluralism: Buffalo, New York, 1825–60* (Urbana: University of Illinois Press, 1989).

7. Laurence Glasco suggested that caution should be used in assuming that the absence of an occupation listed in the 1855 New York state census for Buffalo indicated unemployment. Following his lead, those listing no occupation were checked against city directory entries. Most of those listed without an occupation in the census could not be found. Those who could be identified through the city directory were listed in unskilled occupations. Significantly, a number of those listing no employment appeared in the census in white households with relationship to the head of the household listed as servant. Thus it may be true, as Glasco argues, that those listed without occupations in the 1855 census were not necessarily unemployed, but the author believes that if they were employed, they were likely to hold jobs at lower occupational levels. See Glasco, *Ethnicity and Social Structure*, 89–91.

8. See Gerber, *Making of an American Pluralism*; and Glasco, "The Buffalo, New York, Negro."

9. The problem of providing training for young black workers was a major concern for northern blacks throughout the antebellum period. Unlike their southern counterparts, who were often more-skilled workers who provided apprenticeships to young blacks, northern blacks tended to be less skilled and thus less capable of providing such service. During the 1850s New York state blacks took steps to establish a manual training school that would address this situation. See *Proceedings of the Colored National Convention Held in Rochester, July, 1853* (Rochester, 1853). For information on occupational skill levels of northern and southern free blacks, see Curry *The Free Black*.

10. Perhaps the greater proportion of skilled workers among blacks residing in Buffalo for less than fourteen years reflects the migration to the city of many southern-born black workers during the 1850s. Southern free blacks were more likely to have ben skilled, and their increasing presence in the Buffalo work force would have raised the proportion of skilled employment among more recent arrivals.

11. Gerber, *Making of an American Pluralism*, 124. There appears to be a discrepancy between the figures Gerber reported. Whereas at one point he says, "Only 23 percent of all Irish household heads owned homes in 1855, compared to 56 percent and 54 percent among Americans and Germans," on page 182 he says, "Forty percent of German households heads owned a house or land or both in 1855, compared to 23 percent of the Irish and 43 percent of Americans." Glasco's findings confirm the lower 40 percent figure for Germans. See Glasco, *Ethnicity and Social Structure*, 123.

12. This degree of residential integration was more common in the nineteenth century "walking city" than it may appear to those familiar with the twentieth-century pattern. At a time before improvements in urban transportation made long-distance commuting possible, workers lived within easy walking commute of their jobs. This meant that residential segregation of the type common to the mid-twentieth century was generally impractical. There was not only greater residential integration of the races and the economic classes but also a greater variety of land use, with shops and homes sharing the same ar-

eas. Among the best studies of the "walking city" and its transition to the "modern city" are Sam Bass Warner, Jr., *Street Car Suburbs* (Cambridge: Harvard University Press, 1962); Olivier Zunz, *The Changing Face of Inequality* (Chicago: University of Chicago Press, 1982); Hershberg, *Philadelphia.*

13. Glasco, *Ethnicity and Social Structure,* 145.

14. This study's original figures computed for blacks ranged to 17 percent occupying brick or stone dwellings but this proportion was substantially lowered when controlled for those who resided in masonry institution buildings such as poor houses and other asylums. Similar controls have yet to be imposed on data for other groups in the city.

15. More than half of the Irish population lived either in the First or Eight ward, whereas less than 5 percent of blacks lived in these wards. No more than 8 percent of the Irish occupied any other single ward, whereas no more than 6 percent of blacks occupied any single ward outside of their main neighborhoods in the Fourth, Fifth, and Sixth wards. For information on the residential patterns of blacks and Irish in Boston, see Horton and Horton, *Black Bostonians.* See also Pleck, *Black Migration and Poverty* and Ryan, *Beyond The Ballot Box.*

16. There were certainly more black women employed in these domestic jobs than indicated by the census, which reported only six black female domestic servants out of a total female adult population of more than 250. Although this finding seems consistent with the U.S. Census report of 1850, there was a general undercount of female occupations in most census reports, especially before 1860. One indication of this undercount is the fact that sixty-two blacks listing no occupation in the 1855 census recorded their relation to the head of the household as servant. Forty of these lived in white households. If these servants are added to the register of black workers, they would increase the number of blacks reporting jobs by one-third.

17. Although it is not possible to say with certainty that the black women living in these white households were not boarders, it is likely that the majority were servants. Interracial boarding was not unknown during this period, but it was rare. A random examination of the occupations and property holding of twenty-five of these white household heads strongly suggested that at least twenty-two of the black women living in those households were live-in servants.

18. Among Irish adults, property holding rose from 17 percent for those in their twenties to a high of 29 percent for those in their fifties, but it fell back again to 22 percent for the elderly. See Glasco, *Ethnicity and Social Structure,* 126.

19. Glasco, *Ethnicity and Social Structure,* 189–97. Preliminary evidence suggests that this was a conscious choice perhaps connected to the economic state of black Buffalonians.

20. *Morning Express,* 8 July 1863.

21. *Der Weltbürger,* 4 July 1849.

22. *Newburgh Telegraph,* 14 May 1846.

23. Bruce C. Levine, "In the Spirit of 1848: German Americans and the Fight Over Slavery's Expansion" (Ph.D. diss., University of Rochester, 1980).

24. Robert D. Cross, "The Irish," John Higham, ed., *Ethnic Leadership in America* (Baltimore: John Hopkins University Press, 1978), 176–197.

25. Dale T. Knobel, *Paddy and the Republic: Ethnicity and Nationality in Antebellum America* (Middletown, Conn.: Wesleyan University Press; distributed by Harper & Row, 1986).

26. *Der Weltbürger,* 10 February 1854.

27. *Der Weltbürger,* 10 March 1855.

28. Gerber, *Making of an American Pluralism,* 135.

29. *Morning Express,* 7 July 1863. The quote is taken from *Fincher's Trades Review* in Benjamin Quarles, *The Negro in the Civil War* (Boston: Brown, Little, Brown, 1969), 238.

30. See Gerber, *Making of an American Pluralism,* 186.

31. Iver Bernstein, *The New York Draft Riots: Their Significance for American Society and Politics in the Age of the Civil War* (New York: Oxford University Press, 1990). The quote is from the New York *Commercial Advertiser,* 16 July 1863.

32. See Gilje and George Rude, *The Crowd in History, 1759–1848* (New York: Wiley, 1964). Some have advanced the argument that individual violence is an integral part of the Irish culture and that Irish Americans were likely to turn to violence to address personal and political issues. The use of such arguments here has been resisted. Although these cultural explanations cannot be completely discounted, they are often extremely complex and difficult to prove. Further, they are not necessary in trying to make this point. For the cultural explanation of Irish violence see McWhiney, *Cracker Culture;* Wyatt-Brown, *Southern Honor.*

33. See Donald Black, "Social Control as a Dependent Variable," in *Toward a General Theory of Social Control: Fundamentals,* vol. 1, ed. Donald Black (New York: Academic Press, 1984); Max Gluckman, *Custom and Conflict in Africa* (Oxford: Blackwell, 1955); Elizabeth Colson, "Social Control and Vengeance in Plateau Tonga Society," *Africa* 23 (July 1953): 199–212.

34. Roberta Senecha, "Social Location of Anti-Black Violence: The Springfield, Illinois Race Riot of 1908" (Paper delivered at the American Association of Criminologists, 8 November 1989), 17; Allen D. Grimshaw, "Urban Racial Violence in the United States: Changing Ecological Considerations," *American Journal of Sociology* 66 (September 1960): 114–15.

CHAPTER 9: RACE, OCCUPATION, AND LITERACY IN RECONSTRUCTION WASHINGTON, D.C.

1. American Freedmen's Inquiry Commission, "Preliminary Report Touching the Condition and Management of Emancipated Refugees: Made to the Secretary of War by the American Freedmen's Inquiry Commission, June 30, 1863," p. 33, National Archives.

2. Constance Green, *Washington: A History of the Capital, 1800–1950* (Princeton: Princeton University Press, 1962), 298.

3. Ibid., 298–99.

4. In 1867, eighty-two hundred whites and seventy-two hundred blacks were registered. For an unofficial count of registered voters, see Washington, D.C., *Intelligencer,* 23 March, 1, 5, 15, 20 April, 7 May 1867.

5. First Annual Report of the Education Commission, March 1863 (Boston, 1863), 11.

6. *Minutes and Proceedings of the Second Annual Convention for the Improvement of the Free People of Color in These United States* (Philadelphia, 1832) in Bell, *Minutes of the Proceedings,* 34.

7. Lillian G. Dabney, *The History of Schools for Negroes in the District of Columbia, 1807–1947* (Washington, D.C.: Catholic University of America Press, 1949).

8. Melvin R. Williams, "Blacks in Washington, D.C., 1860–1870" (Ph.D. diss., Johns Hopkins University, 1975).

9. Walter Dyson, *Howard University* (Washington, D.C., 1867), 56.

10. The comparison is 15 percent of all whites to 14 percent of all blacks. Compiled from the *Census of the District of Columbia, 1867*, report of Dr. F. B. Hough (Washington, D.C., 1867). The increased emphasis on black adult education for citizenship was reflected in the increase in night schools for blacks from five in 1861 to fifteen in 1867. See Dabney, *Schools for Negroes*.

11. *The Report of the Board of Trustees of the Public Schools of the City of Washington, 1871–2* (Washington City, 1872), 94–97, National Archives.

12. *Report of the Board of Trustees*, various years between 1870 and 1880, National Archives.

13. John Eaton, *Grant, Lincoln and the Freedmen* (New York: Longmans, Green, 1907).

14. For a detailed account of the circumvention of the Republican-sponsored political and constitutional guarantees, see Foner, *Reconstruction*.

15. Fredrickson, *The Black*, 235.

16. Maud Wilder Goodwin, "The Antislavery Legacy," in *The Literature of Philanthropy*, ed. Frances A. Goodale (New York: Harper & Brothers, 1893), 156–57.

17. Green, *Washington*, 297.

18. Sayles J. Bowen was elected mayor of Washington in 1868. Representing the left wing of the Republican party, he embarked on several progressive, publicly financed construction projects that increased the city's debt and did not endear him to many white voters. He was severely criticized by conservative whites, who also claimed that his efforts to provide public-works jobs for blacks were laced with big payoffs for corrupt contractors. Bowen's position was further undermined by his inability to secure adequate federal funding for public education in the district. See Green, *Washington* and David L. Lewis, *District of Columbia: A Bicentennial History* (New York: W. W. Norton, 1976).

19. Goodwin, "The Antislavery Legacy," 151.

20. Compiled from Bureau of the Census, *Census of the District of Columbia, 1870* (Washington, D.C., 1870); *Census of the District of Columbia, 1880* (Washington, D.C., 1880).

21. A special census in 1867 found that 51 percent of white and 58 percent of blacks had come into the district after 1860. Bureau of the Census, *Census of the District of Columbia, 1867*, 27.

22. For a detailed explanation of how this estimate was arrived at, see Lois E. Horton, "The Development of Federal Social Policy for Blacks in Washington, D.C., After Emancipation" (Ph.D. diss., Brandeis University, 1977), 183.

23. In 1870 and in 1880 the percentage of the population who could read was less than 5 percentage points greater than those who could both read and write: 72.4 percent and 67.7 percent in 1870, and 79.9 percent and 75.4 percent in 1880.

24. Fredrickson, *The Black Image*, 198–216.

25. Goodwin, "The Antislavery Legacy," 150.

26. Melvin R. Williams, "A Blueprint for Change: The Black Community in Washington, D.C., 1860–1870," *Records of the Columbia Historical Society* 48 (1971–72): 359–93.

27. Quoted in Du Bois, *Black Reconstruction*, 195.

Index